Casing ORGANIZATIONAL COMMUNICATION

EDITED BY

JASON S. WRENCH

SUNY - New Paltz

Kendall Hunt
publishing company
www.kendallhunt.com

Kendall Hunt
publishing company

www.kendallhunt.com
Send all inquiries to:
4050 Westmark Drive
Dubuque, IA 52004-1840

Copyright © 2012 by Kendall Hunt Publishing Company

ISBN 978-0-7575-9684-1

Printed in the United States of America
10 9 8 7 6 5 4 3 2

CONTENTS

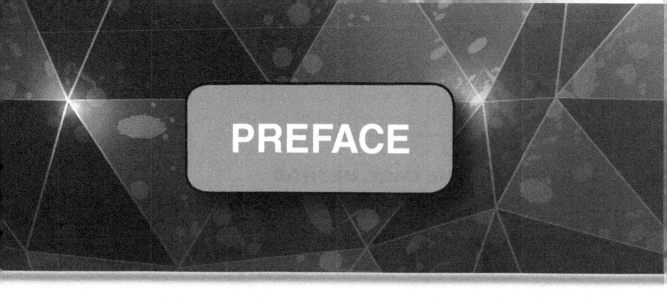

PREFACE

WHY CASES?

Recently, I was engaging with a group of students in my Introduction to Organizational Communication course. The topic of the day was social media, and we were discussing the problems many organizations were facing because their internal policies had not kept up with the quickly moving pace of social networking. My students, who had all grown up using the internet, thought it was farfetched that organizations did not have social networking policies. As one student put it, "That really doesn't happen anymore."

Of course, as a professor of organizational communication and someone who reads trade journals and academic journals alike, I'm acutely aware that Web 2.0 was a topic in almost every issue of the *Harvard Business Review, Wall Street Journal, BusinessWeek,* and so on. One of the biggest challenges I face as a professor at a traditional college (where most of my students range in age from 18 to 21), is most of my students have minimal or no corporate experience at all. As such, showing students how to apply the theoretical content of organizational communication, or how to employ the skills discussed in organizational communication, is quite difficult because they do not immediately see the utility. Every time I attend academic conferences with other organizational communication scholars, this topic of helping students see the applicability of what we study in organizational communication in the "real world" is eventually broached.

Thankfully, over the last hundred years, a method has been devised in schools of business around the globe to help students see the applicability and utility of course content. This method is called the Case Method. The book you currently hold in your hands represents the culmination of a century of understanding about how students learn and apply business related concepts, skills, and theory.

The Case Method is a fun and active way to learn about a wide range of different topics, but is a method of teaching that definitely takes preparation on the part of both the instructor and the student. In the next few pages, I am going to briefly introduce you to the Case Method, including the history, types of cases, and benefits of the Case Method. In the next chapter, I will walk you through a process I recommend for analyzing a case that is based on a wealth of research written by a range of business related scholars from accounting, industrial psychology, management, organizational behavior, organizational communication, and so on.

HISTORY OF THE CASE METHOD

In 1870 Christopher Columbus Langdell was asked to take over as the Dean of the Harvard Law School.[1] Prior to his taking the helm at Harvard Law School, the primary method for teaching law students was a practice called the Dwight Method, which required students to memorize information about the current status of law and regurgitate this information in front of their peers. Langdell believed that this method was not the best possible method for teaching students, so he set out to develop a method based on his own personal learning experience. As a law student, Langdell read every legal precedent that was handed down by the various state and federal courses. These legal precedents, known as case law, generally included the facts of the case and a judge's decision and application of law to the specific case. Instead of having students memorize and regurgitate facts, Langdell believed that it was important for students to not only know the basic concepts of law, but to also be able to apply those concepts in a meaningful manner. Langdell put together a set of diverse legal cases into a single volume, which students would read and analyze prior to coming to class. During class, Langdell would pose questions related to the case and then randomly chose a student to answer the question, which ultimately became known as the Socratic Method.

In 1908 the Harvard Business School was founded, and the original dean, Edwin F. Gay, tried to implement a similar method to that of the Harvard Law School, which he deemed the problem method. Unfortunately, the problem method wasn't really developed, so faculty ended up spending more time lecturing than actually discussing problems. In 1919 a former lawyer who had gone to Harvard Law School and had been teaching corporate finance at Harvard, Wallace P. Donham, was appointed the Dean of the Harvard Business School. As a former student of the Socratic Method, Donham saw the immediate benefit in learning by legal cases. However, businesses provided a fundamental difference from law—there is not business precedents written in the form of case law for students to digest. To help fill this gap, Donham created the Bureau for Business Research and encouraged faculty to spend time creating case studies about specific businesses and business leaders as a form of scholarly research.[2] These early cases were transcriptions of interactions between the professors and business leaders related to a specific decision or a set of decisions the individual had made. Ultimately, this form of teaching practice became known as the Case Method, and quickly became one of the primary tools for teaching business students at all major business schools.

Today, the Case Method is taught around the world in a variety of different educational contexts. Every field from graphic design to surgery has employed some version of the Case Method crystallized by the Harvard Business School. However, the Case Method is still mostly widely used in those fields related to various aspects of organizations: business, industrial psychological, management, organizational communication, organizational sociology, public relations, and so on.

TYPES OF CASES

Before we can delve into the various types of cases that exist, we really need to examine what we mean by the word "case" in the organizational context. Obviously, we do not have case law as lawyers have in the legal profession. As such, our use of the word "case" in the organizational context refers to a "description of an actual {or fictional} situation, commonly involving a decision, a challenge, an opportunity, or a problem or an issue faced by a person (or persons) in an organization. A case allows you to step figuratively into the position of a particular decision-maker."[3] In essence, a case is a story about a real business situation and how people could theoretically act and communicate within that situation. Most importantly, cases do not arrive at a specific decision for the reader. As Wallace Donham wrote when he first popularized the Case Method, a business case "contains no statement of the decision reached by the businessman {or business woman}...and generally business cases admit of more than one solution...{Business cases} include both relevant and irrelevant material, in order that the student may obtain practice in selecting the facts that apply."[4]

Ultimately, cases have three basic characteristics: significance, sufficient information, and no conclusions.[5] First, a case must contain some kind of significant issue or a series of significant issues in the business world. Four our purposes, a good organizational communication case must take on some facet of organizational communication that is relevant in the modern world. While examining how an organization uses the telegraph would not be significant in today's world, seeing the trials and tribulations of how corporate America is communicating with people via Twitter would be significant. Second, a case needs to provide the reader sufficient information to draw possible outcomes. While all cases will provide sufficient information, not all possible relevant information is presented in every case. As often happens in the real world, people must make decisions based on limited information. Lastly, cases will not clearly spell out what the most appropriate decisions should be for a specific case. One of the goals of the Case Method is to enable readers to examine the facts, in light of their own knowledge and research, and arrive at a possible decision. Could your decision be wrong? Yes. Could your decision be right? Maybe. Obviously, the Case Method is ultimately dealing in the world of hypotheticals, so you will not know the ultimate ramifications of making the decision. The results, while important to consider, are secondary to the Case Method. The goal of the case is the learning experience and the application of course content to the case. One of the more fascinating parts of using the Case Method as a teacher is how different groups of students can arrive at radically different decisions for equally valid reasons.

There are often many possible decisions that could be arrived at when analyzing a case, so some students often become frustrated because they want to know the "best" way to solve the case. If you ask 100 different scholars for an answer to a case, you're likely to get 100 different answers. While not every possible outcome is equally valid, every outcome can be examined and discussed

(I'll discuss more on this in the next chapter). Ultimately, there are two types of cases that you may encounter if you're a student of organizational communication: profile cases and fictional cases.

What I refer to as "profile cases" are cases that actually profile actual organizational phenomena and show how various real people in real life handled those situations. These cases tend to be lengthy because they must provide a great deal of detail about real organizational occurrences. For example, let's say we were going to write a case about the communication British Petroleum engaged in after the Deepwater Horizon explosion of the coast of Louisiana in 2010. In this case, you'd have a few pages about the deep water drilling; then you'd explain in detail the actual accident and the resulting crisis; then you would have a section on the initial response from BP; and then you would have a detailed retelling of the various communication strategies utilized by BP. As you can well imagine, covering all of this information could result in a book if you really get into the detail. These cases resemble the original form of the case created by Harvard Business School in the 1920s.

Fictional cases, on the other hand, are shorter cases that are based in actual organizational problems but have been fictionalized in an effort to make the case more succinct. This method of case writing was popularized in the *Harvard Business Review,* which concludes each issue with a short fictional case and then asks a handful of notable experts to weigh in on the case itself. For the text you have in your hand, I have chosen to utilize fictional cases because they are great for undergraduates or lower graduate student engagement. Furthermore, because these cases are more focused on a specific communication issue, readers can more easily apply organizational communication content, skills, and theory to the cases when determining possible courses of action.

BENEFITS OF THE CASE METHOD

By this point, you may be wondering to yourself why anyone would want to use the Case Method. And you'd be remiss if you didn't question the utility of this teaching technique. Besides the fact that the Case Method has been shown to be a highly flexible and meaningful learning experience for both undergraduate and graduate students alike, there are five basic reasons that the Case Method is beneficial.[6-7]

Lend reality to indirect experience.

While the best form of learning is to learn something directly yourself, there is definitely reason to learn from the insights, strategies, and mistakes of others. As such, we can learn from others and the experiences they have had in the real world, which will ultimately make us all more prepared for handling situations. In terms of case studies, the case is an easy way to see what types of situations others have found themselves in, and then think through how we would behave in that same situation.

Focus on concrete problems.

One of the biggest problems that many undergraduates face when learning business related concepts is no frame of reference. What I mean by "no frame of reference," is that your average undergraduates (and many graduate students) have limited or no corporate experience. As such, when we talk about theoretical ideas or how some corporate offices function, the only frame of reference many have is what they've seen through their parents or on television. These viewpoints may be slightly skewed, if not completely inaccurate. By delving into a specific case, you have the opportunity to engage a story based on real occurrences that happen in modern organizations. While the cases have been fictionalized in this book, the cases are based on a range of real-world problems that organizations have faced. Fictionalizing the cases helps the authors make them more concrete and easily understood.

Develop skill in decision making.

Decision making is one of the most useful skills you will learn in the Case Method. In the next chapter, I'm going to walk you through a highly formalized way of analyzing an organizational communication case. The tips and strategies we employ for analyzing a case can be applied to any type of decision-making enterprise, so this skill will be very useful in all parts of your life.

Broaden student insight.

The fourth reason that the Case Method is useful for students is that it helps you broaden your own insight into a complex decision. While the decision you arrive at on your own may seem very logical, when you start to examine the decision in great detail you start to see that there are a wide range of possibilities inherent within a decision. For example, when you think about a simple decision like purchasing a hamburger from one restaurant over another, you may think that you're just purchasing a hamburger. The Case Method asks you to go further than just your taste buds and really delve into the ramifications of your decision. How does purchasing a hamburger from one fast-food restaurant over a second one impact the world around you? If one uses Styrofoam to place its burger in and the other uses paper, the second burger joint is actually going to have a smaller negative impact on the environment. Often when we make decisions, we fail to take into account all of the possible risks and long-term outcomes associated. The Case Method is designed to help you more thoroughly think through how decisions are made and evaluated.

Help students see varying points of view.

When you read a case study, you'll undoubtedly come to some kind of decision that you believe is the best one. One of the fascinating parts of the Case Method is the interaction that occurs during a class that uses the Case Method. When you have the opportunity to discuss a case with your peers, you'll quickly see a broader range of possible decisions that you didn't even think about while reading the case. Furthermore, you'll be asked to defend your own perspective and find the flaws in other's perspectives as well. While the Case Method is not a formalized debate, there are definitely parts of the Case Method that rely on an individual to think logically and systematically when arguing for a specific decision alternative. One of the goals of the case method is to help you see a wide variety of points-of-view. However, do not just assume that because your ideas and someone else's differ that the other person is always right. Instead, think logically and really analyze both your argument(s) and the other person's argument(s). While examining all sides of a case can help you see and understand varying points-of-view, the process can also help you sharpen your own argumentative skills.

CONCLUSION

In the past few pages, I have briefly presented the history of the Case Method, explained what a case is and the types of cases, and lastly explained how the Case Method can help you become a better student and a more functional member of an organization. In the next chapter, we are going to examine the Case Method process put forth in this book.

[1]Garvin, D. A. (2003). Making the case: Professional education for the world of practice. *Harvard Magazine, 106*(1), 56–107.

[2]Donham, W. B. (1922). Business teaching by the case system. *The American Economic Review, 12*(1), 53–65.

[3]Mauffette-Leenders, L. A., Erskine, J. A., & Leenders, M. R. (2007). *Learning with cases* (4th ed.). London, Ontario, Canada: Richard Ivey School of Business.

[4](Donham, 1922, pp. 61–62)

[5]Ellet, W. (2007). *The case study handbook: How to read, discuss, and write persuasively about cases.* Cambridge, MA: Harvard Business School Press.

[6]Graham, P. T., & Cline, P. C. (1980). The case method: A basic teaching approach. *Theory Into Practice, 19*, 112–116.

[7]Ford, L. (1969). *Using the case study in teaching and training.* Nashville, TN: Broadman Press.

ANALYZING CASE STUDIES

The types of cases you are going to read in this book are what we call decision-based cases, or cases that require the reader to come to some kind of decision. Every case is essentially laid out in a very similar pattern. First, you will be introduced to the main character of the case. Second, you will be introduced to other individuals involved within the case. Third, you will be introduced to the main communication problem, or a number of communication problems that either the main character or her or his organization currently face. Lastly, you will be left with a character not sure which direction he or she should proceed. In essence, you, as the reader, will need to come up with the decision the main character should make.

DECISION MAKING AND CASE STUDIES

To help you work your way through the decision-making process, I have created a worksheet (Appendix A) that will help guide you through the decision-making process. Please understand that this is a formalized decision-making process based on the work of communication scholars Dennis Gouran and Randy Hirokawa.[1] The functional approach created by Gouran and Hirokawa involves five basic steps.

Step One—Understand the Problem

First, and foremost, someone making a decision needs to make sure that he or she completely understands the issue at hand. If you look at the worksheet provided in Appendix A, you'll notice that the first few questions all involve making sure you understand the decision that needs to be made. First, you're asked, "Who are the important characters within the case?" In some cases you'll only have two or three characters who are important, but in other cases you could have ten different characters, and you'll need to know how each character is important to the case. Second, you'll be asked about the main communication problem within the case. One of the hardest parts of making a decision is understanding what needs to be solved. As such, clearly articulating the communication problem very early in your analysis is essential. Lastly, you'll be asked to look for any causes that you see within the case that has led to the communication problem. No communication problem exists within a vacuum, so clearly articulating what the problems are will help you ultimately select decisions that are useful within the confines of the specific case.

In addition to the basic understandings of the problems and causes of the case, I also think it's important to start thinking about how relevant organizational communication literature applies to the case at this point. One mistake that we can make is to come up with a decision and then to try to find relevant research to support the decision we've already made. However, when we look at research in retrospect, we often miss out on more logical choices.

Step Two—Select Criteria

The word "criterion" refers to a standard by which we can judge something (FYI—"criterion" is singular and "criteria" is plural). Of course, in the case of a decision, we are searching for standards by which we can judge our decisions. Previous research in the area of case study analysis has identified both Quantitative and Qualitative criteria that may help individuals and organizations judge their decisions.[2] Quantitative criteria are called such because they can be easily numerically measured and computed as having an impact on business functioning. Qualitative criteria, on the other hand, are criteria that are not easily numerically measured or computed. **TABLE 1** shows a list of both quantitative and qualitative criteria for organizational communication cases. Please understand that these criteria are not exhaustive, so other criteria could definitely be added to the list. Furthermore, there are some instances where quantitative criteria are qualitatively applied and vice-versa, so this list is intended as a general list of possible criteria to be applied in a decision-making situation. While some of these criteria may be familiar to you, others may not be, so let's briefly explain what each of the criteria mean.

Quantitative Criteria

Profit. The money a business makes after accounting for all the expenses is its profit. At the end of the day, all organizations must be profitable or they will disappear. As such, whether an organization is a for-profit or a non-profit organization, the organization must be concerned with profit.

Cost. If profit is the right hand of an organization, then cost is the left hand of the organization. Cost can be defined as the price paid or required for acquiring, producing, or maintaining a product or service. All organizations have costs. The obvious goal is to ensure that the costs of your organization are less than the profits. However, the old adage that sometimes you have to spend money to make money is also true, but the goal is to ensure that your profits outweigh your costs.

Return on investment. One concept that isn't overly discussed in many communication textbooks is an organization's return on investment (ROI). According to Patricia and Jack Phillips of the ROI Institute, an ROI is the "ultimate measure of accountability that answers the question: Is

TABLE 1 *Decision Criteria*

Quantitative	Qualitative
Profit	Customer Satisfaction
Cost	Competitive Advantage
Return on Investment	Corporate Image
Cash Flow	Goodwill
Inventory Turn	Cultural Sensitivity
Productivity	Employee Motivation
Efficiency	Job Satisfaction
Capacity	Employee Health - Physical - Psychological - Spiritual
Delivery Time	Safety
Quality	Synergy
Quantity	Ethics - Business - Communication
Errors	Innovation
Growth Rate	Obsolescence
Market Share	Flexibility
Risk - Physical - Organizational	Pragmatism
Staff Turnover	Ease of Implementation

there a financial return for investing in a program, process, initiative, or performance improvement solution."[3] The ROI focuses on the benefits and costs gained from a specific endeavor. While the idea of conducting a cost-benefit analysis dates back to an article written by a French engineer named Jules Dupuit in1848, the process of conducting a cost-benefit analysis was practically developed by the United States Corp of Engineers during the 1930s. A basic cost-benefit analysis is simple to calculate:

$$\text{Benefit Cost Ratio} = \frac{\text{Benefits}}{\text{Costs}}$$

The ROI is an extension of the cost-benefit analysis that was developed in the 1970s and 80s, and really became a hallmark of business measurement in the 1990s. Where a simple cost-benefit ratio examines whether the costs outweigh the benefits, the ROI wants to know how beneficial something was once the costs are balanced out of the equation. For example, imagine you invest $1 in a lemonade stand. At the end of the day, the lemonade entrepreneur hands you back $2. Because your initial investment was $1, we automatically subtract that from our profit, which leaves us with a net benefit of $1. Here is how we would calculate the ROI:

ROI (%) = (Net Benefits / Costs) * 100
ROI (%) = (1 / 1) * 100
ROI (%) = (1) * 100
ROI (%) = 100

What this says is that for every $1 we invested in the lemonade stand, we got back $1 after the costs were covered. Obviously, in the business world, the goal is to have much higher returns on investments than an ROI of 100%. Often ROIs less than 300% are considered losses in some organizations.

Cash flow. Another important concept related to the amount of money an organization is taking in and spending is cash flow. Cash flow is the amount of cash a company generates and uses during a period. Cash inflow is money an organization has entering an organization from profits or investments. Cash outflow then is money that an organization has to spend because of expenses or investments. An organization must have enough inflow to balance its outflow. Having enough cash on hand ensures that an organization can meet its basic obligations in terms of expenses. If an organization's money is all tied up in various investments and does not have cash on hand, then the organization may become insolvent because the organization cannot meet its basic financial obligations.

Inventory turn. Inventory turn is very important for organizations that produce any kind of product. Inventory turn can be defined as the number of times inventory is sold or used in a time period (e.g., a month, six-months, one-year, etc.). Obviously, if inventory is sitting on your shelves, then you're not making money off that inventory. Ultimately, the goal of any production oriented organization is to turn the inventory as often as possible.

Productivity. Productivity examines the relationship between the amount of input into a system and the resulting output. Let's say you run a cleaning service and you know that if you hire three workers (input into the system), then you can clean nine office (resulting output). Ultimately, the amount of input into your system should positively affect your productivity.

Efficiency. From a business perspective, efficiency examines the relationship between means and ends, and is closely related to productivity. If a business process is efficient, then the right amount of input is in place to achieve a desired output. If an organization is inefficient, then the organization could either (A) use less inputs to produce the same output (fire people and expect the same amount of work to be accomplished), or (B) the current inputs should produce a greater end result (keep the same number of workers, but expect them to do more). The goal of efficiency is to streamline a process without reaching the point of diminished returns, when the new input level is no longer able to reach the desired output level.

Capacity. Capacity is a concept closely related to productivity, and refers to the maximum amount or number that can be received or contained. Imagine you own a warehouse and supply coffee-related products to the West Coast. At some point, your warehouse will reach a point where you can no longer physically put any more material within the warehouse; this is capacity.

Delivery time. Organizations that deal with products or services must be concerned with their delivery times, or the length of time it takes to deliver a product or service once a customer has ordered the product or service. If you're building a skyscraper, then your delivery time may be seen in years, but if you're delivering a textbook ordered on the internet, your delivery time should be in days. Different products and services will require different delivery times. One way to make your organization stand out is to ensure that you deliver a quality product or service as quickly as possible.

Quality. Quality refers to producing or providing products or services that meet the expressed and/or implied requirements of an organization's customers. While all organizations should strive for a specified level of quality, perfection may not be a realistic ultimate goal.

Quantity. Quantity is one of the easiest criteria to understand because it's a base count of some product or service. More formally, quantity is defined as the extent, size, or sum of countable or measurable discrete events, objects, or phenomenon, expressed as a numerical value.

Errors. Whether we like them or not, eventually errors happen. In this sense, any product or service may lead to a mistake or a deviation from the intended output. The public often doesn't complain about some errors but becomes enraged at other errors when they occur. Obviously, errors that lead to harm are considerably more important than errors that do not cause harm to people. An error that causes a production line to slow down may lose revenue for the corporation, but an error on a production line that causes someone to lose an arm could be both detrimental to the corporation's profit and public image. Furthermore, there is a strong negative relationship between delivery time and quality. Depending on the product or service, you may side on either delivery time or quality. The faster you try to produce a product or deliver a service, the more likely you will have errors. If, on the other hand, you desire a high quality product or service, then delivery time will be slower as quality inspection is built into the system to prevent errors. There is also a negative relationship that exists between quality and quantity. The higher the quantity, the more likely you will have errors along the way. The higher your desired quality, the lower your quantity should be, which will lead to fewer errors.

Growth rate. In an ideal economic environment, an organization will continue to increase its ability to provide products and services at a desired pace. As such, growth rate is the increase in the demand for a particular product or service over time. For growth rate to be effective, the organization needs to balance the requirements for new raw materials, employees, and so on, into the organization (input), and the processing of those inputs in the creation of products and services (throughput), with your customer needs and desires (output). If an organization has too many new inputs and no outputs, the organization will become insolvent over time. If an organization doesn't have enough inputs or the throughput process is too slow, then the organization will not meet its obligations to its customers, which could lead to insolvency as well. Ultimately, an organization wants to ensure that it is able to increase the amounts of input and increase the throughput process in direct relationship to the demand from customers.

Market share. Market share refers to the percentage of total industry sales that are made up by a particular company's individual sales. If you're in a very niche industry (e.g., canine acupuncture or knitted pencil cozies), you may have 100% of the market share. On the other hand, if you're a fast food restaurant specializing in hamburgers, then you may be competing with a large number of other organizations for the same market share.

Risk. For our purpose, risk can be defined as the chance that something negative will occur. We can break risk down into two categories: physical risk and organizational risk.

- **Physical risk.** Physical risk is the likelihood that an individual will suffer loss of life or be injured in some fashion. As mandated by federal law, all organizations must be somewhat aware of the types of physical risks their employees are exposed. Some organizations innately have more physical risks associated with the organization (e.g., fishing industry, timber industry, etc.), and so considering the importance of risk becomes very important when making all kinds of decisions.

- **Organizational risk.** Organizational risk, on the other hand, examines an organization's return on investment. Whether the investment is in a new employee, product, service, or financial investment, all organizations take risks when they invest. Often these investments do not turn out in favor of the organization. While having some risk will definitely help an organization grow, too much risk can end up sinking an organization if all of the returns on investment are lower than originally anticipated.

Staff turnover. The final quantitative criterion is staff turnover, or the rate at which an organization gains and loses employees (includes both voluntary and involuntary turnover). Voluntary turnover occurs when an employee quits her or his job, whereas involuntary turnover is when an employer must ask an employee to quit (either in a firing or downsizing context). If you have too much staff turnover, the costs of hiring and training new employees may go through the roof. If you don't have any staff turnover, you may end up with a stagnant employee base that doesn't innovate. Most organizations attempt to hire and cultivate a working environment that keeps employees satisfied and engaged in their work, to avoid voluntary turnover while ensuring that "new blood" is regularly integrated into the organization.

Qualitative Criteria

The word "qualitative" refers to the relating to, or the measurement of or by, the quality of something rather than its quantity. In this respect, the word "quality" then is an examination of a degree or standard of excellence related to something. When we discuss qualitative criteria we are examining how organizations can excel within a specific category, but these categories are innately more arbitrary and not immediately numerically measurable. For example, the first criterion we'll examine is customer satisfaction. While most people can intrinsically understand what is meant by "customer satisfaction," there is no clear quantity immediately associated with the idea of customer satisfaction. While there are metrics that have been designed to attempt to measure all of the qualitative criteria discussed below, the qualitative criteria are innately non-numerical. Let's look at all of the qualitative criteria discussed in **TABLE 1**.

Customer satisfaction. Most organizations understand that making sure you have customers who are satisfied with the product or service is extremely important for ensuring that current customers become repeat customers. As a criterion, one must always question whether a decision being made is likely to increase customer satisfaction, maintain current satisfaction levels, or possibly decrease customer satisfaction.

Competitive advantage. Competitive advantage is the superiority gained by an organization when the organization compares itself with products and services of other organizations within its target market. There are two ways an organization can make itself competitive. First, the organization can provide the same value as its competitors but at a lower price. In this case, the organization is figuring out how to manufacture a product or deliver a service in a fashion that is cheaper than its competitors. Another way an organization can set itself aside competitively is to set itself up as a luxury option and then charge more for the base product but sell less of the actual product. In essence, you're creating the myth that your product is a luxury product to be desired. While you may not sell as many products or services, the increased price offsets any value you lose and makes you competitive within your target market.

Corporate image. Corporate image refers to the representation which an organization creates about itself for various stakeholders (employees, stock holders, customers, etc.). While an organization's ultimate image is based on the perceptions of various stakeholders, organizations can help foster a specific image through both internal communication and external communication. Common thematic areas involved in corporate image include the prestige of the organization, quality of its products and services, reputation of organizational leadership, perception of the organization in terms of its relationship to the environment, and so on.

Goodwill. Goodwill, as an organizational criterion, relates to an accounting concept that has been around for many years. In this respect, goodwill is seen as the intangible value of the organization that goes beyond the physical and non-physical assets of the organization (e.g., people, property, finances, etc.) and is generally based on stakeholder perceptions of the firm's reputation. From a communication perspective, goodwill refers to an individual's perception of another's perceived caring.[4] In this case, do you, as an organizational stakeholder, believe that an organization cares about you as an individual both as a stakeholder and as a person? Ultimately, the accounting and communication perspectives on goodwill are not mutually exclusive. While the accounting perspective tries to determine how organizations can quantify goodwill and make it an asset that can have clear value, the communication perspective lends itself to understanding how an organization actually develops goodwill. Organizations can build perceptions of goodwill, but these perceptions are built over a lengthy period of time. Ultimately, goodwill is built through four basic functions: (1) expenditures on public relations and marketing; (2) products and services that meet and exceed customer expectations; (3) investment in the creation of long-lasting customer-provider relationships; and (4) organizational leadership that is perceived as ethical. Once an organization has built goodwill, generally the only way to negate that goodwill is through some kind of indiscretion by organizational leadership.

Cultural sensitivity. Cultural sensitivity is the degree to which an organization is aware of the differences and similarities of different cultures and how culture impacts individual attitudes, values, beliefs, and behaviors. In the United States, there are a ton of different cultures represented, and organizations should be sensitive to their employees' needs and their customer needs with respect to those cultures. Often organizations must balance various cultural needs that conflict, so organizational decision-makers should tread thoughtfully when making decisions that relate to cultural issues.

Employee motivation. Motivation, generally speaking, is the force that drives an individual to achieve her or his goals.[5] For organizational purposes, employee motivation then is the force that drives individual employees to achieve both the employee's goals at work and the organization's goals. Generally speaking, we break employee motivations into two basic categories: internal and external. Internal motivators are those forces that exist within an individual and drive her or him to achieve a goal. An example of an internal motivator could be work ethic. If someone believes in a strong work ethic, he or she may be more motivated to help achieve an organization's goals. If another person has a weak work ethic, he or she may be unmotivated to achieve an organization's goals. The second category of motivators is external, or factors outside an individual that can influence the individual to strive towards achieving a goal. One of the most common external motivators is monetary reward. If you're told that you'll receive a bonus if a product is produced on time, you'll be more motivated to achieve the organization's goal because you see a direct personal benefit.

Job satisfaction. Job satisfaction, like employee motivation, is a concept that is very intangible and ambiguous. Job satisfaction is the emotional reaction that an individual has about her or his job. If people have a positive emotional reaction to their jobs, they will be satisfied and content; whereas individuals who have a negative emotional reaction will be unsatisfied. Ultimately, an individual's job satisfaction will impact her or his attitudes, values, beliefs, and behaviors on the job.

Employee health. Employee health looks at the totality of an individual employee's physical, psychological, and spiritual well-being. In an ideal world, people would be able to disassociate their work life from other parts of their lives, but that is not realistic. As such, there has been an increased focus in considering employee health.

- **Physical health.** Physical health refers to the physical well-being of an individual. When individuals are sick and unhealthy, they miss more work and are not as productive as when they are healthy. As such, many organizations are now investing a great deal of money to ensure that employees maintain their physical health, because it is actually a very good return on investment.[6]

- **Psychological health.** Psychological health is the extent to which an individual is cognitively and emotionally well. Not only can a decrease in someone's psychological health be problematic for the individual, but her or his work performance can also be greatly, negatively impacted as well. While there are some characteristics that can negatively impact an individual's psychological health that are outside the organization's control (e.g., divorce, ailing parent, mental disorder, etc.), there are others that are clearly based within the organization and can be curtailed by a vigilant organization (e.g., excessive stress, bullying, charlatanism, incivility, etc.).

- **Spiritual health.** The notion of spiritual health is a fairly recent one for many organizational academics. As such, many organizational communication textbooks do not really broach the subject. Spiritual health can be defined as the "the enhancement of spiritual oneness with whatever a person considers to be more than oneself as an individual with reason, experience, and intuition; the ongoing development of an adherence to a responsible ethical system."[7] As with both physical and psychological health, when individuals do not feel spiritually healthy, their work performance can be negatively impacted to the organization's detriment.

Safety. One of the basic needs anyone has in a modern workplace is the feeling of safety. Whether this is safety as a result of being exposed to an organizational hazard (e.g., chemicals, heavy machinery, etc.) or safety from being exposed to workplace aggression and violence, people have an inherent need to be safe. You will never get people to work at their optimum levels within an organization if they don't feel safe.

Synergy. The notion of synergy stems out of systems theory and basically states that the sum of the whole is greater than the sum of its parts. Practically speaking, synergy is the idea that individual actors, dynamics, materials, objects, processes, or systems will not help an organization as much as all of those parts working harmoniously with one another. For organizational optimization, all parts within an organization need to be working together to produce an optimal organizational outcome.

Ethics. Ethics, at its most basic level, is the discussion of whether a set of means justifies the desired ends. Ethics can be further explained, as a "critical analysis of cultural values to determine the validity of their vigorous rightness or wrongness in terms of two major criteria: truth and justice. Ethics is examining the relation of an individual to society, to nature, and/or to God. How do people make ethical decisions? They are influenced by how they perceive themselves in relation to goodness and/or excellence."[8] For our purposes, we divide ethics into two basic categories: business and communication.

- **Business ethics.** Business ethics is defined as the determination of various business practices, processes, and outcomes as right or wrong. Owen and David Cherrington[9] discuss twelve common ethical lapses that happen in modern organizations:

o   Taking things that do not belong to you (stealing);

o   Saying things that you know are not true (lying);

o   False impressions (fraud and deceit);

o   Conflict of interest and influence buying (bribes, payoffs, and kickbacks);

o   Hiding versus divulging information;

o   Unfair advantage (cheating);

o   Personal decadence;

o   Interpersonal abuse (physical violence, sexual harassment, emotional abuse, abuse of one's position, racism, heterosexism, ageism, and sexism);

o   Organizational abuse (inequity in compensation, performance appraisals that destroy self-esteem, transfers or time pressures that destroy family life, terminating people through no fault of their own, encouraging loyalty and not rewarding it, and creating the myth that the organization will benevolently protect or direct an employee's career are all examples of how organizations abuse employees);

o   Rule violations;

o   Accessory to unethical acts;

o   And moral balance (ethical dilemmas).

- **Communication ethics.** Communication ethics is defined as the determination of various organizational communication practices, processes, and outcomes as right or wrong. W. Charles Redding[10] created a typology of six different types of ethical problems commonly seen in organizational communication:

  o   Coercive (intolerance of dissent, restrictions of freedom of speech; refusal to listen; resorting to formal rules and regulations to stifle discussion or to squash complaints, etc.);

  o   Destructive (insults, put-downs, back-stabbing, character-assassination, using the untruth as a weapon, and not providing expected feedback);

  o   Deceptive (evasive or deliberately misleading messages, bureaucratic-style euphemisms designed to cover up problems, and 'prettifying' unpleasant facts);

  o   Intrusive (hidden cameras, the tapping of telephones, and the application of computer technologies to the monitoring of employee behavior, etc.);

  o   Secretive (hoarding information and sweeping information under the rug);

  o   And Manipulative-Exploitative (hiding one's true intentions and demagoguery).

Innovation. Innovation is the creating of something new. In the organizational realm, innovation can come in two distinct forms. First, innovation can be viewed as the extent to which an organization creates new and improved products and services. Second, innovation can also be organization's ability to strategically streamline processes, increase one's market share, increase one's competitive advantage, and so on. Organizations that value innovation will be able to adapt more quickly to changing environments than organizations that do not value innovation.

Obsolescence. Obsolescence is what every organization should fear and is often the result of a lack of innovation. Obsolescence occurs when there is a significant decline in customer desire for an organization's products or services. Obsolescence occurs for a variety of different reasons: availability of alternatives that perform better or have new features; availability of alternatives that are of equal quality and cheaper; product or service is no longer viewed as necessary in the current market; and changes in customer preferences or requirements. Over the years many organizations die out because they sunk all of their capital into creating one product or service that eventually became unnecessary or passé. Two classic examples (you may never heard of) are Genera Sportsware Company's Hypercolor clothing line (popular in the early 1990s, bankrupt in 1992) and the World POG Federation (popularity hit peak in 1993, bankrupt in 1995). While both of these organizations had numerous problems, one of the largest problems was that their income was based on a fad that quickly became obsolete.

Flexibility. The next qualitative criterion is flexibility, which refers to whether an organization, process, or decision can modify or adapt within a certain range and given timeframe. In environments that are highly chaotic, you need considerably more flexibility to adapt to changes than in environments that are highly stable. Ultimately, if you're in an organization where flexibility is very important, then a decision being made should be equally flexible.

Pragmatism. One of the hardest questions for some to answer is whether or not a given decision is actually pragmatic. Is the decision being advocated realistic or practical given the organization or the environment? When discussing some larger issues like innovation, sometimes decisions that are arrived at may be very lofty but not overly pragmatic. For example, if you're a small business, running a million dollar advertising campaign may be a great way to raise your market share, but it clearly wouldn't be pragmatic for most small businesses.

Ease of implementation. The last qualitative criterion is ease of implementation, which refers to the speed and the simplicity to which a decision alternative can be enacted. If an organization is making a decision in a highly chaotic environment, then having a decision that can be easily and quickly implemented becomes very important. If, however, your organization can take the time to implement a decision, then ease of implementation may not be a criterion your organization is overly concerned with at all.

Using Criteria

In the previous sections we've discussed the quantitative and qualitative criteria that can be used for making organizational decisions. Remember, criteria are tools that we use, as decision-makers, to help us evaluate or judge potential decisions. As such, the selections of the criteria we view as the most important, given a specific decision, are very important. **FIGURE 1** contains a short organizational communication case; before proceeding with this section please read the case.

Paternity Leave Shakedown

"Donald, bad news," Gerald Hardy said over the phone to his vice-president of Human Resources, Donald Lawrence, "I just spoke to our lawyer Marilee Marcus, and this sexual harassment lawsuit is definitely going forward."

"Gerald, I'm really sorry to hear that. I thought we were protected by our employee handbook, but I guess I was wrong," Donald responded with a clear sense of sincerity in his voice. "What do we do now?"

"Well, Marilee recommends we initiate immediate sexual harassment training for all employees, and she does mean ALL employees."

Two months ago, Jonathan Jeffries had come into his office asking for paternity leave, as he and his wife were adopting a child from China. Jonathan and Samantha Jeffries had been trying to have children for years with no success, so hearing that Jonathan wanted to use the paternity leave offered him through Ellet-Roe, a multi-media consulting firm, wasn't that big of a surprise.

The trouble started not in Human Resources, which was on board with the paternity leave program, but with Jonathan's immediate supervisor, Patricia Booth. The harassment started almost immediately. Patricia, who had three grown children of her own, thought Jonathan's desire to use paternity leave was a slap in the face to women. She started saying derogatory things in meetings to Jonathan, and even questioned Jonathan's manhood. Jonathan quickly went from one of the shining stars of Patricia's department to receiving a number of negative evaluations in the span of one month.

When Jonathan finally set up an appointment with Donald, he was clearly at his wit's end. Donald thought the meeting went pretty well. During the meeting, Donald explained to Jonathan that Ellet-Roe was progressive and purposefully had a progressive maternity/paternity leave to encourage the long-term stability at the company. As Donald frequently said to new employees, "We want to invest in both you and your family. When you have a strong, happy family at home, you'll be more satisfied and productive at work."

After the meeting, Donald contacted Patricia Booth and explained to her the corporate policies related to paternity leave and that Jonathan had every right to take the paternity leave. Donald thought his discussion with Patricia had been a little tense, but nothing in the conversation led him to believe that she didn't understand Ellet-Roe's position on the matter.

Unfortunately, Donald's conversation with Patricia led to an even tenser working environment for Jonathan. The final straw was when Patricia took Jonathan off of a project he'd been managing for the greater part of the year telling him, "Well, since you're going to be off in baby-land, let's let the grownups do the work around here." Instead of coming back to Donald or someone else in HR, Jonathan went to an attorney and filed a sexual harassment lawsuit against Ellet-Roe.

The day Ellet-Roe was served with the legal papers, Donald placed Patricia Booth on administrative leave pending an internal investigation. Donald tried to talk to Jonathan about the matter, but Jonathan informed Donald that he'd been advised by his legal counsel only to discuss matters with his counsel present.

Donald started talking to the people in his office about the legal suit. Upon further investigation of the matter, Donald came to realize that this wasn't an isolated problem. At least two other individuals who had attempted to take paternity leave had faced so much resistance that they had ultimately decided to quit. *Why hadn't anyone told me about this before now?* Donald thought to himself.

———

"Got it, Gerald, I'll contact one of our external vendors and find someone who can come in immediately and deliver this training." Donald hung-up his phone and wondered how this crisis had gotten this far.

Donald spent the next few days calling a range of external vendors he knew trying to get quotes for sexual harassment training. Donald finally zeroed in on two possible choices. One firm would charge $1,000 for the training, but the training was pre-designed, focuses primarily on male-to-female sexual harassment, but the firm could conduct the training immediately. The second firm would charge $5,000 for the training, but the training would be specifically tailored for Ellet-Roe addressing their specific problems. Unfortunately, the second firm could not have the training program ready for a few weeks (because of the time it takes to design the training).

Donald sat back in his chair evaluating the two proposals. He knew Gerald wanted a decision that afternoon. He reread the proposals, picked up the phone, and dialed Gerald's extension.

FIGURE 1 *Sample Case*

In any business-related decision, the types of criteria can vary. In some decision cases, all of the criteria could be theoretically applicable. For this reason, we recommend limiting the number of criteria you select to three (total—not 3 from quantitative and 3 from qualitative). Depending on the criteria that you select, you may end up with radically different types of decisions.

From the case, we learn that Donald, the HR VP from the case, finds two vendors who provide sexual harassment training. One firm will charge $1,000 for the training, but the training is pre-designed, focuses primarily on male-to-female sexual harassment, and can be conducted immediately. The second firm will charge $5,000 for the training, and the training is tailor-made for Ellet-Roe, addresses their specific problems, and will not be ready for a few weeks (because of the time it takes to design the training). Let's evaluate each of these decisions through a few different criteria.

The first criterion you could select would be cost. This criterion is easy to apply to this decision—one training package costs $1,000 and the other $5,000. If your primary criterion for evaluating this decision is cost, then selecting the training package that is $1,000 is the obvious choice.

Another possible criterion you could select could be staff-turnover. In the current case, Donald is feeling like he's being harassed by his manager, Patricia. If Donald believes this harassment is substantial and the working environment becomes too toxic, Donald may decide to voluntarily leave the firm (as two other employees have done in the past). If the organization's goal is to keep talent like Donald, then ensuring that all employees understand all facets of sexual harassment, which is clearly provided by the more expensive training firm, makes more sense. While the first firm may be cheaper, that firm really doesn't cover the current needs of the organization. If our goal is to prevent people from quitting because of sexual harassment, then making sure that the sexual harassment training is appropriately tailored for our organization is the more prudent decision.

Lastly, let's examine the case using a third criterion, communication ethics. One of W. Charles Redding's six types of organizational communication ethical lapses involves deceptive communication. Under this classification, we can argue that picking the cheaper sexual harassment program, while monetarily beneficial, actually doesn't fit the situation and is therefore just "prettifying" the current problem. One common problem with many organizations and training stems from a desire to actually train employees versus being able to say the employees have been trained. Actually training employees requires an organization to thoughtfully engage employees and ensure specific learning outcomes from training sessions. Being able to say employees were trained on the other hand is more like a check-list mentality to training. In this case, there is very little concern about actual learning outcomes, but rather the focus is on being able to say that the training has occurred. From this perspective, choosing the $1,000 option is akin to a façade, and really does not meet the employee learning needs. The $5,000 option has the potential of ensuring that the learning needs of Ellet-Roe's employees are met.

Hopefully, you can see how, depending on which criteria you select, you can end up with very different conclusions. Ultimately, the criteria that you select for evaluating possible decision alternatives will guide the decision-making process.

Once you've selected your three decision criteria, you also need to think about your criteria in terms of how you will measure these criteria. One of the goals of any decision criteria is to help guide the decision-making, but you need to have the ability to think through how these criteria will be achieved through the decision. For example, if one of your criteria is customer satisfaction, you need to ask yourself how a decision alternative will improve customer satisfaction. But you need to take this a step further and think about how will you know when customer satisfaction has been increased because of enacting your decision alternative. In other words, how are you going to measure customer satisfaction?

Obviously, the quantitative criteria have a pre-built-in measurement tool; that's why they are quantitative criteria. Qualitative criteria, on the other hand, still must be measured, but you, as the decision-maker, need to really think through how you will measure the specific criteria. In the case discussed in Figure 2, how would you measure whether or not a specific decision is communicatively ethical? While using Redding's six criteria for ethical organizational communication is one tool you could use to measure the ethicality of a decision, it's not the only way of evaluating communication ethics.

Overall, when it comes to selecting and using decision criteria, you need to really think through the selection, use, and measurement of the criteria you select. The last part of the worksheet discussed in Appendix A asks you to then rank the three criteria you've selected. We ask you to do this because often we have to make a determination of which criterion is the most important. If we had selected the criteria cost, staff turnover, and ethics as our three criteria for the case in Figure 2, we clearly need to know which criterion is more important to our decision making process. If we value cost more, then we would select the cheaper training program. If we valued staff turnover or ethics more, then we would select the more expensive training program.

Step Three—Identifying Solutions

The third of Gouran and Hirokawa[11] five basic steps of decision-making is identifying possible solutions. Some decision cases will come with pre-determined decision alternatives, but most cases will require you, the reader, to come up with possible decision alternatives. For the purposes of the Case Method, most case scholars generally agree that you should develop at least three well articulate decision alternatives. Nils Randrup[12] recommends four possible tools for determining possible solutions: visualization, experience, knowledge of other solutions, and academic discipline/theory/models.

Visualization. The first way to come to a possible decision is to really put yourself in the position of the main decision making character within the case. Really try to see the different issues and possible decisions from the main character's position within the story. Often when we put ourselves into the shoes of the main character, decisions will become very apparent.

Experience. A second way of generating possible alternatives comes from our own experiences in life. Maybe an organization you've worked in faced a similar dilemma. If so, how did your organization proceed? Maybe your organization made a good decision or maybe your organization made a horrible decision. Either way, using your own experience in various organizations can help you think of possible decision alternatives.

Knowledge of other solutions. We often hear about how organizations handle various situations through the modern press. Maybe you heard about a specific decision on the nightly news, or read about a decision in a business magazine like *Business Week*. In either case, we can use the decisions we hear or read about and apply them to the cases in this book.

Academic discipline/theory/models. The last way you can arrive at various decisions is through the application of academic content. Whatever textbook your professor uses in your organizational communication course, the book is filled with all kinds of theories and models that can lead to actual decision alternatives. One of the great things about the Case Method is the ability to take the course content you are learning and clearly apply that content to the decision-making process. I would recommend trying to find at least one decision alternative that clearly stems from your course readings. However, your professor may have other guidelines, so make sure you always follow your professor's guidelines.

Once you've created a list of possible alternatives, you really need to filter them into a list of practical and realistic guidelines based on the context of the case. Here are some helpful hints when creating and selecting decision alternatives:

- **Be realistic!** First, and foremost, the decisions that you arrive at should be realistic given the context of a given case. While it may be fun to ship all of your annoying coworkers to the moon, there are no cases where that would be a realistic alternative. Instead, really think through what types of decisions you think the main character could make in a given case;

- **Avoid overlap!** One problem that many new case analysts have is a problem with overlap. In other words, their decisions tend to overlap one another, making each decision fairly indistinguishable from the next. The goal of writing three different possible alternatives is to have three different alternatives. So try to make sure that all of your alternatives are mutually exclusive;

- **Decisions mandatory!** One copout that some people will try to use is just not to make a decision. Not making a decision is not allowable in a case-based class. You need to make a stand and really make a decision. While there are definitely some decisions that are better than others, not making a decision is generally going to get you nowhere in life;

- **Status quo!** While not making a decision is not a viable decision making option, keeping the status quo can be a viable decision alternative. There are some cases where not changing one's behavior or course of action can be appropriate. While I recommend you use this method of decision-making sparingly, you can definitely argue that the status quo is better than other possible decision alternatives in some cases;

- **Don't sandwich!** When I use the word "sandwich" here, I'm talking about taking two really weak decisions and then placing the one decision you like between the two weak ones. All three of the decision alternatives that you create for a given case should be strong and viable. While different decision alternatives may prove problematic when you evaluate them using your criteria, all of the decisions you create should be viable given the context of the case;

- **Think implementation!** At some point the actors within a case will have to implement the decision you have selected. Think through any possible risks or obstacles that could interfere with selected decisions. If a decision is ultimately not pragmatic given the confines of the case, then it's probably not a viable decision.

While these six strategies will help you think through the alternatives you come up with, there is no single best way to arrive at your three decision alternatives.

Step Four—Reviewing Decision Alternatives

Once you have created your list of decision alternatives, it's time to start evaluating those decision alternatives. First and foremost, we evaluate all of our decision alternatives using the decision criteria we selected prior to creating the decision alternatives. One reason why it is important to select your criteria first is because it prevents you from selecting criteria that specifically lead to one decision alternative. Think logically as you apply your criteria and really think through how each possible criterion either supports or doesn't support a given decision alternative. If you examine the Case Study Worksheet provided in Appendix A, you'll see that the various parts of analyzing the decision alternatives is broken down to help you take each criterion and see how it either supports or doesn't support each decision alternative.

Step Five—Selecting the Best Decision Alternative

Ultimately, you will select the decision alternative that you believe best supports the context of the case and is most supported by the decision criteria that you have selected. Once you've selected the criteria, then you need to start thinking about how the decision will actually play out as it is implemented. For our purposes, I broke down this section into two basic areas: goals and action steps.

Goals. The first step in the post-decision selection process is to think through the ultimate goals of the decision. What are the basic goals or outcomes that you hope to achieve by implementing your decision alternative? Additionally, based on how you decided to measure your criteria, think about how you will determine if your goal is being met? If your goal is to ensure that you are reducing problems of sexual harassment (as seen in the case in Figure 2), how will you determine if the training package you've chosen leads to a decrease in sexual harassment problems?

Action steps. Most decisions do not happen in a vacuum and often require a series of short-term and long-term action steps to fully implement the decision. Ask yourself, "What short-term and long-term steps do you feel are necessary to completely implement your chosen decision alternative?" In the case example we've been evaluating in this chapter, a short-term step may be the actual implementation and evaluation of the training program. A long-term step may be bi-annual training, or at least ensuring that the corporate policy is fairly implemented over a longer period of time. Most decisions involve some level of long-term monitoring to ensure the overall effectiveness of the decision made.

CONCLUSION

In this chapter I have introduced you to the basics of the Case Method. At first, the Case Method may seem a little clunky and hard to manage as you start evaluating cases and discussing the cases in your organizational communication course. As with any new skill, learning how to evaluate and discuss cases takes time and effort. If you really work through the case method before, during, and after class, you will quickly see how important a formalized decision making process is for the business world and in your own life.

---

[1]Gouran, D. S., & Hirokawa, R. Y. (1983). The role of communication in decision-making groups: A functional perspective. In M. S. Mander (Ed.), *Communication in transition: Issues and debate in current research* (pp. 168–185). New York: Praeger.

Gouran, D. S., & Hirokawa, R. Y. (1996). Functional theory and communication in decision-making and problem solving groups: An expanded view. In R. Y. Hirokawa & M. S. Poole (Eds.), *Communication and group decision-making* (2nd ed., pp. 55–80). Thousand Oaks, CA: Sage.

[2]Mauffette-Leenders, L. A., Erskine, J. A., & Leenders, M. R. (2007). *Learning with cases* (4th ed.). London, Ontario, Canada: Richard Ivey School of Business.

[3]Phillips, P. P., & Phillips, J. (2005). Return on investment (ROI) basics. Alexandria, VA: ASTD Press, p. 1.

[4]McCroskey, J. C., & Teven, J. J. (1999). Goodwill: A Reexamination of the Construct and its Measurement. *Communication Monographs, 66*(1), 90–103.

[5]Latham, G. P. (2007). *Work motivation: History, theory, research, and practice.* Thousand Oaks, CA: Sage.

[6]Berry, L. L., Mirabito, A. M., & Baun, W. B. (2010). What's the hard return on employee wellness programs? *Harvard Business Review, 88*(12), 104-112.

[7]Giacalone, R. A., & Jurkiewicz, C. L. (2003). Toward a science of workplace spirituality. In R. A. Giacalone & C. L. Jurkiewicz (Eds.), *Handbook of workplace spirituality and organizational performance* (pp. 3–28). Armonk, New York: M.E. Sharpe. (p. 8).

[8]Parhizgar, K. D., & Parhizgar, R. (2006). *Multicultural business ethics and global managerial moral reasoning.* Lanham, MD: University Press of America. (p. 77)

[9]Cherrington, J. O., & Cherrington, D. J. (1992). A menu of moral issues: One week in the life of the *Wall Street Journal. Journal of Business Ethics, 11,* 255–265

[10]Redding, W. C. (1996). Ethics and the study of organizational communication: When will we wake up? In J. A. Jaksa & M. S. Pritchard's (Eds.), *Responsible communication: Ethical issues in business, industry, and the professions* (pp. 17–40). Cresskill, NJ: Hampton Press.

[11]Gouran & Hirokawa (1983, 1996)

[12]Randrup, N. (2007). *The case method: Roadmap for how best to study, analyze and present cases.* Rodovre: Denmark: International Management Press.

ABOUT THE AUTHORS

Jason S. Wrench (Ed.D., West Virginia University) is an assistant professor in the Communication and Media Department at the State University of New York at New Paltz. Dr. Wrench specializes in workplace learning and performance, or the intersection of instructional communication and organizational communication. His varied research interests include workplace learning and human performance improvement, computer-mediated communication, empirical research methods, humor, risk/crisis communication, and supervisor-subordinate interactions. Dr. Wrench regularly consults with individuals and organizations on workplace communication and as a professional speech coach for senior executives.

Dr. Wrench has published five previous books: *Intercultural Communication: Power in Context, Communication, Affect, and Learning in the Classroom* (2000, Tapestry Press), *Principles of Public Speaking* (2003, The College Network), *Human Communication in Everyday Life: Explanations and Applications* (2008, Allyn & Bacon), *Quantitative Research Methods for Communication: A Hands-On Approach* (2008, Oxford University Press), and *The Directory of Communication Related Mental Measures* (Summer 2010, National Communication Association). Dr. Wrench is currently working on a series of book projects including a Public speaking book with Flat World Knowledge, a book on communication apprehension with Allyn & Bacon, and a two-volume series on organizational communication with Praeger. Dr. Wrench was the editor of the *Ohio Communication Journal* from 2005–2007, and has served as an associate editor for *Communication Research Reports* from 2007–2010. Furthermore, Dr. Wrench has published over 20 research articles that have appeared in various journals: *Communication Quarterly, Communication Research Reports, Education, Human Communication, Journal of Homosexuality, Journal of Intercultural Communication, Southern Communication Journal, The Source: A Journal of Education,* and *The NACADA Journal* (National Association of Campus Advising).

Le'Artis W. Allen, II (B.A., Kentucky State University) studied Mass Communication and Journalism at Kentucky State University. He focused his Bachelor of Arts in Public Relations, because it allowed him to use his planning experience for the overall benefit of the program. Mr. Allen currently is looking into graduate programs so that he can pursue a Master of Arts in Communication. Also, he is looking for a full-time position with a corporation so that he can get started with his career. His motto is, "Go forth and be great."

Carolyn M. Anderson (Ph.D., Kent State University, 1992) is a Professor in the School of Communication, The University of Akron. She teaches and researches small groups, leadership, health, and organizational communication at the graduate and undergraduate levels. She has taught in China and studied in Cuba and Poland. Publications include a textbook and several book chapters. Research articles have appeared in national and international journals. Several convention papers have earned top awards. Prior to the doctorate, she worked as a member of organizational teams and assumed leadership roles. She serves the community as a public speaker, trainer, and consultant.

Colin R. Baker (Ph.D., Michigan State University, 2007) is in his sixth year as a faculty member in the Communication Studies Area in the Department of Communication. Colin teaches graduate and undergraduate courses in Organizational Communication, Group Communication, Leadership Communication, and Research Methods.

Shannon M. Brogan (Ph.D., Ohio University, 2003) is an Assistant Professor of Speech Communication at Kentucky State University. Much of her research emphasizes Interpersonal, Instructional, and Organizational Communication. Dr. Brogan currently teaches undergraduate courses in Interpersonal Communication, Public Speaking, Institutional Communication, Interracial/Intercultural Communication, Oral Interpretation, Persuasive Speaking, and Group and Debate.

Audra T. Buras (M.A., Arizona State University, 2011) is a marketing and communications professional predominantly focused on corporate social responsibility, health communities, and other areas of philanthropy. Her current research is centered on the translation of organizational dissent research into instructional materials to be used in university courses and professional training.

Allison P. Burritt (B.A., State University of New York at Cortland, 2010) is a full-time student and working towards earning her Master's in Communications at the Roy H. Park School of Communication at Ithaca College.

Heather J. Carmack (Ph.D., Ohio University) is an Assistant Professor of Communication in the Department of Communication at Missouri State University. Her research focuses on communication produced by and surrounding health organizations as well as the different ways in which health is organized. She also focuses on organizational cultures and the different ways new organizational members are socialized. She has published articles in a variety of communication, education, and interdisciplinary health journals, including *Health Communication, Management Communication Quarterly, Qualitative Health Research, Qualitative Communication Research Reports,*

Journal of Medical Humanities, Communication Teacher, and others. She has also authored and co-authored several book chapters and case studies.

Danielle Clark completed her undergraduate degree at Keuka College, majoring in Organizational Communication with a minor in Applied Computer Applications. She received many honors at Keuka College including, the Maxwell Plaisted Award in Journalism and the Charles Wallis Memorial Prize in Humanities. She was also a member of the Keuka College President's Leadership Circle and the President of Lambda Pi Eta National Communication Honor Society. She is currently completing her Masters of Science in Communications at Ithaca College and she plans on obtaining a career in Public Relations or Human Relations upon graduation.

Lynn Cooper (Ph.D., University of Illinois) is an associate professor in the Department of Communication at Wheaton College. Dr. Cooper has taught courses in Organizational Communication for Wheaton College (IL) for over 30 years. Her students have successfully completed consultations for campus programs, for-profit businesses, and nonprofit agencies.

Robyn Fink, Caitlin Hamryszak, Adrienne Sliz and **Sarah Upperman** (M.S. candidates, Ithaca College 2011–2) are currently graduate students in the Roy H. Park School of Communications at Ithaca College. Each has a strong interest in the influence that communication can have on interpersonal relationships, in addition to interests in crisis communication, online collaboration best practices, and marketing in higher education. Fink, Hamryszak, Sliz and Upperman will finish their coursework over the next year and graduate with a M.S. in Communications. They will pursue careers in the communications field.

Shireen Kaur is a graduate student at Ithaca College in the Department of Strategic Communication. I grew up in New Delhi, India—a city which is very intriguing and famous for its diverse culture, traditions and cuisine. After getting a Master's degree in Clinical Research, I worked in the Clinical Research industry for 2 years. Not satiated with current level of education, I took up the idea of getting another Master's degree, this time in the field of Communications. My pursuit brought me to Ithaca College which is renowned for its program in communications. This master's program gave me the opportunity to reinforce my existing communication knowledge with a full academia education that I need for my career growth. Being an international student, I was thrilled to attend Ithaca College as it has all the benefits of the American educational system within a community that values diversity and promotes cross-cultural understanding.

Erin E. Gilles (Ph.D., University of Kentucky, 2009) is an Assistant Professor of Journalism at Kentucky State University. Her research areas examine entertainment media, health communication and advertising through a critical theory lens. Dr. Gilles currently teaches undergraduate courses in journalism, news editing, public relations campaigns, event planning, and digital photography.

Kris Grill is a doctoral student in the Department of Communication Studies at the University of Kansas. Her research interests are located at the intersection of Organizational and Interpersonal communication. Specifically, Kris investigates issues concerning mentoring in organizations as well as work-life issues affecting stay-at-home father/working mother families.

Brent A. Hogan (B.A., Southern Utah University, 2009) is working on receiving his Master's in Communications at the Roy H. Park School of Communication at Ithaca College. Majority of his research and studies have been within the communications realm. As a graduate student, he has been involved in courses such as: designing communication strategies, communication theory, communication campaigns, and research methods in communications.

Kimberly M. Hutchins (M.A., Arizona State University, 2011) is a marketing and communications professional in the Public Affairs Office at Arizona State University. Her primary line of research involves multiple facets of organizational dissent expressed on behalf of employees. Specifically, her current research concerns the translation of organizational dissent research into instructional materials to be used in university courses and professional training.

J. Jacob Jenkins received his B.A. in Architecture from Drury University, and his M.A. in Organizational and Interpersonal Communication from the University of Arkansas at Little Rock. Jenkins has traveled throughout China, Japan, Zambia, Zimbabwe, Botswana, Great Britain, and the United States fulfilling humanitarian work. He has studied abroad in France, Germany, Italy, and Holland. Jenkins is currently a doctoral student of Communication at the University of South Florida. His major areas of study include organizational and interpersonal communication, applied communication research, and qualitative research methods. His specific research interests include organizational purpose, identity, and leadership; organizational learning; and positive organizational change.

Lauren Jensen (B.A., SUNY New Paltz, 2011) is an undergraduate student in the department of Communication and Media at SUNY New Paltz. She studies organizational communication within the department.

Doreen Jowi (Ph.D., Ohio University, 2005) is an assistant professor in the Communication Studies and Theatre Arts Department at Bloomsburg University. Dr. Jowi specializes in Organizational Communication and Organizational Health Communication with particular interests in job attitudes, physician job dissatisfaction, and communication climate in supervisor-subordinate dialectics. Dr. Jowi is a coauthor of the forthcoming book *The Directory of Communication Related Mental Measures* being published by the National Communication Association.

Jeffrey W. Kassing (Ph.D., Kent State University, 1997) is Professor of Communication Studies at Arizona State University. His primary line of research concerns how employees express dissent about organizational policies and practices. Dr. Kassing teaches organizational, applied, and environmental communication courses, as well as research methods.

Michael W. Kramer (Ph.D., University of Texas, 1991) has researched the socialization/assimilation process for the last 20 years including his dissertation which won the ICA Charles Redding Dissertation Award in organizational communication and his recently published book, *Organizational Socialization: Joining and Leaving Organizations* (2010). He has published in journals such as *Communication Monographs, Journal of Applied Communication, Human Communication Research, Management Communication Quarterly, Academy of Management Journal*, among others. He has published chapters in the *Handbook of Communication Science* and *Handbook of Decision Making*, in addition to a number of other case studies.

Elizabeth Kranz is a native of Sayre, Pennsylvania and the only child of Michael and Mary Kranz. She graduated from Ithaca College in May 2010 with a B.S. in Communication Management and Design and a minor in Women's Studies. During her undergraduate years she received the honor of being inducted into the Lambda Pi Eta, Sigma Iota Epsilon, and Phi Kappa Phi honor societies. The passion she had for her undergraduate program compelled her to remain at Ithaca College for graduate school; she will be graduating in May 2012 with her M.S. in Communications. After graduation Elizabeth aspires to work in the field of Event Planning.

Anastacia Kuyrlo (Ph.D., Rutgers University) is Assistant Professor of Communication Arts at Marymount Manhattan College in New York City. She teaches courses in Interpersonal Communication, Advanced Interpersonal Communication Theory, Gender and Communication, Organizational Communication, Principles and Theories of Communication, Public Speaking, Intercultural Communication, Stereotypes and Communication. In her twelve years of teaching she has taught at numerous colleges including Borough of Manhattan Community College, Marymount Manhattan College, New York University, Pace University, Rutgers University, and St. John's University. Her research interests include the examination of stereotypes communicated in interpersonal, intercultural, and organizational contexts and the implications of these for stereotype maintenance. She also studies pedagogy and mentorship as well as emotion and culture. She has published five teaching activities, four book chapters, and her work on stereotypes appears in Qualitative Research in Psychology. She is a former President of the New Jersey Communication Association and serves as a reviewer or Editorial board member for several journals. She enjoys spending time with her family, creating mosaics, eating in cafes, and working on her research (especially with her undergraduate students).

Yao Li is a graduate student at Ithaca College in the Department of Strategic Communication. My undergraduate college is located in Tianjin, a city that has multi-cultural environment. And I always have the dream of exploring diverse culture experience, and be prepare for the economic and cultural globalization. I choose the Communication program in Ithaca College because it provides me a great opportunity to practice the knowledge that I learned from the class. Moreover, I am enjoying meeting people with different personalities and different cultural background. As an international student, it is exciting to experience the cultural shock and study the theoretical reasons behind the phenomenon as well.

Corey Jay Liberman (Ph.D., Rutgers University, 2008) is Assistant Professor of Communication Arts at Marymount Manhattan College. His research interests include the effects of organizational identification on work processes and job satisfaction, organizational and societal communication networks, social influence in interpersonal relationships and during the small group process, and persuasion in the context of health communication. Some of his most recent work differentiates cognitive social networks from behavioral social networks, examining both the theoretical and practical implications of both. He routinely teaches courses in interpersonal communication, small group communication, and organizational communication, focusing primarily on the role of social influence and communication networks in these three areas.

Rui Liu is a graduate student at Ithaca College in the Department of Strategic Communication. After finishing my B.A in French in China, I came to the U.S. for graduate school and to accomplish my rebel dream of leaving my hometown to a place far away, so that I can observe, explore, communicate, and understand a bit more of this world. Currently, I am a first-year graduate student in the Roy. H. Park of Communications at Ithaca College. Coming from a middle-sized city in China, Ithaca has all I want: cultural diversity, various cuisine and gorgeous waterfalls. I learned a lot of cool things in my program that I enjoy wholeheartedly, not to be polite. My research interest includes international students' adaption to their new life abroad and the role of ethnicity-based student organization in helping/hindering this adaption.

Franziska Macur is an Associate Professor for Communication Studies at Edgewood College in Madison, WI. Dr. Macur received her Master in Media and Communication studies and her Ph.D. in Communication studies from the University of Bonn, Germany. Dr. Macur teaches organizational communication and research methods classes. Her research centers on group dynamics and facilitation; and case studies in organizational communication.

Alfred G. Mueller II (Ph.D., University of Iowa, 2000) is Professor and Chair in the Department of Communication Studies at Mount St. Mary's University in Emmitsburg, MD. His research interests lie in the areas of political discourse and the rhetoric of the early Church Fathers. He has served as a Fulbright Scholar in Armenia and as a member of a bridging project with Moscow State University sponsored by the Ford Foundation. Dr. Mueller currently teaches undergraduate courses in the history of rhetoric, rhetorical criticism, persuasion, nonverbal communication, rhetorical leadership, and intercultural communication.

Nhung Nguyen is a graduate student at Ithaca College in the Department of Strategic Communication. I am coming from a village in the Central of Vietnam. After finishing my undergraduate program in the Academy of Communications and Journalism in Hanoi, the capital of Vietnam, I spent one year struggling to get the governmental scholarship to go to the U.S for the graduate program of Communications at Ithaca College. When I put my first step in Ithaca, I knew that my everlasting dream lastly came true. It was the dream that grew up with me day by day to fly far beyond the mountain ranges in front of my village to see the world and to learn from the adventure. One year and a half studying at Ithaca College really helps me broaden my vision and deepen my knowledge on my communication program; especially, it helps me to explore what I really want to do and who I would like to be. Now I am focusing on doing research on business coaching under the support of my advisor. I hope that this research would provide the employers with a better approach to enhance their employees' working performance, and for me, I long for its application to the business that I will set up for myself in the near future.

David R. Novak (Ph.D., Ohio University, 2006) is an Assistant Professor in the Department of Media and Communication at Erasmus University Rotterdam in The Netherlands. His research focuses on organizational communication. Specifically, he studies social change organizations in light of democratic values and community life. Dr. Novak currently teaches courses in organizational communication, applied communication and research methods.

Leah Omilion (Ph.D. Candidate, Wayne State University) specializes in organizational communication with an emphasis in behavioral research and crisis communication. She is also a marketing communication specialist in a Detroit area hospital.

Timothy M. Pearce (B.F.A., Binghamton University, 2010) is pursuing a Master's in Communications at the Roy H. Park School of Communication at Ithaca College. Tim is currently working with an advertising firm based in Binghamton, New York, and aspires to work within strategic communication planning.

Caryn E. Quinn (B.A., State University of New York at Geneseo, 2010) is pursuing a Masters in Communications at the Roy H. Park School of Communication at Ithaca College. She is currently working for a marketing firm based in Syracuse, New York, and is interested in a career in public relations.

Juliann C. Scholl (Ph.D., University of Oklahoma, 2000) is Associate Professor of Communication Studies at Texas Tech University. Much of her research emphasizes interpersonal interactions as they are influenced by organizational structures, health care communication, and crisis management. Dr. Scholl currently teaches undergraduate and graduate courses in leadership, organizational communication, business and professional communication, small group communication, health communication, and training and instruction.

Melissa Smith B.A., Kentucky State University) studied Mass Communication and Journalism at Kentucky State University.

Jiuzhen Shen is a graduate student at Ithaca College in the Department of Strategic Communication. My hometown is Beijing, the capital of China. City-born and city-bred, I can surely tell that I'm a pure city animal. But, deep in my soul, I like adventure. There was one time that I rode to Nanjing—7 days, 1200 Km—with two of my friends. There was another time I caught a thief without any help. After getting my B.A. in material modeling and engineering, I chose to work in an advertising company. This job is not as exciting as I expected, so I decided to take a bigger challenge—coming to Ithaca College to learn communication. 10,000 Km away from my family, totally new major, different culture, small town, occasionally I felt like my head was overheated. In fact, I was wrong. I learned a lot from all of these above, even the weather—how cloud is gathered and what is happening inside the rain. Now, I am a poised communication graduate student with a multi-culture background and a rational mind, feel fearless to the future.

Lara C. Stache (M.A., Northeastern Illinois University, 2009) is a Ph.D. student of Communication at the University of Wisconsin—Milwaukee. Much of her research focuses on alternative communities and the creation of a group identity, with an emphasis in rhetoric. Lara currently teaches undergraduate students in interpersonal communication and has taught organizational communication courses during her Master's study.

Marlane C. Steinwart is an assistant professor in the Department of Communication at Valparaiso University. She earned a Bachelor of Arts in Communication in 1988 and a Master of Arts in Liberal Studies in 1991, both from Valparaiso University. In 2009, she completed a Doctor of Management in Organizational Leadership from the School of Advanced Studies at the University of Phoenix Online. From 1989 until 2000, Dr. Steinwart worked in Information Technology in the area of user support. She quickly learned that the most rewarding part of the job was helping non-technical people understand technical things. The realization that she enjoyed teaching led her to accept a fulltime faculty position. Dr. Steinwart is very interested in technology and how it continues to shape the lives of humans. Watching first-hand how college students were addicted to technology caused her to wonder how it would affect them as the next generation of workers. Ultimately, this curiosity led to her dissertation: *Can You Hear Me Now? A Phenomenological Study of the Net Generation's Workplace Communication Skills.*

Elizabeth Tolman is an Associate Professor at South Dakota State University. She serves as Director of Graduate Studies for the Communication Studies Master's program and is also Coordinator of the Women's Studies program. Her research interests include gender and communication, service-learning, and online instruction. She completed the first Online Instructor Certification Program (Basic Level) at South Dakota State University in the fall 2010. Finally, she received a Service-Learning Teaching award for her contributions to service-learning at South Dakota State University in April 2011.

Diana L. Tucker (Ph.D., Southern Illinois University, Carbondale, 2003) is a member of the Core Faculty in Communication for Walden University's Centre for Undergraduate Studies. Her research has focused on areas of sport, gender and organizational rhetoric. She has taught mainly in public relations and organizational communication in past positions, but currently is co-administrator for Walden University's basic communication courses and teaches these courses (introduction to communication, public speaking, interpersonal, mass communication and intercultural) as well.

Thomas R. Wagner (Ph.D., Kent State University, 2005) is Assistant Professor of Communication at Xavier University. His research explores persuasion in interpersonal contexts and interpersonal processes in various settings. Dr. Wagner teaches courses in interpersonal communication, persuasion, organizational communication, and research methods. Co-authors **Anne Baker, Bekah Ford, Jenna Giorgione, Mary Kniffin, Maria Konerman, Nathan Locklear,** and **Laura Wallace** were undergraduate Organizational Communication majors at Xavier University.

Heather L. Walter (Ph.D., State University of New York at Buffalo, 1999) is an Associate Professor and Graduate Coordinator in the School of Communication, The University of Akron. She teaches and researches conflict and organizational communication at the graduate and undergraduate levels. Publications include several case studies, book chapters, research articles that have appeared in national and international journals, and dozens of conference presentations, the most recent earning a top three faculty paper distinction.

Robert Whitbred (Ph.D., University of Illinois) is an assistant professor in the School of Communication at Cleveland State University. His research interests include investigating the dynamics of emergent communication networks and understanding how mission statements facilitate or inhibit organizational effectiveness.

Jeff Youngquist (Ph.D., Wayne State University) teaches organizational communication and interpersonal communication classes at Oakland University. His primary research focus is on the influence of language and sex on perception. His research has also explored student resistance to diversity-related topics when taught in homogenous classroom environments.

—PART I—

ORGANIZING COMMUNICATION

CHAPTER

1

Status Update:
The Ethics of Facebook Checks in the Hiring Process

*Thomas Wagner, Bekah Ford, Mary Kniffin,
Maria Konerman, and Nathan Locklear*

XAVIER UNIVERSITY

ABSTRACT

Ed is a college senior who has worked hard as an intern with a medical supply company and hopes to be a new hire. He is also eager to share his wild party life with the world on Facebook. This case study examines the ethics of Facebook checks as a tool for making hiring decisions.

"I saw what you posted on Facebook last night!" Laura says to Ed with concern, "Aren't you worried that John might check our profiles? We are trying to get a job here!"

"You really think John is going to Facebook-stalk me? Come on! What I do on my time is my business." Ed replied with a nervous laugh.

"If the page is set as public, then there's nothing about the information on those pages that isn't public, right?" Laura questions.

"Well, no I hadn't really thought of that. Wouldn't that be prying?" Ed tries to ignore Laura's comment and buys her another drink.

Ed and Laura are two college interns at Ohio Medical Affiliates (OMA), a large health care provider that provides a wide array of services including urgent, pediatric, and elder care. The company also has a large medical distribution branch that supplies many hospitals and health care facilities across the Midwest.

Ed and Laura work in the company's medical supply distribution division. The company boasts a strong internship program that attracts many students because of the variety of career paths OMA offers, but also because OMA hires many of its interns to full-time positions upon graduation.

The company would love to hire Ed and Laura as full-time employees upon their graduation. Initially, both interns were told that they were likely to obtain full-time positions; however, the distribution division has taken several hits including increased competition and new federal regulations that limit the amount of interstate medical sales. The division is forced to make cuts and there simply isn't enough money or work to hire two new employees.

Ed and Laura have been exceptional interns, performing well above normal expectations. Ed took the lead on a project to develop new delivery routes for drivers, while Laura came up with excellent marketing and advertising ideas. In addition to their scheduled time, the two interns put in an average five to six hours of extra time every week to finish projects. Their accomplishments make it clear that both Ed and Laura take their positions seriously and work hard. It is evident that they equally deserve the open position.

Ed and Laura are good students with very little difference in grade point average and academic achievements. Ed earned a 3.6 GPA and was on the dean's list five times and Laura is an honors student with a 3.3 GPA. They are both very active in the university. Laura is one of the chairs on the student events planning committee. Ed has served as president of the club swim team since his sophomore year. He is also a member of the school's senior board.

"Laura, what was on my Facebook page that made you bring this up?" Ed asks.

"Ed, are you kidding me?" Laura laughs as she grabs her phone to access Ed's page and reads, "Status Update: 'The coach is an idiot! He needs to wake up and play Robinson!' Status Update 'Going to Charlie's Pub for two dollar drafts and partying hard till the sun comes up!' Status Update: 'Blame it on the a a a a a alcohol baby!!!' Ed, come on, what were you thinking posting this stuff?" Laura then scrolls through her smart phone looking at the numerous pictures of Ed at wild parties and bars, drinking and clearly intoxicated. Ed is passed out drunk in embarrassing and sometimes inappropriate positions in several images.

"You gotta admit, it's funny right?" Ed says with an embarrassed smile. "What's on your page anyway?"

Ed tries to grab Laura's phone and she quickly puts it in her purse and says with a smile "No, no, you have to buy me another drink if you want to see my profile."

After spending another four bucks for Laura's micro-brew, Ed asks again for her phone. He reads her page, "Status Update: 'Huge term paper due…looks like it's going to be an all nighter.' Status Update: 'Come to the student union today and show your support for Students Against Child

Violence.'" After reading the posts aloud, Ed starts scrolling through the pictures Laura has on her Facebook page. Instead of excessive drinking, Laura and her friends just appear to be hanging out. Many are with her family and pets. There are also pictures of her volunteering at a local children's center and helping out at different service events. Her status updates are usually about schoolwork or her volunteer efforts. Ed is amazed at the difference between the two pages. While Ed knows his performance hasn't been lacking, he worries that his personal life could affect the hiring process. "Wow, didn't know someone's Facebook page could be so G-rated. You're practically a Disney character here."

"It's all about creating a personal Brand," Laura replies. "If you want to be viewed as professional, you need to present yourself professionally."

One week later, Ed receives the news, via e-mail, that Laura was hired for the full time and he has to move on. After receiving the bad news Ed is extremely upset. He believes he has done everything he can to be the best employee for the organization. Although Laura is also qualified, he really feels he deserves the position because of the leadership he has shown through his extensive work on internship projects. Unsure as to why Laura was chosen over him, he decides to go to the office and ask John, his supervisor, for an explanation.

As Ed enters the office, John welcomes him, "Hello Ed. How are things going?"

"Not so good," Ed admits. "I wanted to talk with you about the full-time position. I'm really not sure why I didn't get it, and wondered what more I could have done to earn it. I've worked so hard here. Is there anything I did wrong? I just don't understand your decision."

"Well, honestly, I was having a lot of trouble deciding between you and Laura," John replied before briefly pausing and then saying , "until I looked at your Facebook pages. Frankly, both of you were equally qualified, but the content of your page and your conduct on the weekends is not consistent with our values here. We don't want to promote a 'party' image as acceptable at OMA. Your personal life could catch up with you and affect work performance. And to be honest, making such portrayals of yourself publicly available makes me question your judgment."

"What I do at home has nothing to do with my work. I've never let it affect my work and I know my limits. Look, I know that there is a time and a place for certain things. I'm sorry, but what right do you have to look at my private information?" Ed asks, stunned at the invasion of privacy.

"The information wasn't private, Ed," John counters. "All I did was type in your name. Any client could see the same things."

"That still doesn't give you the right to pry into my personal life," Ed argues. "Even though the pictures and text are public, they represent a personal part of my life that isn't related to work."

"If you really feel that way, you should have made your page private. I'm sorry, Ed, but I just have to look out for what's best for the company and your Facebook page has given me evidence that you may not be it."

Upset about what he thinks is an unfair decision; Ed goes to visit his mom to vent some of his frustrations. As Ed's mom pours him a cup of hot coffee, he tells her the bad news about his job.

"I didn't get the full-time position at OMA."

"What?!" his mom asks, surprised. "I thought you were both practically guaranteed the job. What happened?"

"Well, there's not enough money and work for them to hire us both," Ed explains.

"But you've always worked so hard. Did they explain why Laura got the job over you?"

"Well, apparently now what you do on your personal time is used to assess job qualifications," Ed replies, his voice rising in anger.

"What do you mean?" his mom asks surprised.

"They looked at our Facebook pages to make their decision. They said all the pictures of me partying and drinking made them worry that it would affect my work." He pauses and tries to calm himself down with a sip of coffee. "I don't understand. It never has before! Isn't that ridiculous?"

"I've warned you that it was a bad idea to post those pic—"

"But it's none of their business!" Ed interjects before his mom can finish.

"Hold on, let me finish," Ed's mom replies calmly. "I understand why you're upset, but you're the one who made the information public with a Facebook page. Think of it as a background check."

"I understand that background checks with past employers and criminal records are necessary," Ed concedes. "But first of all, a background check is work-related information and second of all, you are told before they do it! They should tell people if they're going to check Facebook pages."

"Do you tell your friends before you look at their Facebook pages?" his mom challenges.

"Whatever, I didn't want to work there anyway," Ed says as he grabs his jacket. "I'm going to Andy's to watch the game."

Ed is still upset and disappointed that he did not get the support he expected from his mom. He plans to talk to his friend Andy about Facebook snooping. Andy is working as an intern at a public relations firm. Ed believes that if anyone knows how it feels to put in long work hours, it's Andy. What he probably doesn't know is what it feels like to have all of the hours go to waste because of his personal life.

"So what kind of pictures did you post on your Facebook?" Andy asks during a commercial break. "Were there any that were worse than the ones I've seen?"

"Andy, my pictures are just of our weekends," Ed responds defensively. "I am not doing anything that bad. If I haven't already proven that my work was better than anyone else and that my personal life doesn't affect my work, I'm not sure how to prove it."

"I know," Andy replies, shaking his head. "I mean, your Facebook page is for your friends. You post those pictures because they're for us to look at, laugh, and remember good times, definitely not for an employment decision!"

"My mom said I should have taken all of the pictures down," Ed recalls. "But I think I should have been forewarned that my personal life was going to be judged. After all, they tell me every other aspect of the hiring process. Why should this part stay a secret?"

"It shouldn't," Andy agrees. "If they are going to probe into your private life, your friends, and your weekend whereabouts, I agree you should be warned. I was told that I was going to have my Facebook page checked for my internship so I took down that album from spring break. I'm sorry Ed. I really don't think it's fair either. I don't know what to say. We can go drinking tomorrow night after work if you want to talk more about it."

"I think I'll be fine, man. Maybe I should go through and remove some pictures and posts from my Facebook tonight, though," Ed proclaims as the game resumes.

Later that night, Ed goes through his Facebook and untags the pictures he wouldn't want potential employers to see. Despite his mood, he chuckles and remembers the good times captured in the pictures. Some of them make him cringe, though; until now, he hadn't realized how frequently he was drunk and how evident it was in his photos. Still, he thinks he should have been warned about the check. As he finishes untagging pictures, he receives a text from Andy:

"Hey dude. Time to cheer you up! Come out to Lana's for a drink. No cameras, I promise."

Ed decides that it might make him feel better to get out. As he enters Lana's, he notices Laura with her friends. He approaches her to congratulate her on the full-time position. As he gets closer, he notices she is visibly intoxicated.

"Yeah, girls! Let's take another shot!" she yells so that the whole bar can hear.

Ed laughs to himself and offers his hand to Laura. "Congrats on the promotion, Laura. I think you'll do great."

"Awww, thanks, sweetie," Laura responds as she gives Ed a hug. "Let's get a picture of you and me. OMA interns! Lucy, take a picture of us!"

Lucy looks at Laura reproachfully and says, "I'm sorry, Laura. You know our rule: no pictures of us girls on the weekends. They could end up on Facebook."

"Oh, that's right. Gotta keep it professional! I only put the goody, goody stuff on my Facebook you know," Laura tells Ed with a wink.

"Hey, well congrats again. It was nice seeing you. Good luck at OMA," Ed says as he walks away to find Andy sarcastically wonders if he should take some pictures of Laura tonight and send them to John. Ed is challenged to determine if it is right to hide a personal life for the sake of a job and at what point a person's behavior outside of work is a company's right to scrutinize.

DISCUSSION QUESTIONS

1. Do you consider it an invasion of privacy if an employer checks a candidate's public Facebook page? Why or why not?

2. Under what circumstances is it okay to use a Facebook page as part of the hiring process? For example, is it acceptable if applicants are notified that their page is going to be viewed?

3. Is Facebook effective in determining a person's professional character or would it be impossible to determine a person's work qualifications based on the personal life a Facebook page presents?

4. Does an employer have the right to check a public Facebook page in determining qualifications, or is the duty of the applicant to make it private if he/she really wishes for it not to be judged?

KEY TERMS

Web 2.0, hiring process, organizational socialization, work-life balance

CHAPTER 2

Bad for Your Health Organization

Heather J. Carmack

Missouri State University

ABSTRACT

An employee at the Office for Patient Satisfaction decides to file a hostile work environment claim against her manager when the department director refuses to take action. Several independent conflict mediators determine that the manager is creating a hostile work environment, but no changes are made to the organization. How far should the employee go to deal with a hostile work environment?

Amelia sat in the large conference room, anxiously drumming her fingers on the table. As the communication coordinator at the U.S. Department of Health and Human Services' Office for Patient Satisfaction (OPS), Amelia had dealt with her fair share of conflict between patients and providers. However, she never thought that she would be involved in a conflict. She glanced down at her watch. 7:40 AM Twenty minutes to go before she met with the Department Director, her manager, and the lawyers. Amelia thought to herself: How did it get to this point?

A CHANGE COMES

Everything was going well at OPS. As a communication coordinator, Amelia's job was to organize and run all of OPS's public events and medical workshops. Four years ago, Amelia was promoted to the chief communication coordinator of OPS's new program, Medical Team Training (MTT). The OPS director also hired Dr. Ted, a cardio-thoracic surgeon, to head up MTT. The MTT program was designed to teach doctors and nurses how to better communicate with each other in order to prevent conflict and medical mistakes. Wanting an interdisciplinary team that would truly represent interdisciplinary cooperation and communication, the OPS hired another physician and two nurse educators to work with Amelia and Dr. Ted. For two years, the 5-person MTT team flew across the country, training doctors and nurses on effective communication strategies. The MTT program flourished, becoming the crowning achievement of the OPS.

But then, two years ago, everything changed. The OPS Director, Dr. Patrick, decided to replace Dr. Ted. Amelia enjoyed working with him, he was well-liked and respected by the hospitals the team visited, and his job reviews were outstanding. Whatever the reason, Dr. Patrick decided that Dr. Ted was out and Dr. Lora was in. Because Dr. Patrick made the decision to replace Dr. Ted unilaterally, Amelia didn't know much about Dr. Lora when she arrived. On her first day, Dr. Lora held a "get to know me" MTT meeting. Amelia was hesitant about the new manager and how she would connect with the government physicians. Dr. Lora had not practiced her specialty, obstetrics and gynecology, or any medicine in almost twenty years. Instead, for twenty years she had been "consulting." However, Amelia trusted Dr. Patrick. He must have made this decision because Dr. Lora was outstanding and would be a wonderful asset to the program.

It didn't take long before Amelia realized that was not the case.

FEELING THE HEAT

For the first few weeks, everything seemed to be going well. Because she didn't know anything about the program, Dr. Lora observed the team working on coordinating site visits and presenting to physicians and nurses. One of Amelia's primary jobs on the MTT program was to coordinate logistics of site visits. This often involved calling the hospital and working with hospital staff to organize the visit, finding and reserving rooms and technology, and creating different communication elements to advertise the visit. Because nurses and physicians are both important participants of the program, the calls often involve the team and several physicians and nurses from the hospital they are visiting.

Amelia first started to notice a problem on a site call with a Boston hospital. Halfway through the phone conversation, the hospital's surgical nurse manager began asking questions about the role of the program in helping nurse-nurse conflict. She explained, "For us, one of the biggest problems we have is with nurses' conflicts. I am interested in how the program helps—"

Dr. Lora cut her off. "This program is about making doctors the best doctors they can be."

Amelia looked up from her notes, shocked. "She just means that the program's focus is on helping doctors and nurses communicate better with each other. What we discuss in the program is about the two groups. We don't really focus on nurse-nurse conflict. But, that would definitely be something to think about incorporating." She quickly wrapped up the call and walked back to her office, disturbed by the fact that she would say that when the program was all about bringing the two groups together. Dr. Lora's disregard for nurses and their concerns continued in other site visit calls, and Amelia found herself constantly smoothing over potential conflicts.

And the nurses noticed. At each hospital, the physicians and nurses filled out comment cards about the team members. Nurses from several hospitals commented on the fact that Dr. Lora was ignoring them. One comment card said bluntly, "She doesn't seem to like nurses very much. Why is she here?"

Once home, Dr. Lora decided to make some changes to the program. At the team's next meeting, Dr. Lora announced, "Well everyone, after attending several programs, I have some ideas to really streamline the program. There are a lot of what I would call 'useless' sections in the program. So, I've decided to cut the section on nurses and the section on communication."

Amelia looked at Dr. Lora, puzzled. "I'm sorry, Dr. Lora. I don't understand why you would cut those sections."

"Well, I don't think the physicians really care about those topics."

Kylie, a nurse on the team, injected, "But Dr. Lora, the program is about medical teams, and nurses are an important part of the medical team. And we are trying to get the groups to communicate with each other."

Dr. Lora sighed slightly, "Look, I know you both want those sections because you present those, but I've decided we don't need them. We need to focus on the physicians. This is not up for discussion."

"But what will Kylie and I do at the presentations? Are we not going anymore?"

"That's not my problem, Amelia," Dr. Lora snapped.

Amelia left the meeting with an uneasy feeling. If she wasn't doing the MTT presentation anymore, was she still working with MTT?

Dr. Lora's changes didn't stop with eliminating Amelia and Kylie's sections. Amelia noticed that Dr. Lora's behavior started to change. Now relegated to setting up the technology and running the registration table, Amelia noticed that Dr. Lora had stopped helping with the presentation step up. Instead, Dr. Lora sat in a chair and watched the other team members set up. During the presentations, Dr. Lora would cut off speakers during their sections and make changes without informing the team. Physicians and nurses at the presentations became frustrated when Dr. Lora changed all the examples to her medical specialty, and recommended the staff do things that contradicted with hospital policy. The comment cards continued to express a frustration in Dr. Lora's lack of medical practice and knowledge of contemporary medical procedures.

Back at the office, Dr. Lora began yelling and cursing at team members. She treated Amelia as her personal assistant, demanding that Amelia performed secretarial tasks for her. When Amelia pointed out that several of the assignments were not part of her job, Dr. Lora screamed, "You work for me!" Dr. Lora also began to withdraw from the team. She started requesting to stay at different hotels than the team. She would leave presentations early to go to the airport to get earlier flights. She insisted that the team eat meals together, but created a list of places they "just couldn't eat at" because she didn't like the food.

The workplace became a battleground, Amelia unsure when Dr. Lora would start yelling at her or calling her names. She would yell at the office receptionist when she couldn't get a flight that she wanted or when she was not approved to stay at a different hotel. In meetings, she began questioning the "competence" of "non-doctors" like Amelia to even participate in MTT.

Noticing the tension between Dr. Lora and the team, Dr. Patrick named Dr. Shane, the other physician on the team, co-manager of the MTT program. Unfortunately, Dr. Shane's new appointment did not help the situation. Dr. Lora would engage in yelling matches with Dr. Shane. She started to openly dismiss team members, telling Kylie that she was not needed in meetings anymore because "she didn't contribute anything." The other nurse educator was told she was no longer allowed to attend meetings. Dr. Lora decided that Amelia, who did not have a medical degree, was not allowed to attend meeting, telling her in an e-mail, "You are intellectually beneath us." After a week, Dr. Shane asked Amelia to attend the meetings because she was the only one who knew the procedures for calling and organizing with hospitals.

TAKING A STAND

A month passed and the tension in the office kept mounting. Dr. Lora continued her office yelling matches with Dr. Shane. Amelia began to feel very uncomfortable at work, dreading each day when she turned off the alarm clock. Amelia decided to take action after one meeting in early February. Amelia, Dr. Shane, Dr. Lora, and Kylie were on a phone call with a hospital in Georgia, finalizing the dates for their visit in March. When she rose to get a drink of water, Dr. Lora dropped a pile of papers on the floor. Dr. Shane, who had gotten up to get a drink, bent over to pick up the papers. As he did, Dr. Lora said, "I like a man on his knees."

Amelia's eyes widened with embarrassment, stunned by the comment. Did she mean that in a sexual way? Dr. Shane's face reddened and he quickly sat back in his chair, tossing the pile of papers to Dr. Lora's side of the table. Amelia turned her head when she heard a throat clearing and realized that the phone was still on speaker; the entire organizing staff in Georgia heard Dr. Lora! Flustered, Amelia wrapped up the phone call.

The next day, Amelia, Kylie, and Reese decided to file a formal complaint with Dr. Patrick. At the meeting, Amelia spoke about how Dr. Lora's behavior changed. "It's like she's a different person, Dr. Patrick. She doesn't contribute to the team at all."

"It's not even a team anymore," added Reese, a nurse educator. "She's kicked us all off the calls and cut our parts of the presentation. It's as if she just wants to run the program herself."

Recounting the most recent event with Dr. Shane, Amelia continued, "I think she is creating a hostile work environment."

Dr. Patrick leaned back in his chair. "Interesting. Dr. Lora told me that you three were being hostile to her. I know it's been a rough transition, but I think you three just need to learn to adapt to Dr. Lora's leadership style."

Amelia wasn't sure what she was hearing. "So, what are you saying, Dr. Patrick?"

"I'm saying that I think this is just a little growing pain."

To help defuse the situation, Dr. Patrick asked Brian, a former physician with whom he had practiced, to serve as an independent conflict consultant. Dr. Patrick asked Brian to observe the group working and see if he could identify who and what was causing the conflict. Brian spent two weeks in the office, observing the team work together and sitting in on meetings. He also interviewed each team member. A week later, Amelia found a copy of Brian's memo in her mailbox. She steeled herself to what it might say. Surprised, her eyes zeroed in on two sentences:

> "After observing and speaking with the team members, I believe that Dr. Lora does not know how to communicate and work effectively with the team. I would recommend that Dr. Patrick reassign Dr. Lora to a different project that does not involve dealing intimately with other people."

Amelia took a deep sigh of relief. Brian agreed with the rest of the team! Amelia walked quickly down the hall to Kylie and Reese's stations to see if they had read the memo. Knocking on their office door, Amelia's smile immediately vanished when she saw their faces. "What's wrong? Did you guys see Brian's assessment?"

"Yes, we saw it," said Kylie. "So did Dr. Patrick. He just sent out this e-mail."

Amelia leaned over Kylie's shoulder to read the e-mail. Titled "The Assessment", Dr. Patrick's e-mail said, "As you may have read, Brian's assessment suggests that Dr. Lora be reassigned to a different project. However, after my meeting with Dr. Lora, I have decided that she will stay on as co-manager of MTT."

Amelia looked at the computer screen, deflated. "So he's not going to do anything." She paused. "So, what is our next option?"

MAKING IT OFFICIAL

Frustrated with Dr. Patrick's decision, Amelia and her teammates decided to file a formal hostile work environment claim against Dr. Lora, listing Dr. Patrick as a secondary offender. As government employees, everyone at OPS is in a union. After meeting with their union representative, Amelia, with the help of Dr. Ted and Dr. Shane, compiled a 75-page complaint, complete with a 20 page appendix of e-mails, correspondence from others outside the office, comment cards from presentations, and the original consultation report from Brian. Dr. Lora and Dr. Patrick received a copy of the complaint. A dispute resolution specialist assigned by the Department of Health and Human Services read over the complaint, interviewed all parties and arranged a meeting among Amelia, Kylie, Reese, Dr. Lora, and Dr. Patrick.

Amelia looked up from her watch as the dispute resolution specialist entered the conference room. The dispute resolution specialist opened his folder and turned on his tape recorder. "Alright. Thanks everyone for coming to today's meeting—"

"We can't start yet," Dr. Patrick interrupted. "Dr. Lora isn't here yet."

The specialist looked down at his watch. "Oh. I have 5 after 8. Do you know when she is going to get here?"

"No. I told her the meeting started at 8."

The group sat in silence, waiting for Dr. Lora to arrive. Amelia looked at her watch. 8:20. "I think we should get star—" began the specialist, only to stop because Dr. Lora arrived. She entered with her attorney. Not apologizing for her tardiness, Dr. Lora sat down. "I want to start with a response to the claim." Dr. Lora's attorney pulled out a few sheets of paper.

The specialist paused. "Okay, I guess we can start with your response. I was going to provide a brief overview of the situation so that everyone is on the same page."

Dr. Lora sighed loudly. "Fine! But I want to make sure my response gets on tape."

"Of course. I am tape-recording the whole session. Anything you say will make it into the transcript of today's meeting," said the specialist. "I was just about to explain why we are meeting here today. Amelia, Kylie, and Reese have filed a hostile work environment claim against Dr. Lora and Dr. Patrick. I have interviewed all parties, so today's meeting is about talking through some of the issues I noted in the interviews. Dr. Lora, do you want to read your response?"

Dr. Lora cleared her throat. "The first claim Amelia, Kylie, and Reese make is that I don't acknowledge nurses. However, in the conversation from December, I clearly acknowledge a nurse. From their own document, and I quote, 'Dr. Lora: Good morning, Dr. Dean. Dr. Dean: Good morning, Dr. Lora.' This example clearly illustrates that I talk to nurses."

"Excuse me a minute Dr. Lora," the specialist interjected. "Isn't that example of you saying hello to another doctor?"

Dr. Lora paused. "Oh. Well, then it's an example of how I am nice to people." Dr. Lora continued for several minutes, providing two more responses for why she was not creating a hostile work environment. "In closing," she read, "I believe that Amelia, Kylie, and Reese are merely trying to get Dr. Ted back. I've already notified Dr. Patrick that if I am removed from the position I will file a discrimination claim."

Surprised, the specialist looked at Dr. Patrick. "Dr. Patrick, are you aware of this?" the specialist asked.

"Yes. Dr. Lora and I have had many conversations about this situation. However, I don't believe the claim that Dr. Lora has created a hostile work environment. I think these girls have simply not been able to adapt and are upset that Dr. Lora cut their parts of the presentation. I also don't believe that all of that evidence is real."

Amelia's eyes widen at the comment. Before she could comment, that specialist jumped in. "Okay, this is good start, but the purpose of this meeting is to provide some responses to comments made in the individual interviews. So, everyone received copies of the interviews I did. Does anyone have any questions or comments about things said in the interviews?"

Amelia spoke up. "I have some questions about comments made by Dr. Patrick in his interview. First, Dr. Patrick, you said, and I quote, 'Amelia and Kylie are illiterate girls who are only doing this to get Dr. Ted back. I believe they were both engaged in a sexual relationship with Dr. Ted.' You also said, 'Once this situation is over, you will rectify the problem.' I am curious, Dr. Patrick, why you would say that two women, both with Masters Degrees, would be illiterate? What is it that we can't read? How could two illiterate 'girls' put together a 95 page document? Also, when you say you will rectify the situation, are you suggesting that you will fire us for filing this claim?"

"Uh, well, uh," Dr. Patrick stumbled. "I didn't mean that you were illiterate. Of course, you can read. I think that might be a typo in the transcript."

"Well, that's what it says," Amelia continued. "Neither you nor Dr. Lora actually addressed our concerns. You didn't say anything about her elitism, the name-calling, or yelling. Dr. Shane even said that he thinks she is being hostile and he's the co-manager of the program."

Dr. Lora spoke up. "You are just trying to get me fired because you are threatened by the fact that I am a woman in a leadership position."

Amelia interjected, "If you read over the document, we never once ask that you be fired. We are simply asking that you be moved to another project, as recommended by the first consultant."

After an hour, the specialist ended the discussion, noting that he had all the material he needed to make a decision. Amelia left the conference room feeling emotionally exhausted.

A week later, Amelia received the specialist's decision. His executive summary and decision were succinct:

> "Based on my assessment of the original claim, the individual interviews, and the responses provided by the Dr. Patrick, Dr. Lora, and the claimants, it is my conclusion that Dr. Lora is creating a hostile work environment. It is also my conclusion that Dr. Lora has on several occasions sexually harassed members of her team. It is my recommendation that she be removed from the MTT program and assigned work that does not involve members of this team."

Amelia collapsed in her chair, relieved. Dr. Lora created a hostile work environment. The specialist thought she should be sent to work on a different project. Her relief was tempered, however, by several sentences near the end of the report. It read, "I have provided my recommendation for this claim. If Dr. Patrick decides not to reassign Dr. Lora, the claimants may file another grievance with Dr. Patrick's superior at the Department of Health and Human Services."

Amelia thought about that last line. Dr. Patrick could still refuse to make any changes? They might have to go through the process again? Amelia sighed. It was still a victory, she thought as turned the page to read Dr. Patrick's addendum. Her excitement deflated, she read Dr. Patrick's decision to not take any action recommended by the conflict specialist. Dr. Lora would remain in her position as the MTT program manager and there would be no disciplinary action.

Amelia leaned forward, hanging her head in her hands, thinking about her next step. She could continue to pursue the case, filing a claim with the Department of Health and Human Services. *But am I emotionally ready for a continued fight, she thought?* She could take the small victory, drop the claim, and hope that Dr. Lora would change. *I don't see that happening,* she thought as she smiled to herself. Or, Amelia thought with trepidation, *I could just resign and find another job myself.*

DISCUSSION QUESTIONS

1. What should be Amelia's next step? What are the reasons for this decision?
2. If you were in the director position, what would be your decision? What are the reasons for this decision?
3. How do issues of power in superior-subordinate relationships impact Amelia's case?
4. How do the different components of the Circle of Conflict help to make sense of Amelia's conflict?
5. What kinds of conflict styles are used by the employees of OPS? How do these conflict styles contribute to the outcome of Amelia's conflict?

KEY TERMS

Organizational conflict, harassment, dispute resolution, power

CHAPTER 3

A Snapshot of Ethics:
Managing Sensitive Information

Erin E. Gilles, Shannon M. Brogan, and Melissa Smith

KENTUCKY STATE UNIVERSITY

ABSTRACT

The marketing director of a small technology company, EcoSnap, recently arrived with his marketing team at an ecology-focused technology conference. While at the conference, he received a call from the CEO informing him of a company merger to happen that day. The marketing team had been working for months to launch a new product, and was going to unveil it later that afternoon. After learning that the whole team was going to be fired, the marketing director wondered if his team should still present the new product, and when he should tell them that they had been let go.

Gwendolyn Talbot, the marketing director of EcoSnap, a leading innovator of recycled cameras and tech gadgets, was just waking up in sunny San Antonio before the upcoming Recycle Mania Expo at the downtown convention center. It was 5 AM on the first day of the three-day expo, and her company was scheduled to unveil their new product in a presentation at 3 PM As the sun rose, Talbot booted up her laptop to go over the presentation. She looked at her cell phone, wondering if it was too early to call Team Eco, the team in charge of launching the new Eco50, a digital camera made of 50% post-consumer waste. Talbot knew that there was nothing like it in the industry, and the conference would be buzzing about it in a few hours.

After her morning jog, shower, and breakfast, Talbot was the second of the foursome to arrive on the golf course at 8:47 AM She was jittery, knowing that this meeting with major distributors could make or break the first year's retail sales. Brushing aside her nerves, Talbot stepped forward and grabbed a club out of her golf bag.

An hour later, Talbot was two under par and hitting it off with the executives. As they approached the fourth green, the cell phone in her pocket vibrated letting her know she had received an e-mail. Fearing a problem from Team Eco, Talbot hit the button linking her with her e-mail account. To her surprise, the new message was from Darrell Hightower, the CEO of the EcoSnap. Talbot felt apprehensive, as this never meant good news. The subject of the e-mail was less than reassuring, "Possible Management Restructuring." Talbot heard her golf companions joking behind her, but her concentration was on the contents of the e-mail. With a shaking hand, Talbot opened the e-mail. Her mouth dropped open; she was not prepared for this information.

Despite her jangling nerves from the contents of the e-mail, Talbot managed to put the swirling questions out of her mind as she rejoined her fellow golfers.

"Anything amiss, Gwendolyn?" Pauline Frazier, head technology buyer for a major retail chain, asked.

"Just an e-mail from my husband, Trevor, asking where he can find the spare package of diapers," Gwendolyn said, laughing. "Mitch, it's your turn," she said with a bright smile.

TEAM ECO PREPARES

Ansel Fox pulls his suitcase behind him at 8:25 AM as he heads to his room on the 17th floor of the hotel. His nerves were frazzled after the multiple connecting flights to San Antonio from Los Angeles, where EcoSnap was headquartered. Fox was the leader of Team Eco, and he had been fielding text messages, phone calls, and e-mails all morning. The team was ready to make their 3 PM presentation at the Recycle Mania Expo. Per their company policy, the presentation group was coming in on different flights. They planned to meet Fox in the hotel restaurant for breakfast at 9:30 AM

Fox entered the restaurant and saw his group at a corner table overlooking beautiful downtown San Antonio. They were smiling and joking, and seemed confident about the upcoming presentation. Fox felt proud of his team, and was looking forward to unveiling the Eco50 camera. He greeted his team and joined them at the table.

Twenty minutes later, as the waitress was refilling Fox's orange juice, his phone buzzed as Talbot's name appeared on his caller ID. Fox felt a moment of panic when he saw Talbot's name. Fox knew that Talbot was spending the morning wooing distributors on the golf course. As Fox answered the phone, the tension in Talbot's voice was a clear indicator that something was wrong.

"Ansel, Gwendolyn here. We've got a problem. I just received a cryptic e-mail from Darrell Hightower. There's been an unexpected merger, and news is going live at noon."

Fox felt like he had been punched in the stomach. He took a breath, and tried to maintain his composure. "Gwendolyn, we're launching the new product at 3, and the team has been killing themselves to prepare. Is the presentation still on?"

By this time, the laughter and chatting at the table had subsided, and the team was staring at Fox. They knew something serious was happening. The team strained to hear Gwendolyn's part of the conversation.

"Listen, Ansel. I can't say much more at this point, I'll meet up with you after I finish golfing. Let's plan to meet at 12:45 in the hotel lobby."

As Fox disconnected the call, he looked at the three expectant faces of his team members. Fox realized that he had asked Talbot about the upcoming presentation, but had failed to realize that more than the product launch at the Expo was at stake. There was no guarantee the product would ever hit the market now, due to this unexpected merger. For that matter, there was no guarantee that any of them would still have their jobs.

With a sense of dread, Fox explained to the team what Talbot just communicated to him on the phone call. Although he was fighting panic, Fox knew that as the team leader he had to remain calm to keep morale high.

THE MERGER BEGINS

Fox and the rest of Team Eco had been pacing around the hotel lobby since 12:30 PM It was now 12:56 PM, and Talbot was never late. At 1:05 PM Talbot appeared with an official press release in hand.

Talbot approached the team and removed her sunglasses. The team noticed the worry etched around Talbot's eyes. "I've got news, guys, and it's not good," Talbot said. "The press release version says that we are merging with TechnoSavvy, Inc., the software giant out of Cupertino, CA. However, this basically amounts to a hostile takeover, and these guys play hardball. We still don't know much at this point, so let's get some coffee and focus on the presentation."

Two espressos later, Fox's team was sitting in an empty conference room with Talbot at 2:30 PM The mood was subdued as the team ran through their parts of the presentation. They had just begun gathering their things to head to the presentation room when Talbot's phone beeped with a new e-mail. Talbot didn't recognize the name Diane Callahan, but the e-mail's subject, "Update from the new Director of Human Resources," certainly caught her attention. As she opened the e-mail, Callahan's memo said that effective immediately, the team working on the Eco50 digital camera is being cut due to the merger. While she was reading that, the screen flashed indicating another message. This e-mail came from the new CEO, Harry Hine, and Talbot feared that it was more bad news.

Dear Mrs. Gwendolyn Talbot,

As the new CEO of TechnoSavvy, Inc., formerly known as EcoSnap, I would like to thank you and Team Eco for your service and dedication to the Eco50 product line. I know that the launch of the new recycled digital camera will be a success based on your hard work. Although we are not able to provide positions for you within our organization, I know that such consummate professionals will have no trouble finding work. Although I know that this unfortunate news comes at a bad time, I have no doubt that your professionalism will ensure that your presentation will not be affected by the organizational changes occurring.

Sincerely,

Harry A. Hine
CEO of DigiSoft

MORALS IN QUESTION

Talbot exited the e-mail, and wondered what she should do. After all of these months of hard work preparing to unveil the new camera, TechnoSavvy was about to reap the rewards and steal the glory. There was nothing that Talbot could do to salvage the situation. The team had been working overtime together for months, and they had started to feel like family. As the marketing director, she needed to make a decision with them in mind, as well as herself.

With just minutes to spare before the presentation, Talbot wondered if they should still present the new Eco50 recycled digital camera. There were a million thoughts racing through her head. Should she call Ansel now before the presentation?

Should she tell her team now that they have all been let go? She knows that she must tell them; however, will this add too much stress before their presentation? Should they have the right to make this decision as an individual and/or as a group? She felt torn between her loyalty for the company that had provided a stable life for her and her family for so many years, and the personal relationships she had established with her coworkers. Talbot wonders if they should all just call it a day, since they have been let go. Talbot knows that the team members' names are printed in the Expo program for the launch, so skipping the presentation could damage the team members' reputations and possibilities for future employment. Many key decision-makers in the technology field were attending the conference. The countdown is on, and her final decisions as marketing director could end up being the most important of her career.

DISCUSSION QUESTIONS

1. If you were in Gwendolyn's position, would you tell your team about their impending downsizing?

2. Do you think it is ethical for Gwendolyn to wait until after the presentation to break the news?

3. Was it ethical for Harry A. Hine to expect the team to proceed as if nothing was happening in the organization?

4. Do you think firing someone via e-mail is an ethical way to let someone know they've been terminated?

5. If you were Harry A. Hine, how would you have handled this situation differently?

KEY TERMS

Business ethics, technology, internal communication

Learning the Job

Michael W. Kramer

UNIVERSITY OF OKLAHOMA

ABSTRACT

Jamie's faces challenges trying to learn a new job as a department manager for a large store. There is the need to ask for information and a need to appear competent. In addition, there are the problems of how to respond when things are not as expected.

Jamie had only been working for the big box department store for a few months. It was not the ideal job for a recent college graduate, but at least it was a management position—albeit manager of the shoe department. Times were tough and many recent graduates were still looking for jobs. At least money was coming in and with a little experience there would be advancement opportunities either within the company or, hopefully, somewhere else.

The first few days had been taken up with training sessions. The store manager, Chris, had given Jamie some surprising news the first day on the job. "Jamie, it's company policy that all new employees, regardless of their position, have to complete the video training program. I know you don't really need it, but around here policy is policy. Besides, you'll get paid your full salary while you're doing it."

With that, Jamie was led to the back training room/break room with other new employees to sit through some rather slick corporate videos that presented a rather idealized picture of the company image, its supportive and diverse culture, its career opportunities for employees, and its programs that supported the community through volunteering and donations. Jamie actually felt pretty good about the company after viewing these videos. There were also a few videos on safety and loss prevention, code words for preventing employee and customer theft. Jamie was surprised at how inattentive most of the other new employees present were. They seemed to see little value in watching the videos. Jamie wondered if they would have even turned on the videos if someone from management had not been there.

Once the video training was over, the training got a lot more interesting since it involved other department managers and store management. Chris introduced Jamie to the two most experienced department managers, Pat in electronics and MJ in household goods. Chris told them, "This is Shawn's replacement in shoes. I expect you two to mentor Jamie on the job of department head. You know, the usual things like procedures for hiring and firing employees, maintaining and ordering sufficient inventory, and maintaining the store appearance. And of course, Jamie, my door is always open if you have questions these two can't answer." That turned out to be one of the longer interactions with MJ, who always seemed to be too busy when Jamie wanted to talk about some issue. As a result, Pat became the only reliable source of official policy.

Jamie found that Pat was reasonably helpful explaining how to read the memos and reports from corporate headquarters, showing how to use the computer system to accomplish most of the simple tasks, and providing advice on how to manage some of the more common employee problems like scheduling employees, most of whom were part-time. Pat suggested, "You'll be tempted to try to please everyone by working around their schedules. If you do that, you'll go crazy. Give it a decent effort and then just fill in the schedule. It doesn't matter if they're happy. It matters that you have enough employees to serve the customers. But remember, it's important not to have too many either. You want customers served, but you don't want employees standing around with nothing to do either."

Jamie learned most of the job by observing other department managers as they interacted with employees or from just by doing the job. Within a couple weeks, the inventory issues were under control because there was enough information in the computer system from previous months, quarters, and years to make that easy enough. That course in college on inventory management actually applied here, too. When it came time to change the seasonal line up to include more winter boots and accessories (it seems that the "shoe department" included a lot more than shoes), Jamie felt comfortable asking for some additional help on this new task from Pat, who provided valuable information on discounting and displaying the going-out-of season items to make room for the new products.

Jamie felt a lot less competent when it came to the continuing problem of having the right number of employees on the job at all times. One Saturday, he thought he had the right number of employees scheduled based on the volume of sales the previous two Saturday, but he forgot that there was a big game in town that day and no one came shopping. Of course, Chris came by the department that day and commented, "There seems to be a lot of employees with nothing to do."

The next Saturday, Jamie cut back, but it seemed like every grey-haired person in town came in the store that day. They all wanted individual help, even though most of them didn't buy much. It turned out that all the seniors received their social security checks that Friday. That time

Chris remarked while passing by, "It looks like you should have scheduled a few more people so customers don't have to wait. Remember, customer service is what sets us apart."

And of course, Jamie couldn't do anything about the weather. If the weather was too nasty or too nice, people would stay away, but if it rained just the right amount, it seemed like everyone headed to the store.

For the first couple months, Pat patiently answered Jamie's questions and provided additional suggestions for managing this staffing problem. But no matter what Jamie tried, something always seemed to happen that made it turn out wrong. Having already asked Pat for help so many times, Jamie felt that the grace period was over and it was time to quit asking questions to give the impression of competence. Recently, Jamie realized that the flexibility to assign employees to organize the storeroom or get out on the floor help to make it look like the staffing was correct even when it wasn't. Recently, Jamie concluded to himself, *maybe the real secret to staffing is just making it appear as if it's right by moving employees around, but I better not ask anyone in case I'm wrong or in case I should have figured this out sooner. I don't want to get a big "Duh" from someone.*

In considering the situation further Jamie thought, *I'd feel a lot more comfortable asking Pat questions if I had a chance to talk informally. The experienced store managers seem to go out to happy hour after closing about once a week, like almost every Saturday when the store closes early. How come none of them ever invites me to join them? I've been here over three months. Maybe it has something to do with Shawn quitting after just four months. Maybe they're waiting to see if I'll last. Or maybe I just ask too many questions.*

There were some other surprises, too. For example, it turned out that the diverse culture heralded in the corporate training videos was more of a mirage than a reality. At entry-level positions, which were mostly part-time, there was a rather diverse set of high school and college age students in the company, but after that, when it came to full-time positions, it seemed that it was a pretty homogeneous group. Jamie wondered if anything could be done to change that. Hopefully, the reason for the disparity was something other than bias, but it was hard to tell after such a short period of time. Optimistically, the lack of diversity had more to do with the location of the store than anything more disturbing.

Just this evening Jamie stumbled onto a new problem while working in the back of the storeroom. Two employees who were organizing the front of the storeroom talked without realizing they could be overheard. They discussed store closing procedures. Each night after the last customer was out of the store, the employees did a "walk-through" with either the store manager or one of the department managers. This involved all the employees walking together through the store to make sure everything would look good when the store opened the next morning. If something was wrong, they all worked together to fix it. Jamie was surprised to hear one of the "best employees" talk to a recent hire about this procedure.

"I hate store closings. Last night we were here until almost 10. At nine o'clock I want to get out of here."

"What were you all doing? Following what that stupid video said you were supposed to do?"

"I guess so."

"Hasn't anybody explained how we really do things here?"

"I guess not."

"Well, let me tell you the trick on closings."

"Okay. I've got places to go at 9."

"Here's the secret. The managers only walk down the main aisles. They never go down the smaller ones. And they only look at the first few feet of each aisle. If that looks good, they move on. The middle of the aisles don't have to look that good and the side aisles can look like crap and they'll never notice if they can't see it from the main aisle. So during the last half hour, just make sure the last 10 feet along each main aisle look good and you'll be out in no time."

"I wish I had known that sooner."

"And one more thing—always pick out one end-cap to leave messy. That way the manager finds it and gets to frown at everybody while you fix it. It makes him think he earned his pay for the evening. And it only takes about two minutes. And if he doesn't notice it, then you didn't do any extra work."

"Thanks for the tip."

"Spread it to the rest of the newbies. We can't be working until 10. I got places to go, too."

Jamie was in shock. Here was one of the best employees, who won "employee of the month" last month, teaching a new employee how to cut corners. But the bigger problem was what to do and whom to talk to about it. No one, including Jamie, liked getting out late and it wasn't like this was a career job.

DISCUSSION QUESTIONS

1. What different types of uncertainty does Jamie face in learning a new job?
2. What were some of the main surprises or unmet expectations that Jamie experienced?
3. How should Jamie balance the need to ask for information to do the job effectively with the need to appear independent, competent, and informed?
4. What are some of the ways that the organization's official values, policies, and practices differ from the organization's informal norms?
5. What should Jamie do after finding out that one of the best employees was teaching other employees poor work habits?

KEY TERMS

Socialization, uncertainty management, unmet expectations, group norms

From Paris with Love:
A Communication Case Study of Organizational Learning

J. Jacob Jenkins

UNIVERSITY OF SOUTH FLORIDA

ABSTRACT

Dunlop & Dunlop hired Mia to rescue them from the brink of bankruptcy. After eighteen months with the firm, Mia has accomplished just that. Despite increased revenue and productivity, however, she still wonders whether true Organizational Learning has occurred. Can Mia leave Paris with her head held high? Will the organization continue to adapt and grow even after she is gone, or will it stagnate and eventually die?

DECISIONS, DECISIONS

She would miss the wine, that much was certain. Mia made a mental checkmark in her head beneath the column: "Reasons to Stay." She would also miss *Le Grenier a Pain,* her favorite bakery. Parisian pastries were unlike anything Mia had ever tasted in America. Moving back to the states would mean no more chocolate tarts for breakfast or almond bread with dinner.

On the other hand, Mia thought, accepting the new job in Los Angeles would mean being closer to her sisters. She made a check under the column: "Reasons to Go." It would also mean a promotion, a better work schedule, and a considerable pay raise. Check, check, check.

What concerned Mia more than anything though—what truly made her decision difficult— was whether Dunlop & Dunlop was ready for her to leave. As a specialist in Organizational

Development, Mia was hired to help the advertising firm become a Learning Organization. Dunlop & Dunlop had certainly made progress during Mia's tenure, however, had the firm learned *how* to make progress? Had it become a truly adaptive system, capable of change after she left, or had Mia merely dragged the organization from Point A to Point B? Dunlop & Dunlop had spent the previous twenty years at Point A. Would it spend the *next* twenty years at Point B?

Mia glanced at her phone. She had less than ten minutes until the afternoon staff meeting, a meeting at which Mia's boss planned to award her recent accomplishments. Little did anyone know that Mia's acceptance speech might also be her public resignation. She exhaled audibly and swiveled to face the window. Beyond the mansard skyline of Paris stood Sacre-Coeur Basilica in the distance, its white silhouette prominent against a blue-rich sky. "Reasons to Stay:" check.

BEYOND POINT B

Nathaniel Dunlop leaned his body into Mia's office, offering to usher her toward the afternoon staff meeting. Mia had made the mistake of calling her boss "Nate" when she first arrived in Paris. She had walked into the conference room with an outstretched hand, "It's an honor to finally meet you in person, Nate. I'm excited to work alongside you and the other employees of Dunlop & Dunlop." Her greeting was not well received. She later tried "Nathan," but that didn't seem to work either. She eventually settled on "Nathaniel," like everyone else.

Needless to say, Nathaniel was a conventional man. He had inherited the firm from his father, who inherited it from his father, who inherited it from his father. He was not about to let some fresh hire call him "Nate." After all, there were customs to uphold and traditions to maintain. This sense of tradition, ironically, was one of the main reasons Dunlop had hired Mia to begin with. Nathaniel's resistance to change was also the primary reason she now found herself concerned about leaving the firm. Had Nathaniel truly come to see himself as a learning team member? Would he still allow margin for negative feedback, even after Mia had left? Would he encourage his firm members to reassess their own goals, without Mia there to keep him accountable?

Questions continued to swirl in Mia's mind as she entered the conference room. Other employees soon began to spill in. A long, mahogany table plugged the space, seating well over twenty people. Latecomers stood around the room's edges, leaning against wood paneled walls. It was a full house.

Nathaniel called things to order, silencing the pre-meeting talk. "As you all know," he began, "it's been a banner year for Dunlop & Dunlop. We've brought an entirely new philosophy to the Dunlop firm. In the process, we've increased our clientele, opened two new divisions, and raised revenues by nearly 30%." A polite applause filled the room.

Nathaniel continued, "It's impossible for me to discuss our recent success without acknowledging the work of Mia." He stepped from behind the podium to place his hands on Mia's shoulders.

"Before Mia arrived, we'd been trying to break into the television market for years. We'd tried everything we could think of; we'd spent millions courting FOX and MSNBC. With Mia's help, we took a step back and reassessed our goals. By doing so we realized online advertising was what best suited our firm's abilities. Not television. We've since integrated viral promotion into our ad campaigns. We've begun using interactive and contextual marketing. And as a result, our advertisements are reaching more people than ever before."

As another round of applause began to fill the room, Mia continued to contemplate her decision. She had witnessed several positive changes in the organization and, yes, quarterly revenues were up nearly 30%. Yet Mia was still concerned. After all, Nathaniel was not the only employee of Dunlop & Dunlop who was resistant to change. There was also John sitting across from her, who only seemed concerned with his own performance. Every time Mia introduced a new idea, John always wondered aloud how it would affect his sales numbers. He never asked about the impact her ideas might have on the firm as a whole. Not once. Then there was Samantha. Samantha was consistently offering excuses for why she had not implemented the changes Mia suggested, blaming everything and everyone. Other than herself.

Of course, there were bright spots among the staff as well. The creative department, for instance, had begun working alongside the production team. Meanwhile, account services had begun checking with research and development before making major decisions. Dunlop & Dunlop had also created a unified vision for its future, centered around the concept of "Live More. Live Creative." As a result, many of the firm's employees had reinvigorated their personal lives. Nick had finally proposed to his long-time girlfriend. Libby had finally booked that hike to Machu Picchu she had been planning for years. This newfound passion had spilled over into Nick and Libby's work lives as well, resulting in deepened goals and focused energies.

A third applause filled the room, breaking Mia's chain of thought. Suddenly, she realized people were looking at her. They were waiting for her to take the podium and offer an acceptance speech— or else, a resignation.

MOMENT OF TRUTH

Mia swallowed her face with a gulp. She stood and walked to the vacant lectern, gripping its margins with white knuckles. She glanced around the room, from John to Samantha, Nick to Libby, still unsure of what her final decision would be.

"Thank you for your kind words, Nathaniel. But I can't take all the credit for myself…" Mia paused, allowing Nathaniel a moment to reply.

"Please," he said, "call me *Nate.*"

A grin leaked across Mia's face, as she considered what her final decision might be.

"Reasons to Go": checkmate?

DISCUSSION QUESTIONS

1. Do you think Mia will choose to leave Dunlop & Dunlop? Why or why not?

2. If Mia does leave, do you think the organization will continue to increase revenue and productivity without her? Why or why not?

3. Within this story, can you identify at least one of Senge's (2006) five disciplines of a learning organization?

4. How is double-loop learning exemplified in this story?

5. What common obstacles for organizational learning are represented by the employees John and Samantha (Common, 2004)?

6. What positive consequences of organizational learning are represented by the employees Nick and Libby (Senge, 2006)?

KEY TERMS

Organizational learning, adaptive systems, double-loop learning, second-order learning

Organizing for People without Homes:
How Does Structure Impact the Organization?

David R. Novak

ERASMUS UNIVERSITY ROTTERDAM

ABSTRACT

This narrative takes place at the offices of StreetNews, which is a street newspaper that is sold by people without homes or people at-risk for homelessness. The story takes place in a major American city. In this story, James feels the need to go speak with Denise, the Executive Director of StreetNews about some organizational issues that he and some other vendors find troubling.

It was a hot, sunny July afternoon as James sat in the break area of the air-conditioned *StreetNews* offices with a few other vendors. Most of them were escaping the heat of the sweltering summer day. Water, ice, and fruit were available on a nearby table. The vendor break room at the *StreetNews* office was located centrally on the first floor of the three-story *StreetNews* building. The *StreetNews* building was purchased more than 10 years ago in what was then a run-down part of town; the area is now undergoing significant gentrification. The first floor of the *StreetNews* building contained not only the vendor break area, but also the cage where vendors bought their magazines for the day, the vendor manager office, a very small kitchen, and two bathrooms.

"Did you see that game last night?" Vince questioned.

"No, I'm not a big baseball fan," James responded setting down a stack of magazines at his feet.

"A come-from-behind win in the 9th inning!" exclaims Vince. "Still in 2nd place though."

"That's good. Sorry man, I've got a lot on my mind. I'm about to go upstairs to talk to Denise about some things."

"What kind of things?" asks Vince.

"You know, vendor issues, problems I'm hearing about on the street," says James. "This one vendor told me last week that a panhandler forced the vendor off of his street corner that he's been selling at for over a year. The vendor called the police, but the cops wouldn't help. The panhandler was threatening him, I guess. We've got to do something about this stuff!"

Vince, "You're right, man. The upstairs doesn't know what it's like to be out on that street all day."

James, "Nah, they don't. All they do is write the articles and print the copies. They don't know what it is like out there! They don't know what it is like down here. They never come downstairs!"

"Are you going to talk to her about the vendor representative issue? We've got to get that fixed," says Vince.

"Yeah, I'm going to bring that up. The vendors have no representative now. It can't stay like that. Heck, we should have two or three vendor representatives on the Executive Board. Not just one!"

"You said it," agrees Vince. "They need to start paying more attention to us down here. Heck, without us, there is no *StreetNews*!"

"Yeah," says James.

"Hah, well, have fun talking to her," Vince jokes.

"Thanks."

THE *STREETNEWS* ORGANIZATION

StreetNews is a non-profit organization that seeks to help the city's homeless and near-homeless people help themselves. It does so by offering opportunities to sell *StreetNews* magazine to earn a living and gain valuable skills. *StreetNews* is nationally recognized as one of the top street publications in the country.

Street publications are a widespread medium of news and advocacy on behalf of homeless persons. Nearly every large city in the United States (and many in Europe) have a street publication. Most operate on an entrepreneurial model with the goal of allowing people in poverty to earn some money. Generally, people interested in selling the publication purchase the magazines or newspapers from the organization. Then, vendors are allowed to go into the city, sell that publication for a higher price and keep the profits. Moreover, homeless organizations like *StreetNews* offer important services and help to enhance civic life by fostering discussion about homelessness as a social issue.

Currently, *StreetNews* has an Executive Director as well as six full-time employees and two part-time employees. In addition, a 21-member Executive Board drawn from local businesses and community organizations oversees *StreetNews*. All Executive Board members volunteer their time.

Another body of personnel at *StreetNews* is the vendors. The official *StreetNews* vendors are bound by a set of rules that are published in every edition of the magazine. Among these "rules of the street" are using a legitimate *StreetNews* ID badge, selling only the current issue, selling issues for $2.00, using professional language, being courteous when dealing with all members of the public, refraining from asking for donations, cooperating with other vendors, and selling the magazine while drug-free and sober.

Together, the employees and volunteers make up *StreetNews'* seven major "departments." The organizational structure places the magazine vendors atop the organizational chart. The vendors have a direct line to the Executive Board which, in turn, connects to the Executive Director. The needs of these three organizational bodies are served by three additional departments: the editorial staff, the advertising staff, and vendor management. Finally, an administrative services department serves the entire organization.

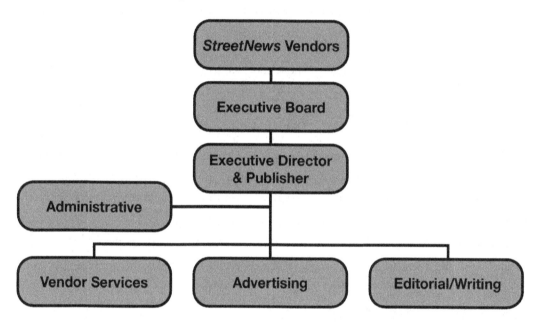

James Garcia sells *StreetNews* magazines for a living. James lives in poverty and, at times, has been homeless. James is one of 450 vendors that sell *StreetNews* magazine annually in the city. James buys the magazine wholesale and sells the publication at retail, keeping the profits. He can buy as many magazines per week as he likes. The new edition comes out every Tuesday.

James has worked for *StreetNews* for around three years and knows the organization quite well, as he is one of the vendors who sells magazines consistently. James often takes his breaks at *StreetNews* office, where coffee, water, and snacks are provided. James has even held a vendor supervisor position, where he walks the streets of the city to count how many vendors are selling the magazine and the locations in which they are selling. James, having previously owned his own business, has some strong opinions about how *StreetNews* is run.

THE ORGANIZATIONAL STRUCTURE OF *STREETNEWS*

After getting permission from Ray, the staff member selling papers by the entrance, James heads up the long staircase to get to the second floor of the *StreetNews* offices. At the top of the stairs, the floor opens up to reveal a few modest desks and a copy room with paper. This is where the articles for the paper are written and edited. Also, the paper is designed on two Mac computers in the corner. A long table with mismatched chairs fills the meeting room next door. A small coffee machine sits on a table in the corner. To the right is Denise's office, with a window to the street below, a small table and chairs, a large plant, and a cluttered desk. Framed copies of *StreetNews* and various awards decorate the walls.

James heads toward Denise's office and knocks.

"Hi James, come in. Have a seat," she said.

"Thanks."

"So what is on your mind?" Denise asks.

"It's rough out there," James starts out. "The vendors are struggling with all the panhandlers and scam artists."

"I know it is. What can I do to help you?"

"Well, it isn't really just about me. A lot of vendors are experiencing the same things. When are we going to get our vendor representative back on the Executive Board?" he asks.

"Well, James, the board has talked about this. You know we've had a hard time keeping someone in that position. The last two vendor representatives showed up for the first few meetings but then they stopped coming," Denise points out.

"The meetings were at 11 AM on Saturday! That is prime selling time," James replies.

"That is true, but there are a lot of people on the Executive Board. All of them have jobs during the week and cannot volunteer during normal business hours."

James responds, "Well, I understand, but we have to work as well. Anyways, has the Executive Board discussed the stipend or about adding more vendors?"

"In the past, the $1,000 stipend that the vendor gets paid for being a board member has been paid at the end of the year term. That's how it has been," Denise tells him.

"But..."

Denise interjects, "You know that we can't have a vendor walking off with $1,000 after just a few meetings."

"That is true, but maybe we can have payments or something. A lot of the vendors can't afford to put in an entire year and wait the whole time for the check."

"Well, all I can tell you is that I will bring it up at the next board meeting," Denise offers.

James inquires, "Have you all talked about having more than one vendor on the board?"

"Not yet, but I'll bring that up as well."

"OK," he responds.

"Anything else, James?" Denise asks.

"No. That's it. Thanks for seeing me."

James heads back down the hall and down the stairs to where the vendors congregate. Returning to the table that he was sitting at earlier, Vince asks how the meeting went.

"I don't know, man. It doesn't seem like upstairs wants to change at all. They think they know how to run things. But they don't know what it is like out there. They need to learn from us vendors," James says.

Vince nods in agreement. "Yeah, they do. I've been at *StreetNews* a long time, man, and the upstairs has always been like that. We're just here to sell magazines."

"You would think they'd want to hear from us! We're the ones dealing with the customers," James responds.

"You would think."

DISCUSSION QUESTIONS

1. How should James proceed with his complaints about vendor representation and participation?

2. Do you think that *StreetNews* vendors need to be included to a larger degree in the discussions of the Executive Board? Why?

3. How are physical organizational structure and symbolic organizational structure intertwined and/or related to one another?

4. What is the significance of language such as "upstairs," "downstairs," "them," and "us" within an organization? How might that type of language reflect organizational structure?

5. Is there any significance to *StreetNews* having the vendors at the top of the organizational chart? Why or why not?

6. How are organizational communication and organizing practices altered when the people who work for your company are also the people you are most interested in helping?

KEY TERMS

Organizational structure, hierarchy, homelessness, social change organizing

—PART II—

INTERNAL COMMUNICATION

CHAPTER 7

The New Guy:
A Case of Organizational Socialization—Politics, Personalities, and Multiple Perspectives

Leah M. Omilion and Colin R. Baker

WAYNE STATE UNIVERSITY

ABSTRACT

Starting a new job can always be touchy, as a new employee tries to avoid the numerous mine fields that exist in corporate politics. When Chris joins Reeds Sports Marketing, he quickly meets Jennifer, who sets out to show him the way to walk the mine field, but is Chris' new friendship with Jennifer one of the mines he should have avoided?

"I'll take the dark blue," Chris told the sales associate.

"Ah, yes, the Striped Oxford suits you well, sir," the associate responded, picking the suit off the rack and holding against Chris.

Chris glanced at the price tag. He cringed at the price, $850. It was nearly a month's rent, but he was the newest member of Johnson and Reed's Sports Marketing firm. He had all of the right credentials, an MBA in business from Harvard's Business School and years of internship experience in sales and agency work, and now he also had the right suit for his first day.

That night he hardly slept, but rose dutifully at 5:30 AM He stumbled sleepily to the kitchen to pour himself a cup of coffee. *Thank God for automatic brew,* he thought as he took a long, slow sip and began to open his eyes, blinking away the sleep from the night before. After finishing his cup of coffee he took a shower, shaved, and put on his suit. While he tightened his crimson tie— the associate told him it was a nice accent to the suit—Chris realized that he still had an extra

45 minutes before he had to leave for his new job. With too much nervous energy to stay at home, he headed to a coffeehouse that was on the way to his new office.

"What'll you have today?" Asked the barista.

"Black coffee. Medium. Thanks." Answered Chris.

"No problem sir. It'll be $1.95 today. By the way, that's a nice suit."

"Thanks. I'm off to a new job today. First day, actually."

With coffee in hand, Chris smiled as he walked to a vacant table. Its legs were uneven and its surface was sticky, but it afforded him a place to collect his thoughts. He began to think about his new job at Johnson and Reed's Sports Marketing firm. He wondered about his boss, his coworkers and the work itself. *I really don't know what to expect. They seemed nice at the interview, but you never really know until you start,* Chris reasoned with himself as he left the coffeehouse and headed to his new office.

MEETING THE TEAM

"Good morning. I'm Christopher Turner," he told the pleasant, auburn-haired receptionist who smiled in front of him. "Today's my first day. Mr. Andrews asked me to check in with you when I arrived."

"Yes, we've been expecting you, Mr. Turner. Please follow me," said the receptionist.

He followed her through what felt like a labyrinth. There were a handful of cubes, but mostly there were hallways that led to office suites for the various teams within the firm. He tried to keep track of the route the woman followed, but after two lefts and a right, Chris conceded.

She stopped at a corner office suite labeled "Strategic Planning and Brand Development." Once inside she waved at the department's receptionist and stopped at the third door on the left.

"Good morning Mr. Andrews. I have your new associate, Mr. Turner, here."

"Yes, thanks for your help Shirley. And remember, you can call me Richard. No need for Mr. Andrews, I feel like you're talking to my dad." Mr. Andrews joked as he motioned for Chris to enter.

"Oh yes, Mr....Oh! I mean Richard. Thank you," she said as she began to leave.

"How are you, Chris? I remember you said you go by Chris, right? Excited for your first day?" asked Mr. Andrews.

Chris launched into his pre-rehearsed response. "I am grateful for this opportunity. It is something that I have dreamt of for a long time. I can't wait to—"

"I'm going to cut you off there. I can tell you're excited and that's why I hired you. We're a little less formal here. I expect you to always do your best, but I want you to have some fun, too. Sound good?"

"Since you're also a Brand Development Specialist, I am going to have you work with Ty who does the same job. I think he's in a meeting until noon though, so why don't you just go over to your office and make yourself comfortable. It's the second door on the right once you leave here. Oh you'll probably meet Jennifer sometime today, too. She does our PR, so a little different from you and Ty but she's still a member of the team," continued Richard.

"Sound good?" he asked Chris.

"Yes, Sir. Oh, I mean Richard," answered Chris.

"That's better! Good to have you on the team," said Richard as he shifted his gaze from Chris to the mountains of paper on his desk.

Chris walked into his dark office and found himself blindly reaching for a light switch. He exhaled loudly from frustration for not being able to locate the light and also for feeling like he was already failing at his new job.

"It's tricky—your light switch is hidden. It's tucked inside this cabinet up here. It's silly, but when they built our suite it was the only way to put adequate storage in this office. Your office. I'm Jennifer, by the way," said the impeccably dressed woman standing in front of him.

"Chris," he replied while extending his hand toward hers.

"I know. Good to meet you, though; we're both Harvard alum," explained Jennifer.

Before Chris could respond with more than a nod, Jennifer continued. "I bet Richard told you to come make yourself at home. I think that's the silliest thing, though. You just got here; you should meet everyone and take a tour. Follow me; I'm going to take you around," said Jennifer.

"I'm supposed to be training with Ty at noon, though," cautioned Chris.

"Ty, Ty, Ty. Don't worry; you'll be back in plenty of time. I promise," said Jennifer.

A wave of relief washed over Chris. He was thankful to have someone to interact with and a tour on top of it. He had actively looked for a restroom when the receptionist walked him to his office, but hadn't managed to locate one. Yet, as he followed Jennifer he was also slightly hesitant too as he felt as though he were disobeying Richard's instructions.

"Is Richard going to be upset? He made it sound like I should stay put until Ty was back," asked Chris.

"I don't see why he'd be upset. He should be grateful that I'm helping to orient you," she responded.

WHO'S WHO?

"Over here is where Mr. Johnson and Mr. Reed work when they're in the office," explained Jennifer.

"Wow! They still come into the office? It says a lot about the firm, I think," responded Chris.

"They're just two old bats, now. Not worth your time, if you ask me. I swear every time that I see Mr. Reed I try to walk the other way. Get cornered by him and you'll kiss a couple hours goodbye."

Jennifer continued. "Listen, I am going to give you a lot of candid advice that I wish that someone had given me when I started. I learned a lot of this the hard way, and I don't want you to do the same."

After looking at Chris, she nodded, turned on her heel and continued the tour. When they would pass others, Jennifer would provide commentary under her breath relaying anecdotes about previous interactions with the individual.

Chris was on information overload. *How can I possibly remember all of this? Who did she say was always late on deadlines? And what department was that man in that I'm never supposed to trust?*

Recognizing the overwhelmed look on Chris's face, Jennifer decided it would be a good time for lunch. Jennifer led him to the cafeteria and paid for Chris's first lunch.

What do I make of this? Wondered Chris as he followed her back to their suite.

As they walked in, he saw Richard engaging in conversation with a well-groomed Asian man. The Asian man couldn't be much older than he was, Chris reasoned.

"Ah, nice of you to join us," exclaimed Richard as he glanced down at his watch. Chris couldn't tell how much sincerity was behind the joke, but it still made him nervous as he looked at the clock that indicated it was 12:25 PM Chris looked at Jennifer, but she didn't return his glance.

"I thought it was nice to show him around. I wish someone had done it for me," retorted Jennifer.

"Well that was good of you Jennifer," responded Richard, "However, I asked Ty to train Chris beginning at noon. Do you remember we talked about it in the meeting this morning?"

"I just think it's really important to orient new associates. I want to make sure that Chris knows what he's getting into," replied Jennifer as she walked past Richard and Ty and toward her office.

"Thanks Jennifer," yelled Chris before she disappeared from sight. She immediately turned and replied to his comment with a genuine smile. He found Richard and Ty staring at him, so he shrugged his shoulders and offered his sincerest apologies for his tardiness.

TRAINING

"You're in great hands," Richard said has he left Chris with Ty before disappearing out of the office.

After spending the past three hours listening and observing Ty, Chris was in complete agreement. Ty worked quickly, but with a precision to his actions and speech that Chris admired. Ty was calm and patient in explaining his daily responsibilities, many of which would become Chris's when he became more comfortable.

"The best advice I can give you, man, is to take your time. This can be an intense industry with all of the athletes and big money franchises. But I just remind myself, they're people too. They put their pants on the same way, both legs at a time while hopping up and down," said Ty with a smile.

He continued to explain all of his actions to Chris until five minutes to 6:00.

"I'm sorry to do this, but it's time for me to hit the road. I need to leave to pick up my daughter from daycare on time," explained Ty as he began to shut down his computer and organize his papers.

"Oh—do you leave at 6:00? Is that normal leaving time?" inquired Chris.

"I always do 7:00 to 4:00, with an hour lunch. So long as you put in eight hours, Richard is flexible."

"4:00? I am sorry to keep you! I didn't mean to," Chris began to apologize.

"No, no, no. Don't worry, man. I'm happy to help. When I started, Richard trained me. He came in early, stayed late, and it made all the difference. I had a much easier time learning the ropes and interacting with other departments when I was confident with my job. Know what I mean?" Ty asked.

Chris nodded his head and extended his hand. He smiled at Ty when they shook and thanked him again.

MAKING DECISIONS

Chris continued in this fashion for the next week. He would come in early to meet Ty, and spend his days with his chair pulled up next to Ty's when he was working at his computer. When Ty went to meetings, Chris did as well. Ty always made it a point to introduce Chris to other organizational members—and he did this whether they were in formal meetings or passing in the hall.

"Hey Carrie, how are you? I have someone I want you to meet," Ty would engage each and every person they passed. "This is Chris, new colleague and friend. Real good guy, and sharp too. He'll be handling branding for basketball and tennis once we get him up and running."

At this point, Chris extends his hand and meets his new coworker. The organizational members liked and trusted Ty. Chris could tell. There was something in their expression when they talked to them; it was like they were talking to a childhood friend and not just a coworker. He felt the same way.

After meeting Carrie, Chris recalled an earlier conversation he had with Jennifer. Jennifer had told him that Carrie was hard to work with, bossy and domineering. Chris decided to ask Ty.

"She seemed really nice," Chris said as Carrie walked away, "It's strange though… I heard that she was overbearing, but she seemed kind. Maybe just when you're working with her," concluded Chris.

Ty stopped walking and Chris followed suit.

"You don't need to tell me where you heard that; I think I have a pretty good idea. Carrie is a good person and about as good of a coworker as you can ask. I really don't want to say too much else about this, but try to form your own evaluations of people before making up your mind. There are a lot of great people around here. I think that the people are what make this such an incredible job."

Chris nodded his head taking in what Ty was trying to say to him. He paused for a second looking at his watch before explaining, "I can't believe it's already 11:30."

"Off to lunch with Jennifer now?" asked Ty as he looked at his watch.

"Yeah. See you at noon?" responded Chris.

"Yeah, just think about what I said. She means well, but you might want to consider asking some other people to lunch once in awhile too," advised Ty as he walked away.

Chris was comfortable having lunch with Jennifer. It was reassuring to know that in the midst of so much uncertainty that he would not have to worry about eating lunch alone. Ty hadn't asked him yet, but maybe that's because he knew he sort of had standing lunch plans. Anyway, lunch was fun. Jennifer would ask whom Chris had met that day and then she would point them out and tell him stories about the person. She would give him her evaluation good or bad of their coworkers, but generally Chris had counted himself lucky to have access to such information. They even went out to have drinks after work one night. While Ty taught him about the job, Jennifer provided his education on the people.

He wasn't sure if Ty was right about Jennifer. He trusted Ty, of course, and he even found himself really liking the guy, but Jennifer was smart too and they both came out of the same school and program.

"Who'd you have lunch with before I came along?" joked Chris one day as he and Jennifer sat in the cafeteria.

"Myself. There was no one competent enough to hang out with before you got here," she joked.

"Ty's smart," replied Chris.

Jennifer agreed. "Yes, he is. I like Ty. I just wish he weren't so close to Richard and everyone else for that matter. I used to think he was a brown-noser, but now I think he's just too nice. I feel like he could get taken advantage of and not even know it."

"He is nice, that's for sure, but he's assertive, too. I can't imagine him letting someone walk all over him." Chris found himself irritated at Jennifer's assessment of Ty.

"Okay. Believe what you like, just trying to help," she said as she grabbed her tray and walked away.

CHOOSING SIDES

The next day, the group got together for a staff meeting. It was the first one that Chris had been to since he began a week earlier. Ty told him that Richard believed in getting together as a team every two weeks to discuss everyone's workload. It gave them the opportunity to help each other out if need be, but most importantly, be on the same page as a group.

"Chris, welcome to your first staff meeting!" exclaimed Richard. "I'm sure Ty has filled you in, but we have them every two weeks so that we know where everyone stands. We get pretty busy in the department, so sometimes we don't realize that you and Ty may have different parts of one project, or Jennifer and Ty and so on," explained Richard. "Since you don't have any solo projects, I'll just have you listen to teammates' status sheets so you can begin to decide which projects you are interested in."

"Great!" exclaimed Chris.

"Ty, why don't you get us started?" prompted Richard.

"Why does Ty always get to start?" asked Jennifer earnestly.

"Jennifer, Ty does not always get to start. Since he is training Chris, I thought it would be good for him to start to provide an overview of his projects." Chris could feel the tension thicken as Richard responded.

"Richard, Jennifer can go first if she likes. I'm fine with that," Ty chimed in.

"No, that is not necessary, but thanks Ty. You're such a team player," Richard replied.

"I'm a team player, too. You just don't give me the same chances that you give Ty." retorted Jennifer.

"Jennifer if you feel the need to begin, please do so. Otherwise, I will expect you to be respectful to me and teammates," Richard said. The smile he usually wore had faded as he reprimanded Jennifer.

"Okay, I'll begin. I just want to make sure that Chris knows about my projects too so that he can decide who he wants to work with," said Jennifer.

Richard took a deep breath and then sighed heavily. His facial expression reflected a mixture of exhaustion and annoyance. "Again, Jennifer, this is not a competition. I just want to expose Chris to all of the services that our department offers. We brought him on because we are expanding and there is too much work for the three of us to handle. Anything that he can help us out on is appreciated."

After Jennifer and Chris stared at each other for several seconds, she began to discuss her projects. As the Public Relations Specialist, many of Jennifer's projects were unfamiliar to Chris. His education and experiences rested solely in Sales; regardless, he took notes on those projects that seemed interesting.

When Jennifer discussed her projects, Chris found himself somewhat distracted by the thoughts running rampant in his head. *What was that outburst? Is that normal? If so, why hasn't anyone warned me? I guess it's inappropriate for Richard to, and Ty's too nice. I wonder if it's bad that I've been spending so much time with her. What does that say about me?*

Ty walked through his list after Jennifer concluded hers, but when he flipped through the pages of his project status sheets, his voice did not reveal anxiety or bitterness for the heavy workload the way that Jennifer's did. He went through the projects matter-of-factly, informing the group of his obligations.

He has some really great projects, thought Chris. *I've always wanted to work on a branding campaign for a new franchise, and for a basketball team, too! What a dream!*

After Ty wrapped up, Richard provided an overview of the department's strategic initiatives. Prior to concluding the meeting he told Chris to think about the projects he was interested in working on and the two would meet briefly after lunch to discuss which would be most helpful for the department and for Chris's development.

As the group began to gather their project sheets, notebooks, and pens and disperse from the conference table, Jennifer broke the silence.

"Hey Chris. It's 11:30, ready for lunch?"

He could feel everyone's gaze shift to him. He was genuinely at a loss for a response.

DISCUSSION QUESTIONS

1. What is the nature of each of the relationships (e.g. positive, helpful, strained, combative), that exist among the actors?

2. What strategies did Chris use to actively seek information about the job and the new people he would be working with?

3. How did the members of the organization formally and informally "show Chris the ropes" in his new position?

KEY TERMS

Organizational socialization, conflict management, mentoring/coaching

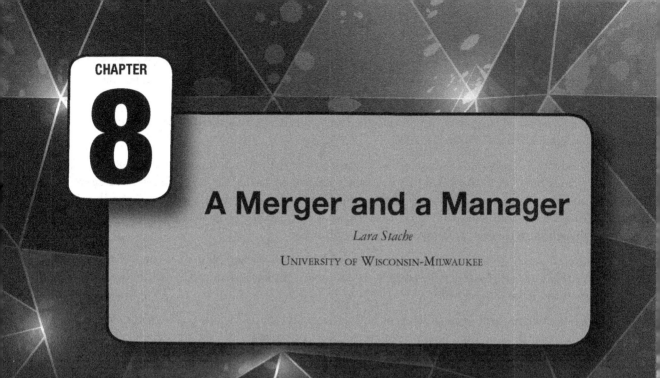

CHAPTER 8

A Merger and a Manager

Lara Stache

UNIVERSITY OF WISCONSIN-MILWAUKEE

ABSTRACT

Wicker Candle Co. has been bought by a competitor and Rebecca Crawford, the new Ecommerce Marketing Specialist sees the writing on wall for her position. She is aware of the office grapevine and, though she suspects everybody's jobs are in jeopardy, she has vowed not to spread her suspicions. As time passes, she grows to really like the other members of the marketing team, and when they believe their jobs are at risk, they ask her what she knows. Rebecca must decide if she wants to hinder Management's optimistic desire to have a strong work ethic and possibly secure her position with the new company, or recommend that everybody start looking for other jobs.

Rebecca Crawford smoothed her skirt and sighed as she opened the front door of the corporate offices for the Wicker Candle Co. She had been working for the company as a part-time Ecommerce Marketing Specialist for two weeks and was already regretting her decision to take the job. During the interview process, she had been thrilled at the prospect of working for Wicker Candles, a store she had visited many times. Wicker Candle Co. was a staple in many towns in every state she had ever lived and Rebecca had been thrilled at the opportunity. Not only was it difficult to find a part-time mid-level marketing position, but also she was a loyal customer and looked forward to helping the ecommerce team increase sales for a product she actually believed in.

"Hello, Rebecca!" called out Suzanne, the Director of Ecommerce Marketing for Wicker Candle Co.

Rebecca smiled and waved as she ducked into her cubicle and started her computer. She groaned inwardly as she noticed a post-it note on her keyboard asking her to come to Suzanne's desk after she got settled.

Rebecca's cubicle neighbor, Christina, smiled and winked as Rebecca walked past her cubicle with a notebook and a slump in her step.

"You wanted to see me, Suzanne?" Rebecca stood at the entry to Suzanne's office and looked around at the personal touches that lined the walls and bookcases. Suzanne's young children were budding artists and had a number of finger-painted portraits on display. It was interesting that Suzanne also decorated with what Rebecca would have called Southwestern home décor, even though she had never lived anywhere but the Midwest.

"Yes, I wanted to have a two-week check-in with you and see how things are coming along. Do you have a status update on the projects we discussed?" Suzanne motioned to the seat opposite her desk and Rebecca sat down.

Rebecca flipped through her notebook and ran down the status of the creative pieces and launch dates. She then updated Suzanne on the progress of the website analytics tool that had been the major reason for her hire. "I have pulled a list of the top drop-off points for customers. Our shopping abandonment rate is quite high and I thought there might be an issue with the coding. I've been running some tests both inside and outside the office to see if there is any reason why so many customers would be dropping off at the same spot, but so far, there are no red flags. I'm going to try a few more tests and see if we can figure this out, but I think you might want to talk to Ed about investing in some site improvements. Maybe adding upsells to the cart will keep people interested and get them closer to the Free Shipping threshold, which will give incentive to submit the order."

"Ed does not want to spend any money right now. CEMCO, our new parent company, is really crunching down as we get into the busy season, and we just are not going to be able to allocate the budget you need," Suzanne said, looking stressed.

"OK, I understand. Suzanne, I know we discussed this last week, but can you explain to me how CEMCO is portioning out the budget? I've never worked for a company that was bought out by a competitor—"

"We were not bought out by our competitor," Suzanne quickly interrupted. "CEMCO only bought Foster Candles nine months ago and then they finally had enough money to buy Wicker. And, now, we are all getting on the same marketing plan, same web platform, and on the same budget; just to get everybody on the same page."

"Yes, of course," Rebecca said unconvincingly.

"Our goal now is to work as hard as we can to show CEMCO how good a team we are and make sure we are seen as invaluable," Suzanne looked straight at Rebecca.

Rebecca was uncomfortable under Suzanne's gaze. She had sat in on an Executive meeting with Suzanne last week and Rebecca felt that the writing was on the wall for Wicker. Why would a big company like CEMCO keep two companies with essentially the same products and run them as competitors? Rebecca had seen both Foster Party & Candles and Wicker Candle Co. in the same strip mall at times, clearly competitors. It just didn't make any sense, and yet every time Rebecca tried to talk about the situation with Suzanne, she was tersely brushed off.

"OK, yes, well, perhaps we should just compile a list of the A & B programming projects so that the web team will know exactly what we need. That way, when we do have the budget, we will be all set to make some changes." Rebecca felt bad about what she was saying when it was clear that nobody would ever care to see the list.

"That sounds like a great idea! Why don't you get Christina to help you since she's been here the longest and probably has some good suggestions for what customers have asked for?" Suzanne shuffled the papers on her desk and tapped them together, seemingly pleased with Rebecca's decision to drop the CEMCO competitive buy-out issue.

Rebecca smiled, got up and walked back to her desk.

THE WATER COOLER

Rebecca was a part-time worker in the office and had only gotten to know the members of the ecommerce marketing team so far in her short time with the company. All the members of the team had started with the company fresh out of college and had been pulled into the duties of marketing and merchandising out of sheer necessity. Christina was the Merchandising Coordinator and filled in occasionally in customer service, when Phyllis was a little overwhelmed. Larry, as the Ecommerce Marketing Coordinator, was the only official member of the team with a title that included a marketing reference, and he had confided to Rebecca during one of their first conversations that he might be ready to try something new with a different company. Rebecca really liked this group and she hoped they were all looking for jobs, in order to get out before the end.

Rebecca watched now as Phyllis came out of the coffee room in whispered conversation with Paul from accounting. *Ah, the days of the water cooler,* Rebecca thought, *I do miss the information from the grapevine with this work arrangement.*

Out of the corner of her eye, Rebecca saw Larry walk up to Phyllis and Paul and motion his head into the break room. The three were in there for a good five minutes before they all came out laughing. Larry looked over at Rebecca's cubicle as he came out of the office and caught her eye. He walked over, "Hello there, how is your second week going?"

"Fine, thanks! Are you telling jokes in the break room without me?"

Larry smiled. "Hey, I just wanted to make sure that our conversation the other day," he lowered his voice slightly, "about me wanting to look at my options, just stays between us. I know you are working closely with Suzanne, but I would really appreciate it if I could trust you with that information."

"Of course you can. I certainly do not have any intention of getting you in trouble." She smiled reassuringly.

"Cool. I figured, but you have to be careful. You know how she can be." He rolled his eyes and went back to his cubicle.

Not really, thought Rebecca, *I'm still new.*

CONTRIBUTING

The next day, Rebecca walked in and could hear Suzanne talking very loudly as she made her way up the hall. She couldn't make out the exact words but she could tell that Suzanne had somebody in her office and was not happy.

"It's Larry," Christina mouthed to Rebecca and pointed to Suzanne's office, as she put her coat on the back of her chair. Rebecca mouthed back, "What happened?" Christina shrugged her shoulders.

About two minutes later, Larry came out of Suzanne's office red-faced and stormed to his desk. Rebecca listened as the ding of instant messaging windows began going off furiously back and forth. Even after only two weeks, Rebecca could recognize the pattern from Larry, Phyllis, and Christina's desks. Within two minutes of aggressive typing and dinging, all three popped up from their desks simultaneously and made their way to the break room. Larry stopped by Rebecca's desk and motioned his head toward the break room for her to follow.

All right, I guess this makes me official, Rebecca thought as she waited a few beats and followed. She glanced into Suzanne's office as she walked by and saw her staring at the ecommerce marketing award the team had gotten for excellent performance just last year.

In the break room, Larry was very upset and Phyllis was patting his back while Christina got him some water. "How is it my fault that the emails that we sent out were three times the estimated cost? I told her that when we increased the list, the price would increase and she OK'd it. And now, she's mad and wants to take it out of my paycheck! I hate her!"

"I'm sorry, Larry," was all Rebecca could think to say. "I heard she's having trouble getting pregnant again and her husband is really pressuring her to have another baby," Christina volunteered.

Rebecca grimaced visibly at this shared personal information. From what she had gotten to know about Suzanne, she was a woman who loved her family almost as much as she loved her job. Rebecca had been in marketing for many years and she knew Suzanne was "corporate" material. She clearly meant to retire as a CEO of a company someday.

"Well, she OK'd the cost of the increased emails. I asked her before I sent them. This is not my fault and she shouldn't have blamed me for it," said Larry.

"One day, we'll all just up and quit and then she'll see where she's at without anybody to do everything that she needs," Christina chimed in.

"Paul, in accounting, said that he overheard Ed tell Suzanne that she needs to double sales and cut costs in half by the end of the year if she wants to keep her job," said Phyllis. "Apparently, CEMCO is really tightening the ropes. I'm sure she is just stressed about that."

"I need out of here. I wish I could just get up the nerve to leave now," said Larry.

"Well, you might not have a choice. Why would CEMCO keep two competitive companies in the first place? Especially since they moved Foster in house. Why would they have two budgets and keep two identical ecommerce teams when everybody is moving onto the same web platform?" Rachel was pouring herself some coffee as she said this. She looked up when everybody was silent and saw that all three people were staring at her. "Uh, but that is just me talking, sorry." Nobody said anything and Rebecca turned and went back to her desk.

The next day, Rebecca was very uncomfortable and had regretted sharing the little bit of information that she had yesterday. She tried to focus on her work, but every time Suzanne sent her an email, she opened it quickly to see if the news had made its way around the office yet. She jumped slightly as she heard Larry's voice whisper behind her, "Meet me in the break room." She turned and Larry motioned for her to follow him.

When Rebecca got into the break room, Larry, Phyllis, and Christina were all waiting for her.

"What do you think is happening with the company, Rebecca?" Christina asked her. "Should we all be looking for other jobs?" Phyllis chimed in.

Rebecca wasn't sure what to say and just looked at Suzanne's marketing team, as they all asked her what she thought was going on.

DISCUSSION QUESTIONS

1. From whom do you tend to hear work-related information while at work?
2. Do you see any potential ethical implications in any of the workers' behavior?
3. In your opinion, what is the best way for a manager to handle a merger? Should he or she express concern if jobs might be in danger, keep team morale up, and/or set realistic expectations among team members?
4. How can office gossip be harmful in the workplace? Can office gossip be helpful?
5. If you were in Rebecca's position, how would you handle this situation? Would you tell your new coworkers your suspicions? Why or why not?

KEY TERMS

Informal communication networks, rumor, managerial control, organizational climate

CHAPTER 9

Behind Closed Doors:
Formal and Informal Communication Networks at FootWorld

Corey Jay Liberman

MARYMOUNT MANHATTAN COLLEGE

ABSTRACT

FootWorld has decided that the use of cross-functional teams would be best for increased organizational effectiveness. However, might the communicative and relational costs of such teams become too much for employees to endure?

"The problem here is that those who have enough power to make change don't, and those who want to make change don't have enough power to do so," Frank complained to Sloane, a fellow coworker.

Frank had been a loyal employee of FootWorld for the past fourteen years and has disagreed about the way the organization has managed issues for as long as he can remember. According to Frank, those in top management positions decide to take the "don't fix it until it is broken" approach, which has plagued both employees and the organization.

Frank continued by saying, "People here do not take my feedback seriously. They assume, because of my potentially demeaning tone, that I am being obtrusively critical instead of offering constructive feedback. For example, did I think that having cross-functional teams would be beneficial? Absolutely not. But those in upper positions decided that this was the best way to fix a broken problem...one that has been broken for a long while. So what did I do? I did what was expected of me, all the while complaining to my friends about those not pulling their weight. Well, apparently I spread informal gossip to the wrong people and, as a result, I feel as though I might now be an army of one. What shall I do, Sloane...what shall I do?"

FootWorld is a corporation dedicated to manufacturing footwear and foot care products that are sold to medical facilities, trained professionals, and retailers. The organization's two main goals are to (a) create, brand, and distribute performance products that are technologically advanced and therapeutically sound, and (b) educate and train professional orthotists and pedorthists about the organization's product line. Recently, those in upper management positions had a meeting to determine why business seemed to be suffering and what could be done about it.

The problem, as many saw it, was the lack of communication between and among departments that needed to collaborate. For example, the manager in charge of the sales department made it quite clear that there was a recent lack of communication between his department and the marketing department. One of FootWorld's new products, a revolutionary insole that provides comfort, support, and flexibility, had just been approved, and the salespeople were ready to begin rolling out a new advertising campaign. However, whereas the insole should have been marketed to both product distributors and licensed orthotists and pedorthists, marketing decided to target the consumer directly. In essence, the marketers bypassed the liaison (the distributor, orthotist, and/or pedorthist) and went right for the consumer. This decision negated the entire vision that both the sales and production departments had.

"How are we supposed to sell our products if the marketing department is not explaining their strategies to us?" the sales manager asked during a cross-departmental forum. Ultimately, the marketing department was forced to redesign its marketing campaign in order to realign itself with the organization's goals.

A very similar incident occurred between the technology department and the production department, where the former created a new athletic sock that had advanced shock absorption and advanced arch support. Unfortunately, however, there was not much dialogue between the two departments and those in production created 1,700 more pairs of athletic socks than requested, ultimately causing an error in the amount of approximately $3,000.

The manager in charge of technology voiced a concern when she said "My tech people need to be in constant dialogue with those in the production and operations departments, but they never are. I am not pointing fingers," she continued, "but I am pointing to the need for more inter-departmental communication."

The salespeople agreed to help remedy the situation and, in the end, were able to convince the organization that originally requested 2,400 pairs of socks to purchase an additional 1,700 at a discounted price. In the end, although the net loss was only $1,200 for FootWorld, this incident could have been avoided had there been more interdepartmental dialogue. Given these two examples, and after much discussion, those individuals part of the meeting collectively decided that cross-functional teams would be a tactic to increase communication and collaboration.

At the next organizational meeting, Lester Charleston, the CEO, made the announcement about the introduction of cross-functional teams. "We are not doing this because we think that you are doing inadequately within your own departments," Lester said. "We are doing this because we see the benefit of having voices from different departments that, collectively, comprise FootWorld. As such, each cross-functional team will consist of a total of nine individuals from the production, technology, shipping, sales, marketing, operations, purchasing, accounting, and customer service departments."

It was obvious that not all employees were excited about this decision. "Talk about micromanagement," claimed Seth, a member of the customer service department. "This is just another way of them saying, covertly, that we are not doing our jobs well enough. I thought that the last microscope that I would see would have been in my high school biology class. I guess not."

Clayton, a member of the shipping department, had a similar complaint when he claimed that "... this is evidence that we truly are only as strong as our weakest organizational link."

Although other employees were also disgruntled by this decision, claiming that they really had little to talk to other departmental members about and that this was going to do nothing but make their jobs more difficult, most saw the inherent benefits of such cross-functional teams.

According to Marc, an employee in the sales department, "having the input from everyone, regardless of departmental membership, will certainly benefit the organization."

Sally, a member of the customer service team at FootWorld, echoed Marc's comment when she said "I cannot wait to make a better informed decision after consulting with others in the purchasing and shipping departments...we probably should be doing this anyway, but we don't."

THE INCEPTION OF CROSS-FUNCTIONAL TEAMS

It was approximately two months after this employee meeting that those in upper management positions decided that it was time for the very first cross-functional team at FootWorld. The technology department had just finished creating its new, state-of-the-art product: a technological device that, by creating a blueprint of one's foot, could provide trained professionals with information about the appropriate footwear product, or orthotic, for a potential consumer. This product took employees nearly 18 months to create, program, and patent, and promised to be a revolutionary tool that would forever change the industry.

However, there was a problem. The members of the technology department needed help. They needed to figure out a price point; they needed to figure out how to market this to professionals and salespeople; they needed to figure out how to sell this product to interested parties; and they needed to figure out the type of warranty to offer the potential customers. This was the perfect time for a cross-functional team. As such, all department heads were notified about this decision and were asked to please nominate one individual for team membership. Employees were chosen based on self-nomination, expertise, or both. Once these members were nominated, they were asked by the department heads to please report to the Blue Room on Monday morning to begin the brainstorming process.

Monday morning arrived and so, too, did the emergent team: Frank from the production department, Amanda from the technology department, Alyssa from the shipping department, Jonathan from the sales department, Loryn from the marketing department, David from the operations department, Martin from the purchasing department, Michelle from the accounting department, and Allen from the customer service department. At approximately 9:00 AM, the CEO walked in to discuss his expectations regarding the team.

"As I mentioned in an organization-wide meeting a few months ago, we at FootWorld will begin using teams as a way of making decisions if the need arises," Lester said. "Well, the need has arisen. As you hopefully know, the tech folks have created the new Foot Master, which provides a blueprint of a patient's foot and then indicates the most useful product based on the spectrometer reading. You will be in charge of determining how this product should be marketed, how this product should be sold, to whom this product should be sold, what this product should cost, and the type of warranty that should accompany the purchase. Although this might seem like an easy task, this decision-making process is likely to span the next several weeks. As such, I expect results. And I expect good results. Now go at it."

At first, the nine individuals were perplexed about two things: how to best approach the task and how to make sure that all of those involved participated. Interestingly enough, not everyone knew each other and, as a result, the first meeting was spent on introductions. Admittedly, some employees found it rather strange that those who worked for the same company did not necessarily know each other.

"Although I knew everyone else, not everyone else knew me," said Michelle, from accounting. "And most of the others did not know each other. It was as though most of us were meeting each other for the very first time."

Allen, from the customer service department, also felt alienated, stating "it is funny to think that Lester thinks of us as a family, yet nobody knows each other, or at least nobody knows each other well." He continued by saying, jokingly, "we are more like an extended family where not everyone is invited to Thanksgiving dinner."

After that first half hour, however, the nine members of the team felt comfortable enough with one another, now that they all knew each other's role in the organization, as well as each member's main area of expertise. For example, all were informed that Loryn's greatest asset to the team was her knowledge of international marketing, and that Frank's greatest asset was his knowledge of turnaround time regarding the new Foot Master. This information allowed the team to understand "who knew what" and how this would ultimately assist the team with its task. The team decided that introductions were enough for one day and called the next meeting for the following morning. The team disbanded and individuals returned to their respective departments.

INFORMAL COMMUNICATION WITHIN NON-TASK-BASED NETWORKS

Nearly two weeks after the introduction of cross-functional teams at FootWorld, the first ad hoc team had completed its task. They had met a total of ten times and were confident that their decisions were fruitful for the organization. Most of the team members were excited about the process and were equally as excited to tell Lester, and others in upper management positions, their ideas. The only member of the team who was not excited, nor proud, was Frank from the production department. The problem was that Frank did not agree with many of the team's decisions, but, since he was the only team member who did not agree with such things as the price point and the warranty, he kept his opinions to himself out of fear of nonconformity and being the sole dissenter.

For example, when discussing how the Foot Master would be marketed to interested parties, the team decided to only market the product to those companies that sell an average of $750,000 worth of orthotics per year: a figure based on sales research. However, Frank did not agree with this marketing tactic and wanted to vehemently disagree with the decision. However, he purposefully avoided conflict and, instead, voiced his concerns to himself. *This is absolutely crazy. In essence, this is taking a 'rich get richer and the poor get poorer' perspective here. Why would we want to market this product only to those companies that already sell a lot of orthotics? Where is the logic in that? Shouldn't we exert our energy attempting to get those companies that don't sell a lot of orthotic products to start doing so? We could create a great pitch here. We could ask the company the following question: have you ever had a customer come in and want advice about the best possible foot product based on his/her foot blueprint? Well, with this new technology, you have the ability to find the perfect foot product for your customer. Enough said. This would work. But if I am the only one who thinks this, what is the purpose of me talking?*

Although he did not voice his opinions to his fellow teammates directly, he did make his opinions known, quite clearly, to his numerous friends he worked with. For example, he routinely went to Catherine, in the administration department, to complain about one of his teammates.

"Alyssa must be the laziest individual I have ever met," complained Frank. "She comes to every single meeting at least ten minutes late and never contributes a darn thing. To be honest, she is pretty much worthless as far as I am concerned."

Frank also complained to Sylvia, from the sales department, about Martin. "Seriously, how hard is it to be a member of the purchasing department," Frank would say time and time again. "The guy is on the phone all day and he was the one nominated to be on this team. I could do a better job than this guy in my sleep."

In addition to Catherine and Sylvia, Frank also routinely complained to Jeffrey, head of the IT department, about Loryn. "I really do not think that Loryn understands the overall goal of marketing," stated Frank. "She has not done anything productive for this team. In fact, I would say that her insight and advice have provided this team with nothing. Absolutely nothing!"

Because all three of these individuals were friends with Frank (Catherine was his fellow smoking buddy; Sylvia was a regular lunch partner; and Jeffrey was a friend who always assisted Frank with his BlackBerry and iPod issues), they would listen to him and offer sound advice. They did not agree with his assessment of Alyssa, Martin, and Loryn, but they each individually offered suggestions so that Frank could relieve some of his anger and disappointment regarding them. Frank, however, was plagued by communication issues. Rather than offering suggestions during team collaboration, he remained quiet for much of the two weeks and never complained about the productivity, or lack thereof, of the others: at least not to the group members themselves. He saved this communication for his friends and assumed that these friends would never disclose this informal gossip. Unfortunately, however, Frank assumed incorrectly. One of the problems with organizational gossip, especially in an organization that is relatively small, such as FootWorld, is that there is very little knowledge regarding who communicates with whom for informal reasons (e.g. gossip groups, lunch groups). Formal relationships are well established and well known, and all that one must do in order to know and understand these formal network ties is to look at an organizational chart. Informal networks, however, because of their very nature, are much more disguised. Because of their disguised nature, they become much more problematic. For Frank, the problem was that he did not know who was friends with whom. Based on the foregoing discussion, Frank routinely went to Catherine to discuss his dislike for Alyssa and her lack of work ethic. Catherine, however, was very close friends with Dante who, like Alyssa, was part of the shipping department. As such, the gossip about Alyssa (from Frank) was communicated first to Catherine, who told Dante, who finally told Alyssa after a department meeting (see Figure 9.1). "You are never going to believe this," Dante said to Alyssa, "but Frank thinks that you are a bad worker with a poor work ethic. He has been complaining about your team performance to Catherine and she just had to tell me about it. She told me not to tell you, but I really have no choice. I felt like I had to let you know."

A very similar thing occurred with Sylvia. Sylvia was friends with Jennifer, who was friends with Jason, who was friends with Martin (see **FIGURE 9.1**). Like the previous network example, Frank complained to Sylvia about Martin, and Sylvia told Jennifer about her correspondence, and Jennifer told Jason, who finally disclosed this information to Martin one day during an informal chat about boating.

"Although I love talking about yachting, there is something important that I must tell you," Jason said to Martin. "Frank thinks that you are a poor team player and that you have very little knowledge about the business. He said that your input has been horrible and that the team is no better off because of your suggestions."

Lester met with the team one last time to discuss his observations and to thank his employees for a job well done. "I want to thank the entire team for their hard work on this project," exclaimed Lester. "I think that you all did a great job and the best part of all is that you are still smiling and joking around with each other and all seem to still be friends. I could not be more thrilled." Like many CEOs in the corporate world, Lester was plagued by one thing: he had absolutely no idea what was going on at FootWorld behind closed doors.

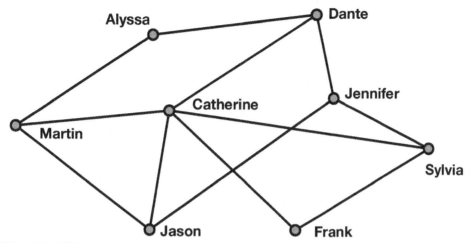

FIGURE 9.1 *The Effect(s) of Communication within Informal Networks*

DISCUSSION QUESTIONS

1. From a communication perspective, what becomes difficult about working in cross-functional teams? Why are cross-functional teams perhaps problematic for organizations? How can cross-functional teams be beneficial for organizations?

2. Although Frank was obviously displeased with his cross-functional team, what communicative maneuvers could he have used to get his points and ideas across?

3. How could Frank have repaired the communication networks that he destroyed after the introduction of cross-functional teams?

4. Assume that Lester found out that certain employees were displeased with his decision to create cross-functional teams at FootWorld. What could he have done to increase motivation and satisfaction for those displeased employees?

KEY TERMS

Ad hoc team, cross functional team, organizational dissent, organizational conflict

When Face-to-Face Communication and Technology Meet

Elizabeth Tolman

SOUTH DAKOTA STATE UNIVERSITY

ABSTRACT

A recent college graduate starts her first job. Should she speak up about multi-tasking during meetings or just let it go?

WELCOME TO THE OFFICE

Jane had just landed her first job out of college. She accepted a position as a marketing coordinator at a credit card company, Canon Credit. As she drives to work on her first day, she feels anxious and excited. She worked hard completing her undergraduate degree in four years and is ready to start her career.

Jane enters the building and her manager, Clint, greets her, "Nice to see you on your first day!" Clint says with a smile and a handshake. Jane appreciates Clint's warm and welcoming personality.

"Thanks, it's great to be here," Jane responds.

Jane and Clint talk for a few minutes about their weekend, Jane's commute to work, and about Clint's dog. Clint shows Jane her cubical and explains some of Jane's responsibilities including, coordinating marketing projects and working with the other coordinator, Bethany.

"As we talked about in your interview, you will be working closely with the other marketing coordinator, Bethany. One of your responsibilities will be providing updates on marketing projects at different meetings," Clint shares.

The rest of the day is spent going over her new duties with Bethany. Overall, Jane's first day on the job went smoothly. After work, She drives home from work thinking about the people she met and how she will decorate her cubical.

Weeks go by and Jane's responsibilities as a marketing coordinator increase. She attends more and more meetings with the Marketing department and other departments such as Customer Service and Credit. She works closely with the other coordinator, Bethany.

During the various meetings Jane must attend, she regularly provides updates on current and upcoming campaigns, products, and creative work. After one meeting, Clint comments that he's glad to see that Bethany has fit so well into the Cannon Credit Family.

During her third week at Canon Credit, Jane is asked to provide an update about a direct mail campaign to senior executives because Bethany is going to be meeting with a vendor out of state.

"Bethany, I don't think I can do this. I'm just so nervous right now. I mean, giving updates in the office is one thing, but this is a formal presentation. I haven't had to stand and speak in front of a group of people since I took public speaking my freshman year in college."

"Jane, I completely understand. I used to get really freaked out, but I ended up joining Toastmasters a few years ago and have really gotten the speaking thing under my belt," Bethany replied reassuringly. "I may not have to give many formal presentations, but at least I know I have the requisite skill set if I ever need to do so now."

"Toastmasters, eh? I remember hearing about them as an undergraduate. Do they have a crash course before Thursday?"

Bethany sighed and laughed as Jane smiled, "No Jane, but don't worry about it. Focus on explaining the tasks we have completed, the research we are using to guide our decisions, and the deadlines we have established. I have complete confidence that you'll do fine. Maybe in the long run Toastmasters may be a good tool, but for now just know that you know this presentation inside and out, and walk into that meeting with your head held high."

Thursday finally arrives and Jane shows up with her PowerPoint presentation and a stack of handouts for the people attending the meeting. Thankfully, Clint is in the meeting and starts by introducing Jane the group. As Jane stands to start into her presentation, the group politely claps putting Jane a little more at ease than she had been just minutes before.

She started with her first slide, and almost immediately knew she was in for on long presentation. Almost immediately, Frank, the senior vice-president of credit, and Kari, the head of customer service, pulled out their cell phones and started texting. At one point, it looked like the two were actually having a conversation with each other. One of them would text a message, and then almost immediately the other could be heard pounding on the keypad a response.

Jane kept going through the presentation pointing out specific charts and figures within the handouts, but the constant distraction of the two on their cell phones really threw her off her "A" game. Not once did either Frank or Kari ever look at her during the entire presentation. *How rude!* Jane thinks to herself.

Thankfully, the presentation ends and takes her seat. Clint pats her on the back and congratulates her on a job well done.

Over the next few weeks, Jane attends additional meetings, and in each meeting she attends she periodically notices people texting during meetings, checking their calendars, or fidgeting with their phones. In addition, she notices a few employees accessing Facebook on their smartphones and laptops.

WHAT'S THE BIG DEAL?

One evening, Jane just decided she had to vent to her husband, John at dinner. After politely listening to Jane vent for about twenty minutes, she pauses to let John react.

"I don't see what the big deal is," he says. "How is texting during a meeting any different from doodling on a sheet of paper? There is still the possibility that the person is not really paying attention."

"Because it just is!" Jane explained. "When I'm talking with someone I expect that they will look at me and show that they are listening. Why attend a meeting and sit there if you aren't going to listen to the person talking?"

Jane thinks about how nervous she is at these meetings with the other staff members. When giving updates on her projects, she expects some feedback from the employees in marketing and the other departments.

Jane ends the conversation with John because he just doesn't seem to get her point. "What should we do this weekend?" she asks in order to change the subject.

After getting nowhere at dinner with John, Jane decides she needs to talk to someone who will understand why the texting is bothering her so much.

"How is your job going?" Kate asks enthusiastically.

"Good," Jane responds quickly without giving it much thought. "I have my own cubical and get to attend meetings with our marketing group and other departments. And I help to coordinate different projects." she continues.

After talking with her husband about how she didn't think people were really listening to her or the other employees during meetings, Jane isn't sure that she wanted to share this with Kate. She doesn't want Kate to think she is being negative about her new job or making a big deal out of nothing.

Jane changes the subject from her new job and asks Kate about her plans for Labor Day weekend.

After she ends her call with Kate, Jane starts to think more about how she may be over-reacting to the cell phone use in these meetings and her expectations for how others should be responding to updates on these projects.

What is the big deal? How is this different from doodling on a sheet of paper while someone else is talking? Jane thinks to herself. Maybe John was right.

Later that week Jane has a one-on-one meeting with Bethany. During the meeting Bethany looks periodically at her phone. Jane works to keep the meeting on task and make it a productive meeting. The two identify the process for the next marketing campaign. The meeting is brief.

DISCUSSION QUESTIONS

1. Are cellphones the modern equivalent of doodling in a meeting?
2. How should Jane handle the frustration she feels about the texting during meetings?
3. Do you think that texting during a presentation could exacerbate a speaker's level of communication apprehension?
4. Can audience members be effective listeners if they are playing with their mobile devices?
5. Do you think Jane should express her frustration with someone higher than her about the inappropriate use of technology during meetings?

KEY TERMS

Computer-mediated communication, effective listening, face-to-face communication, communication apprehension

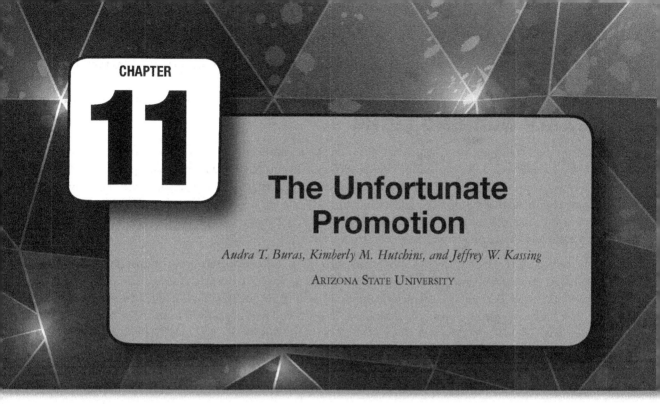

CHAPTER

11

The Unfortunate Promotion

Audra T. Buras, Kimberly M. Hutchins, and Jeffrey W. Kassing

ARIZONA STATE UNIVERSITY

ABSTRACT

A hard-working employee realizes that she has been put in an unfair position at work. Should she resign or should she fight for what seems fair?

Hadley Stokes excitedly gazes around her new office. She is very pleased because she was recently promoted. Hadley has been working at a national non-profit organization that provides youth services for almost four years. With this promotion she believes she has the chance to contribute directly and significantly to the mission of the organization. She is very excited to hit the ground running in her new role.

Despite her enthusiasm, she has some trepidation going into the new position. It will be rewarding for sure, but also very challenging. And because her newly appointed responsibilities were not made entirely clear, she finds herself feeling somewhat uneasy. It seems the responsibilities were not clearly spelled out because she will be working on very sensitive and extremely confidential projects with the organization's General Counsel.

Along with the General Counsel she will support a disciplinary committee, an internal field team, and the internal team located at her headquarters. The disciplinary committee primarily consists of external constituents, who are mostly members of the organization's national board of directors. The organization has many regional offices across the country. Since Hadley works at the headquarters, it is imperative that she quickly familiarize herself with the many different groups she will be supporting in her new role.

EARLY WARNING SIGNS

Although Hadley has yet to finish her training, she is called into an important meeting. On her way to the meeting she bumps into her predecessor Amira Noori. Due to an unexpected family illness, Amira is moving to another state. Unfortunately, this means that Hadley will only have one week to learn about her new role from Amira. While walking to the meeting, Amira explains to Hadley that things often move quickly. She tells Hadley that there is almost no time for "asking questions or evaluating work," so she must "learn fast."

In the meeting Hadley sits next to Amira. She is introduced briefly and the meeting moves forward. Two hours later the meeting wraps up. After a week of sitting through similarly long and disorganized meetings, Hadley finds herself feeling slightly drained. It does not, however, deter her from getting acquainted with her colleagues and her new boss Tonya Proust. In her old department Hadley had no real chance to interact with this group of people. Yet she knew that Tonya had a reputation for being very blunt and hard to work with. Hadley was not too concerned, though. In fact, she welcomed the challenge since she had ample experience working with difficult supervisors before.

After her first week, Hadley comes to the realization that this department operates in a silo, clearly removed from other departments in the organization. And she discovers that everyone, not just her boss Tonya, seems overwhelmed. It becomes clear that there is more work than personnel to accomplish the work. Yet, given the confidential matter of the topics handled, not much of this work can be shifted to other departments.

EXCITEMENT BECOMES CONCERN

Several weeks into her new position Hadley feels empowered as she had expected, actively contributing to the mission of the organization. But the position is completely different from what she anticipated. Like her colleagues, Hadley finds herself overwhelmed with the amount of work she faces. Every minute of every hour she is consumed with work. She struggles to keep up with emails and deadlines even though she is working more than she ever has. She has never felt unable to perform the expected duties in any of her previous positions. She knows she is a hard worker, someone willing to put in the extra effort whenever necessary, but in this new position she just cannot seem to keep up. Hadley begins to wonder if the increasing volume of her workload is due to something other than her own personal work habits. She begins to suspect that something is amiss. She feels reluctant to express her worries about falling behind, but knows she must. Hadley decides that during her next performance review she will raise the issue.

As more time in the position passes, Hadley becomes increasingly annoyed about her pay. She finds it unfair that she is expected to complete so much work for so little compensation. She feels she has been misled regarding what the job actually demands. In effect, she has come to the realization that if she had been properly informed about the demands of the position she would have turned down the promotion.

SPEAKING UP AND OUT

Aggravated but not wanting to look bad, Hadley begins to discuss her concerns with coworkers as discreetly as possible. A recurring theme, "that's just how it is," continues to surface across these conversations. Moreover, she discovers that everyone who has worked in the position prior to her has felt the exact same way. Through these interactions Hadley learns that the organization has created a practice of hiring for this position internally, with the expectation that individuals will remain due to a sense of duty and loyalty, all the while tolerating less pay and an inappropriate job title. While Hadley continues to believe in the organization and the important function it serves, upon learning this she feels manipulated. She also realizes that she cannot continue to consult coworkers about the issues she faces. She worries that as a young employee she will appear unappreciative of the advancement opportunities afforded her, and risk compromising future possible promotions within the organization.

So, Hadley begins to complain about her work situation to friends and family. After many happy hours and cups of coffee with friends she discovers that the nature of what she does is too complex and confidential to share openly with others. As a result she finds little relief or satisfaction when discussing her situation with people outside the organization. Hadley realizes that she must stand by her plan to confront these issues with her immediate supervisor during her upcoming performance review. She understands that this is the best place to raise her concerns if she hopes to see them addressed. Accordingly, she plans to discuss the overload of work she has experienced, the underpaid salary she receives, and the inappropriate title she carries.

The time finally comes for Hadley's performance review, but Tonya unexpectedly cancels it. Hadley proceeds to reschedule it. Tonya cancels again. Hadley reschedules several more times, only to have each and every performance review canceled. Hadley figures she can no longer wait for the appropriate forum to discuss her problems with Tonya. Instead she gathers reports and tracking documents that show the incredible amount of work with which she has been tasked. Additionally, Hadley learns from Amira, who formerly occupied the position, that she was working late every night, through lunches, and most weekends. When she accepted the promotion Hadley had no idea that Amira had willingly put in so much extra time, but now understands that this has put her at a serious disadvantage.

Hadley presents Tonya with this information. Tonya quickly dismisses the idea, claiming that "everyone is this busy" and further explaining that "Amira enjoyed this amount of work." While this may have been true for Amira, Hadley cannot adopt the same work routine. She is enrolled in a graduate program, which consumes much of her time outside of work. Thus, she cannot work late during the week or on weekends. At this point, Hadley is no longer preoccupied with changing her title and pay. She simply wants to have a fair and balanced workload.

Hadley knows her next move is risky, yet she decides she must discuss her frustrations with Tonya's boss. Mike Finn is a top executive at the organization who is known for being very dedicated. He is approachable and well respected by all. Hadley feels confident that a conversation with Mike will likely help her manage the issues that have surfaced with her job. During their visit Mike seems sympathetic to Hadley. Yet he mirrors Tonya's disposition and even utters the same words throughout the discussion, multiple times offering that "everyone is busy." While Hadley believes it was helpful to air her concerns with Mike, nothing actually happens after their meeting.

END OF THE LINE

Hadley feels as though she is at the end of her rope. She knows everyone is busy with very important work. But she has been placed in an unusual position that no one seems to fully appreciate or understand. Furthermore, no one seems willing to take the time to legitimately address the situation. For Hadley it is patently clear that no changes will be made. She believes she has exhausted most avenues for expressing her concerns. At this point she realizes she has two choices: accept and make the best of the intolerable situation, or take a more extreme position demanding change. As the former option is really not a viable possibility for her, she opts for the latter.

Still hoping that she can move the organization to improve the situation, Hadley approaches Tonya once more. With as much composure as she can muster she tells Tonya, "I don't feel this position is well-suited for me or anyone else that may be hired for it. I do not see any room for growth, and unless things are re-structured soon, I may need to leave." Tonya appears completely unfazed and responds, "I'm not surprised you feel this way." She ends the conversation abruptly and offers no solutions for Hadley.

DISCUSSION QUESTIONS

1. Would you consider Hadley's promotion one accompanied by a realistic job preview?
2. Was Amira's attempt at training Hadley helpful or hurtful?
3. How has this organization promoted a culture of employee silence?
4. What dissent strategies has Hadley used in this case?
5. Do you think the articulating of Hadley's dissent was effective?

KEY TERMS

Organizational dissent, workplace learning, employee silence

Dealing with an Emotional Tyrant

Juliann C. Scholl

TEXAS TECH UNIVERSITY

ABSTRACT

Kevin is an office supply sales representative who has enjoyed a reputation as a top performer in company. But lately, it's been getting hard to reach his quota while he's been under the watchful eye of Sylvia, the new sales manager who seems to enjoy tyrannizing him whenever he's in the office. Sylvia's bullying reaches a new low when she makes a comment about Kevin at a weekly staff meeting that completely humiliates him in front of his colleagues. Is this the final straw that motivates Kevin to confront Sylvia's bullying once and for all?

A WORKPLACE BULLY

It is 8:18 AM on Monday. Kevin Wilkins sits motionless in his office cubicle. He has no desire to get up and pour his routine cup of strong coffee. He's fighting a stress headache and is wondering how he's going to muster up enough energy to go out and do the cold calls he had scheduled for that day. He's remembering the argument he had with Julia, his wife, the previous evening. He has since deeply regretted raising his voice to her; he obviously hasn't been himself lately.

In stark contrast to his irritable mood the previous evening, Kevin now feels unenergetic as he hides in his cubicle this particular morning. Except for a phone, desk pad, a few scattered papers, and a pencil cup, Kevin's cubicle is mostly bare. His sales awards are the only decorative artifacts hanging on his cubicle wall. He supposes he needs to see them to remember how successful he was in previous years, but they are of little comfort to him today.

For five years Kevin has been a sales rep for Office Craft, the second-largest supplier of office products in the metropolitan area. The sales manager of the department lured Kevin away from his previous company and mentored him well. It didn't take long for Kevin to earn a place among the top ten percent of the sales force, and then the branch Salesperson of the Year title three years in a row. Until recently, Kevin thrived easily in his work environment. Although he has always loved doing outside cold calls, he treasured "checking in" at the office at the start and end of each day, and he looked forward to bumping into the other sales reps to "shoot the bull" with them. He and his colleagues enjoyed a healthy competitive—yet supportive—spirit, and he was friends with many of the other reps. His best friend at work is Janine Chatterjee. She came to work for Office Craft two years after Kevin and has recently become one of the department's top performers. Kevin and Janine became fast friends, and only with Janine does Kevin feel comfortable discussing his personal life, especially the difficulties he and Julia are currently having with their marriage.

Despite the friendly spirit the department had enjoyed over the years, the tone of the office climate seems to have changed overnight. About four-and-a-half years into Kevin's employment at Office Craft the company hired a new sales manager, Sylvia Flores. She rarely hides her aggressive and domineering managerial style. Most of the staff, especially upper management, thought at first that her style would be a refreshing change, since Office Craft needed to do something about the slumping profits they experienced the previous fiscal year. In the beginning, the staff and sales force, including Kevin, welcomed Sylvia's competitive and no-bull attitude. She was rigid in her expectations as manager, and the company's profits appeared to be on the rise as a result.

Soon, however, Sylvia's attitude turned toxic. At weekly sales meetings, it becomes increasingly obvious who Sylvia's "stars" are, as well as who are her "targets"—usually the lowest-performing reps. The "stars" for a given week are typically showered with verbal praise in front of the entire team and asked to share their secrets of success. Outside of meetings, Sylvia's stars are often invited to join Sylvia for lunch and hang out in her office to chat or share gossip. Conversely, Sylvia has a sarcastic way of singling out the low performers. Sylvia seems most venomous when she has an audience. Moreover, she often alludes to her targets' personal problems during staff meetings or whenever there are other employees within hearing range. Kevin still hadn't forgiven her when, about two weeks earlier, in front of three other workers in the break room she wisecracked, "Why so glum, Wilkins? You and your wife talking divorce again?" Kevin has always been sensitive about references to his personal life, especially his marriage.

These embarrassment tactics appear to be Sylvia's primary method of motivation. Few people in the department are immune to this form of treatment. During the third of Sylvia's weekly meetings, Janine, who was in remission from ovarian cancer, once bore the brunt of this venom when Sylvia quipped, "Janine, I noticed your numbers were a little low last week. We all know about and sympathize with your health problems, but you don't want to let your 'girl-part' cancer get in the way of what you're capable of doing, okay?" Some of the other reps chuckled nervously, but Janine was mortified. As usual, Janine did her best to shrug it off because she reasoned that bullying from the boss was quite common.

BREACH OF PRIVACY

Kevin looks at his watch. 8:27 AM He sighs, and then groans quietly. Every Monday morning at 8:30 the outside sales reps convene for their weekly meeting. Kevin figures he should get moving toward the conference room before his tardiness would be noticed by Sylvia and the other reps.

The weekly meetings are intended to brief the team on new products, go over sales strategies, discuss office policies as needed, and recognize reps who performed well the previous week. Now that Sylvia has been managing the team, the meetings have become less about briefings and policies and more about singling out the top and low performers. These weekly meetings are a source of stress for almost everyone in the department, not only for those who don't meet their quotas, but also for the top performing reps who hope their numbers would keep them safe from Sylvia's embarrassing remarks for yet another week.

When Kevin enters the conference room, he encounters half a dozen of his colleagues lazily finding their chairs on all sides of the conference table and mumbling quietly in side conversations. Kevin finds a seat next to Lamandre Kaffee, who has been with the company for about ten years. Kevin still doesn't know him all that well, but has admired his work ethic and his cunning sales techniques. He wants to say "hi" to Lamandre, but instead just nods his head to him. Kevin also spots Charles Tudor, one of Sylvia's latest stars. Charles was becoming one of the most successful reps on the team, quickly surpassing Kevin's highest numbers. Kevin has always resented the way Charles feeds off of Sylvia's taunts and how he parrots her so-called motivational phrases. But today Kevin does his best to stay out of his way; Charles is known to spread gossip, and Kevin suspects that he often repeats employees' comments to Sylvia.

At exactly 8:30 Sylvia marches into the room with a painted-on smile. The mumbling in the room instantly stops and everyone finds a seat around the big conference table. Just as Sylvia sets down her notepad at the head of the table, Anthony Feldstein rushes in, fully aware that Sylvia is staring him down all the way to his seat. When she doesn't supplement the stare with a comment, Anthony and the rest of the team are silently relieved.

Sylvia begins, "Okay, kids, this meeting is gonna be short. I know you all are just anxious to get out there and grab more business for us." As she says this, her eyes meet Kevin's. Kevin gulps; he begins taking a quick inventory of the rejections he got from prospects the previous week. Sylvia continues, "Okay … please check your emails with my attachment on the updated specs on the new color laser printer we're pushing. I'll leave you to read that on your own. I don't want to waste time here going over it with you."

Without missing a beat, Sylvia's tone turns pleasant. "I'm proud to point out that Charles' numbers were at the top again this week. Good job, Chuck. You more than surpassed our quota this month."

Charles beams, but adds a humble head nod, saying, "Well, it was a tough month ... post-holiday season, you know." The other reps politely clap for him, maintaining neutral faces.

After recognizing two other top performers, Sylvia maintains her pleasant tone and admonishes, "Now, for some of you, your numbers have been lower than I would have expected." Kevin's dread of the morning quickly intensifies. He barely made last month's quota. What he laments more than his low performance is the unwanted attention from Sylvia.

"Okay, I hate to come down on you, but you all know what it means to miss your quota more than two months in a row, right?" Sylvia continues. Turning her head toward Kevin, Sylvia remarks, "Kevin, you scraped by again last month."

Kevin could sense that Sylvia's tone is becoming more patronizing. He decides simply to placate her to save face. He's afraid of what she's going to say next. Nodding, he responds, "Yeah, I hear you, Sylvia. I'm pushing to get those numbers back up."

Sylvia puts both elbows on the conference table, leans forward and says, "Now, Kevin, I'm pulling for you to get those numbers back up to where I know they can be ... Any trouble at home?"

Time seems to stop for Kevin. His face becomes flushed. "Excuse me?"

"If there's anything we can do to help you and Julia with your difficulties, you need to let us know. But trouble in paradise will lead to trouble elsewhere, including your job performance. Okay?"

Kevin is in such shock that all he can say is, "Uh, okay."

The rest of that meeting, although brief, becomes a blur. Kevin's thoughts sway from embarrassment about the reference to his troubled marriage to the dismay of having his private business being the source of gossip among the team. He darts a piercing glance at Janine, who looks as stunned as he feels. As if to read his mind, Jasmine slightly shrugs her shoulders and conveys an expression that seems to say, *I don't know how she got that idea. I'm as shocked as you are.* Kevin turns front and takes a mental inventory to figure out when he might have said anything about Julia, other than the late afternoon when he and Janine talked in the break room with the door closed. After a few minutes, Kevin begins to stare at the wipe-off board on the front wall, slumps in his chair, and tunes out the rest of the meeting.

ASSESSING THE SITUATION

The second the meeting ends, Kevin makes a beeline for Janine. They both have important prospects to visit that morning, but Kevin decides he cannot leave without talking to her about what happened at the meeting. He is anxious about what he told Janine and what may have been leaked from their previous conversation about his marriage. When Kevin reaches Janine, he puts his hand on her arm and sputters, "Parking lot. Now!" Janine is hesitant, but then nods. She grabs her jacket and briefcase, and follows him out of the building.

They make it as far as the front of Janine's car when Kevin angrily whispers, "What happened? How did she know about Julia and me?"

Janine defensively replies, "Don't look at me! It's not like I walked up to Sylvia and said, 'Hey, did you know that Kevin and his wife are having marital problems?'"

"Well, she got it from someone!" Kevin insists.

Trying to calm Kevin's tone, Janine says, "And I don't know who that could be. Look, you know that what we say in confidence stays between us. I would never gossip about you, or about anyone else, even Charles. And what Sylvia did to you just then was just appalling. She had no right." Janine feels herself become increasingly angry.

"I don't even have the energy to get angry anymore. She's already watching me like a hawk since my new sales dropped two months ago. And the way she always has an audience when she makes her snarky comments drives me nuts! This marriage comment is just one more thing I don't need hanging over my head. If Julia finds out I've been airing our dirty laundry—even to you—I might as well start shopping for a divorce lawyer!" Kevin sighs in exasperation. "Why did she go and do that? I was so humiliated. Not only am I sucking as a salesman, but now it's apparent to everyone that I can't keep my marriage together … Honestly, if I were heading up that team I would never dream of berating someone like that."

"I know, I know. But for the moment," Janine advises, "just walk it off and move on. I'm sure Sylvia's spying on us right now, wondering why we haven't dashed off to our appointments. But someone's going to have to do stand up to Sylvia, or go above her head and complain. As for you, this stress can't be helping you sell copiers."

"You think I should do it? Why? Besides, what good would it do? She would probably come down on me even harder. I wouldn't put it past her to switch me to a different territory just to punish me. I can't afford to stick my neck out anymore. Besides, I'd rather put up with her snide comments than discover what she's really made of if I complain." Kevin then looks directly at Janine. "Why not you? You seem to be back in her good graces." Kevin almost sounds resentful with his last comment.

"Hey, don't be mad at me. I'm keeping my nose clean around here like anyone else would. Maybe we both can do something, like go to Sylvia's boss. Do you think we can couch this under some kind of harassment?"

With a little more hope in his voice, Kevin offers, "Well, it certainly feels like harassment. All I know is I won't have the guts to do anything without you to back me up. What do you think?"

"I think we need to decide what's in our best interest. We can confront Sylvia, go above her head and complain, or plow on and improve our sales performance so she doesn't target us at all."

"What I *really* want to do," says Kevin, "is tell Sylvia off in front of the whole team, at one of her precious weekly meetings."

Janine nods. They give each other a look implying that Kevin's dream would not likely be an optimal strategy.

CONFRONTING THE BULLY

As Janine drives off to her first client meeting of the day, Kevin realizes that he has to go back in and get his briefcase. He dreads running into anyone else on the way to his cubicle, but he decides to make it quick. When he gets to his desk, Kevin has an idea. He makes a quiet phone call to the prospect he was meeting that morning and reschedules the appointment. Bypassing Sylvia's office without incident, Kevin goes to Human Resources. He asks to see Pamela Routledge, who handles EEO issues.

"Hi, Kevin," says Pamela, warmly greeting Kevin with a handshake. "What can I do for you today?"

"Hi, Pamela," says Kevin. "Thanks for fitting me in on short notice." Kevin sits down, exhales as if to gather his thoughts, and then says, "I have a problem in my department. I don't know if there's anything that can be done at the organizational level, but I'd sure like to find out what my options are."

"I'm sorry to hear that, Kevin. What's the problem?" Pamela sits more alert in her chair.

"Well, I wish it were just one problem …" Kevin then tells Pamela about Sylvia's treatment of some of the reps over the previous six months, and about the incident that humiliated him at the meeting that morning. Pamela slowly nods her head and jots a few notes in her notebook. Kevin takes notice of this and elaborates on Sylvia's tendency to reward her favorites as well as "punish" employees who disagreed with her or exhibited low performance. When Kevin concludes his story he waits for Pamela to finish writing. "So, what are my options if I don't want to confront her directly?"

"Hmmm … Well, would you consider any of her comments or behavior as sexual harassment?"

Kevin pauses. "No, can't say that applies to any of it."

"What about off-color jokes, or racial slurs? What I'm looking for are blatant violations to our discrimination clause. It would be much easier to identify those kinds of things. You would then have reason to bring up some kind of formal charge or complaint, and then we could address it with training, something constructive …"

"Why?" asks Kevin in exasperation. "Why can't you, or someone, do something to protect me and my fellow employees? You're telling me she's not breaking the law. But I'm walking around on egg shells around here. I can't look some of my colleagues in the eye. I get a stomach ache thinking about coming into this building. And I get so worked up sometimes that my wife avoids me when I come home."

"Look, Kevin," replies Pamela, "you're not the first person to complain to me about Sylvia. I do believe what you're saying, and I feel for you. Really, I do. Right now it's an uphill battle because I know for a fact that management likes what Sylvia's doing for Office Craft. I heard that their numbers are up from last quarter, so it would take a lot for Sylvia to get some negative attention from upper management."

Kevin just looks at Pamela. "But what do I do?" His energy is completely drained, and it isn't even 10:00.

"You do have some power. Try to document all the problem exchanges that already happened, and encourage others to do the same. Continue to log your interactions with her, or anyone else that is causing problems. Perhaps this documentation can be helpful to you if you decide to confront her directly."

Confront her. Kevin thinks about the other times he was advised to do just that. If he never confronts her, he thought, who knows if and when these abuses would be addressed? He reasons to himself that HR is impotent to do anything about it right now.

Kevin slowly gets up, thanks Pamela for her time, and walks calmly out of her office. As he's walking past his cubicle to leave the building, he notices that Sylvia spots him. He recognizes the look on her face—*Why is he still here?* Kevin asks again, but to himself, *What do I do?*

DISCUSSION QUESTIONS

1. How do you define workplace bullying? What examples in this case suggest that workplace bullying is occurring?

2. Kevin is apparently upset about the comments Sylvia makes toward him at the staff meeting. What could be the reason(s) for Kevin's emotional reaction?

3. In what ways might Kevin, his colleagues, or the company be helping to perpetuate the incidences of workplace bullying?

4. What effects does workplace bullying have on its victims? Identify examples from the case study.

5. What advice would you offer Kevin to help him cope with his situation?

KEY TERMS

Emotional tyranny, workplace bullying, productivity

—PART III—
WORKPLACE RELATIONSHIPS

13

Servant Leadership:
The Story of Dr. Dan Damon

Carolyn M. Anderson and Heather L. Walter

UNIVERSITY OF AKRON

ABSTRACT

Ten faculty members cast a vote of "no confidence" in retaining Dr. Dan Damon for four more years of leadership as director in the School of Health Communication. Conversely, Dean Pat Smithering wrote a letter supporting the retention of Dr. Damon. Should the Provost consider the recommendation of the Dean or the Faculty?

Dan Damon sat back in the airline seat, closed his eyes, and began dozing off into a peaceful sleep. He did it! Yes! He was going to be director of the new School of Health Communication at Anderson University. Doris and the girls won't be happy to be moving, but this was the opportunity to bolster his career and add another peg in the climb for presidency of a university someday. Although modest, the Center for Disease Control grant was awarded and the successful fundraising he did with alumni sealed the deal. He had limited leadership experience serving on university committees, but he wasn't worried. Barnes & Noble bookstore's shelves were sagging under the weight of books on how to lead efficiently and effectively, so he picked up a couple to peruse during his flight. His grandmother always said: "If you can read, you can cook." I can read so I should be able to lead, he reasoned. Besides, Dean Smithering offered me all the resources needed to gain national recognition.

A meeting with the Provost later that day was Pat's first opportunity to share the good news. Pat started the meeting, "I am so pleased that we've convinced Dan Damon to join us here as the School of Health Communication Director."

The Provost was pleased, "I know this took a lot of persuasive power on your part, Pat, but this is great news."

"The School of Health Communication can finally start to grow now with Dan as the leader. I am confident that with Dan at the helm, we can finally start to see grant money and alumni donations rolling in to sustain our goals for national recognition. Dan is our shining hope for this program and this college," Pat added.

"Well, then," added the Provost, "Whatever Dan wants, Dan will get. He will have new position lines to hire five researchers to work alongside the five noted faculty members already on board."

"Great," ended Pat, "with Dan's expertise in gerontology research, I see the School soon becoming the number one in research devoted to the aging population around the globe."

THE REIGN OF DAN—YEAR ONE

The first year seemed to fly by rapidly. Anderson University had a large student, faculty, and staff population and Dan was mired in red tape for accomplishing even what seemed routine tasks, such as hiring additional faculty. This process was a new twist for Dan. The time and expense seemed disproportionate to the results. He filled one of the five lines, and this person was a new Ph.D. with only a few research articles out for review. The other candidates had more qualifications but chose other opportunities. As his first year drew to a close, he placed a running ad to snare a new crop of job seekers.

The interviewing process was equally challenging for Dan. The candidates looked good on paper but after the interview began, the conversation seemed to take a downhill slide. One of Dan's practices was to have the final dinner with each candidate for the position. Dan remembered how Dean Smithering convinced him to come aboard. So to follow the Dean's strategy, Dan pulls out and hands each candidate a copy of the rules and norms he created for the department, otherwise known as the Ten Commandments. Dan reported on the latest candidate to the Dean the day after the candidate left.

"Pat, can you imagine, the candidate asked me if he would work as part of a community? Further, he asked if I would grant him all the information from the other researchers and the space to develop his research in partnership."

"What did you say, Dan? At the Dean's conference I think I heard some reference to a leadership style that focuses on those principles."

"Don't worry, Pat, I set him straight. We all do our own work in my department. The expectation would be to produce cutting edge research using his creativity, not letting others do the work so he could slide by."

In self-reflecting on the first year, Dan knew he would have to whip his faculty into shape. He kept his ever-growing stack of leadership books noticeable on his desk, and consulted them every once in a while to help in his leadership efforts. Despite all he was doing to be a great leader, he was increasingly irritated with faculty. Dan was annoyed that most faculty members were not keeping posted office hours. He convinced himself the five noted tenured faculty members seemed to be getting lax in their duties. In the college wide directors' last meeting, he complained to his peers.

"What can I do to make them keep their posted office hours?" Dan quipped. "It's part of their responsibilities as teachers. I created a form they fill out and post the hours on their office doors. Yet, I walk by and only occasionally see anyone in their offices. Every Friday at our mandatory meeting, I keep reminding them."

Dr. Philips from Arts & Sciences offered: "Well, Dan. It may be tied in with the union thing. When you were hired it was the first year of unionization. Maybe they see themselves as the 'punch-in and punch-out' line workers."

"Oh, come on, Phil. Advising is in the union contract."

"That's all well and good, but I hear my faculty members say I don't care about them anymore. Perhaps it's not what we do as leaders; it's how we should not try to control them."

"Nonsense! Every Friday at our mandatory meeting, I keep reminding them. Faculty need to understand accountability," Dan retorted.

"Maybe you can toss in the idea that you are open to new ideas and they have the right to appeal some of your Ten Commandments," Dr. Phillips added.

Dan shrugged his shoulders and left the meeting still not certain about what to do.

THE REIGN OF DAN—YEARS TWO AND THREE

University life moves on. Dan stayed busy running numerous searches for new colleagues, while continuing to build a reputation for the program and raise money. Dan was dismayed by the slowness of filling the new lines and by the sheer number of candidates who interviewed and were offered the position, only to turn down the opportunity. The few who had accepted the positions were also somewhat of a disappointment in not being on the cutting edge of gerontology research.

Relations with faculty seemed to be deteriorating. No one in the department really tried to understand his position and meetings were becoming a drag. Was faculty sinking into the line worker mentality? Several times he overheard faculty discussing how they were being treated not as equals but as children under Dan's Ten Commandments. One was the standard of having to show up for work every single day, five days a week. As if this isn't the expectation for all people in the workforce at any organization, Dan thought.

Despite the fact that his faculty members were very productive with publications and well received by their students, Dan was beginning to think the whole lot of them was just a bunch of ingrates.

At the end of his second year, Dan heard that the faculty union was having a hard time coming to contract agreements with the University administration. After five years of no salary increase due to the unionization process, the faculty were upset that the administration was only offering a 2% salary increase in the new contract. Furthermore, the administration was increasing healthcare costs that would completely offset even that meager increase. Dan and the other Department Directors were called to the Dean's office to prepare for what might happen if the faculty went on strike.

Dr. Phillips voiced concerns about the possibility of a strike. "We have too many faculty members being asked to teach an extra class to fill student needs for classes to graduate."

Dean Smithering sighed, "The State budget has been cut at this late date. We simply cannot hire part-timers."

"You know, I can see where faculty are coming from," Dr. Phillips added. "Most of my faculty are incredibly productive scholars, teaching graduate and undergraduate courses, advising dozens of students, and sitting on many committees. I feel that it is my job to support them and let them make some of the decisions."

Dan piped in, "Faculty are idiots. I can't believe they think it's a good idea to strike in our tough economic times. I'm sure the local community will hang them in effigy. What have they got to complain about anyway? They only work nine months a year, with extra pay for summer classes. Mine don't even hold all of their office hours. They all grumble when asked to come to my weekly Friday meetings."

Dan hoped that the administration didn't budge an inch. Until his department started following all the rules, he didn't think they deserved any additional benefits. Early the next year, when the contract was finally ratified, Dan said to his faculty, "I think you were very lucky to get 2.5% increase considering how much less you seem to be doing than the average non-academic."

THE REIGN OF DAN—YEAR FOUR

By his fourth year, Dan was somewhat nervous but optimistic. The evaluation process covered the four years of his leadership. Evaluations would be by faculty, staff, and the upward chain of command. Standardized forms were on line for the quantitative and qualitative reviews. Dan mused. His motivation in the leadership role was his personal drive to achieve national recognition and make the School of Health Communication into a health center of acclaim. The latter two hires were brought in at the Associate level and they had experience in gerontology research. That success was positive. So, he was confident that Dean Smithering was in his court. He was given the resources he needed, whenever he needed them. However, a new provost was put in place during the last six months, who has been well received. In a welcoming address the provost suggested that leaders are responsible for their followers and those followers have rights.

"Now, Dan. The evaluation process is a routine process we all go through. It takes time to build a new health center of excellence. Granted the provost is new and has made a few changes already, but, in the beginning new leaders tend to tread slowly," Pat said reassuringly.

In meetings with Pat, there were always reassurance and kind words. Now that all faculty positions were filled, the Dean seemed to understand and listen carefully to his list of challenges offered as reasons for not yet reaching goals of national acclaim, and the shortfall in alumni giving.

Just yesterday during his latest meeting, Dan also tried to share with the Dean the unrest of the faculty and to offer his side of the story in seeking support for retention.

"Pat, I just need four more years. It has not been easy to hire top people, as you know. I have paraded lots of top applicants through here. Although we now have ten faculty members, they are slow in action. Ten faculty members should be able to raise our status a lot quicker than they have," Dan pleaded.

"Relax, Dan. The next four years will be different," Pat offered.

"You know, Pat, I still blame faculty. When they talked to stellar candidates during the hiring process and even when they came aboard, they probably gave them an ear full of discontent. You know I don't tolerate mistakes."

"I know. It was disappointing about what happened to Professor Yang."

"She sure made one big mistake. She must have done something wrong. Two years waiting on a grant and we didn't get it. I let her have it! This mistake makes me look bad," Dan said with anger in his voice.

"Now, Dan. I know you are a traditional style leader but you have been working hard at it. Faculty will fill out their evaluations next week. Remember, we have layers of evaluation. After I complete mine, the Provost gets everything. I think you're on the right track here."

"Thanks, Pat," Dan offered. "I truly appreciate the way you listen and understand all the internal politics going on in the School of Communication."

EVALUATION RESULTS—DR. DAN DAMON

Faculty in the School of Health Communication elected an evaluation chair and gathered the comments of faculty and staff following the guidelines sanctioned by the College and University as a whole. The unanimous faculty vote was one of "No Confidence." However, staff members were mixed in their support of Dan's leadership. Dan was taken aback by the evaluations. In consultation with Dean Smithering, he again pleaded the need for more time to fulfill the School's mission entrusted to him. Pat assured him a letter of support would come from the Dean's office to offset lack of faculty support. The faculty had crafted a letter to the provost itemizing issues of concern. Some of the items mentioned were based on the writings of leadership scholar DuPree, who advanced the idea that followers have certain rights in a leader- as-servant perspective. Among the rights faculty listed were the right to feel needed, have work be acknowledged as meaningful, have a say in their own destiny, and have the right to appeal decisions made by the leader that appear irrational to them. Further, they felt that Dr. Damon needed to analyze his own leadership values and behaviors to strive for being more trusting, willing to distribute power, judging fairly, showing concern about them, being open to new ideas, and being more insightful when it comes to building a cooperate community of partnership in research goals. Stress levels were high.

When Dean Smithering read the faculty letter, she felt the faculty was not totally fair in their evaluations of Dr. Damon. Some of the new hires did not have enough time invested to make those types of comments. Perhaps Dan was right about the new faculty being influenced by the original five faculty members. After much thought, a letter supporting the retention of Dr. Damon was submitted by the Dean to the Provost. The letter clearly countered the letter of "no confidence" written by faculty members.

Provost Vance read through Dr. Damon's dossier and was impressed with the amount of work he'd done over the past four years. After reading the glowing letter from Dean Smithering, she thought keeping Dr. Damon on for another four years was a given. Then she read the faculty evaluation letter and really wasn't sure what to do. She could easily follow the advice of Dean Smithering and support the retention of Dr. Damon for four more years *or* accept the vote of the faculty to immediately remove Dr. Damon from the leadership role of the School of Health Communication. As a new provost, she really didn't know any of the parties involved that strongly, so she felt she was between a rock and a hard place. Clearly, Dr. Damon's leadership style violated what she'd been clearly articulating across campus, but he was clearly an effective leader in some sense.

She laid the dossier back on her table and turned back towards her computer. *I could always put this one off for later, but I don't know if later will really help me come to a different decision.* With that thought, she started writing her letter of recommendation on the Dr. Damon's continuing appoint in the School of Communication.

DISCUSSION QUESTIONS

1. The new Provost is charged with either retaining Dr. Damon for another 4-year contract or find a replacement in response to the faculty concerns... if you were in the Provosts position, what would your decision be? Why?

2. What are some of the similarities and differences between the leadership styles of Dean Smithering and Dan Damon?

3. According to the letter from the faculty evaluating Dan's leadership, there are many aspects of servant leadership that Dan has failed to accomplish. Can you find an example for each of the claims made by the faculty? Can you find any examples of Dan showing better leadership than his faculty claim?

4. Can you find examples of a supportive communication climate? Can you find examples of a defensive communication climate?

KEY TERMS

Servant leadership, follower rights, organizational leadership style

Never Again

Kris Grill

UNIVERSITY OF KANSAS

ABSTRACT

Dayna Reynolds has just been asked to join her company's talent development program and start working with her old mentor again. Should Dayna forget about past negative experiences and say "yes" to resuming a relationship with her mentor? What will become of her "high-potential" status if she decides to say "no"?

At 5:00 AM Dayna Reynolds walked outside and took in a deep breath of cool Autumn air. It was the perfect morning for a run so she locked her front door, popped in her ear buds, turned on her favorite playlist, and started jogging. Usually, Dayna loved her morning runs; they were a chance for her to leave all her problems behind and think about nothing but the scenery. Today was different. As much as she wanted to forget about everything, she had an important decision to make by the end of the day and she still had no idea what to do.

Danya decided to flood her head with aggressive music instead of thinking about her impending decision; she turned up her iPod and found her favorite workout song. *If I just focus on my running and the music, I can at least have some peace for the next 45-minutes,* she thought as she quickened her pace down the local jogging trail.

Dayna joined Clarkson Foods, a large multinational food company, three years ago, and has been working tirelessly to make a name for herself. Immediately out of college she was hired as a research-and-development team member, but in no time her project managers began giving her additional responsibilities and asking her to take a more hands-on role in the larger projects her team was working on. Her ambition had been rewarded with merit raises, bonuses, and a few promotions. She quickly became a team leader in the research-and-development department. She was working her way up in the company and knew that joining ClarksonCareers—her company's talent development program—was the best route to an executive position.

She received an offer to join this year's talent development class, but had to decide if she wanted to commit to the program. While it seemed like it should be an easy decision, this one had been haunting Dayna for some time.

As she was finishing up her run, her thoughts raced back to the conversation she and Charles Martinez had had a few weeks back. As she ran through a forest of fall colors she paid no attention to her backdrop. All she could think about was what she was going to do.

THE OPPORTUNITY OF A LIFETIME

Two weeks earlier Dayna had received an email from Charles Martinez, Clarkson's senior vice president of human resources. In the email Mr. Martinez asked Dayna to set up an appointment so they could talk about an opportunity he thought she would be perfect for. Intrigued, Dayna called his administrative assistant that afternoon and set up a meeting for the following day.

Dayna had butterflies in her stomach as she walked across the Clarkson campus to Mr. Martinez's office in the Bailey building. Because of her anxious excitement, the elevator ride to the top floor seemed excruciatingly long and Dayna hoped there wouldn't be a lengthy wait. She needed to know what this opportunity was all about.

Walking into the C-Suite, Dayna was amazed at how plush the offices looked, especially compared to the grey cubicle she called home. The walls were paneled in dark wood; the furniture was mahogany and leather; and the artwork looked like it came from the walls of the Louvre; there were no prints in the executive suite. After she checked in, she took a seat on one of the comfy leather sofas in the common area and waited for Mr. Martinez to call her in.

"Hi Dayna, it's nice to see you, come on in," Mr. Martinez said, "How is everything going?"

"Just fine," Dayna stated, although she really wanted to dispose of the small talk and get right to the matter at hand. Luckily, Mr. Martinez was on the same page.

"As you know, I wanted to talk with you today about an opportunity I think you might be interested in." Dayna nodded, giving him the go ahead to continue. "Every other year we assemble a class of Clarkson's best and brightest to participate in our ClarksonCareers program. I have been hearing wonderful things about you and the work you have been doing for some time now, so it came as no surprise when Joyce suggested that we ask you to join this year's class."

Dayna had heard about the ClarksonCareers program during her orientation. The program was designed to help high-potential women and minorities advance in the organization by pairing them with high-ranking organizational members. These more advanced others served as mentors to the program participants. By agreeing to participate, both mentor and protégé committed to meet on a bi-weekly basis to complete organizational projects. While program participants "graduated" after two years, the expectation was that individuals would continue to collaborate with their executive mentors for years to come.

During her first year at Clarkson, one of Dayna's teammates was participating in the ClarksonCareers program. Because of his involvement in the program, Sundeep would periodically miss group meetings to work with his mentor. Due to the impressive results that he and his mentor produced on their projects, Sundeep became highly visible in the company. By the time he finished the program he had already received a promotion, and within a year he was being groomed for a position at the executive level. This was the opportunity Dayna had been waiting for. She knew that joining the program would make attaining her goal of transitioning into an executive role much easier.

"Here is some information about the program," Mr. Martinez said as he handed Dayna an envelope containing several pamphlets. "Make sure you read through all of that and let me know if you have any questions. We don't need your answer right away—you can take some time to think about it—but I wanted you to know that we all would be very excited to have you join the ClarksonCareers program."

As much as Dayna wanted to accept his offer immediately, she appreciated the opportunity to examine the materials more closely. "Thank you so much," Dayna said as she stood up and prepared to leave, "Let me look over these and I'll get back to you soon."

"By the way," Mr. Martinez interrupted, "we have already been in contact with Michelle Richards, who has agreed to serve as your mentor. She was really excited to hear that you were asked to join this year's class and volunteered to be your mentor. I know you two worked together a few years back and if I recall correctly, you were pretty successful. The moment she suggested it, I knew that this pairing would be great."

"Yeah. Umm. Thanks...thanks again," Dayna stammered as he escorted her out of the room, "I'll be in touch." As she walked back to her cubicle, she couldn't help but feel upset. While she and Michelle had collaborated on a few very successful projects, the experience was less than desirable. As much as she wanted to advance at Clarkson, the idea of agreeing to let Michelle be her mentor again was very troubling. Working with her again would not only be unpleasant, but also, to tell the truth, Dayna didn't know if she could survive it.

A CHANCE MEETING

The clock read 7:45 as Dayna pulled her black Monte Carlo into an open spot in the parking garage. She got out of the car, grabbed her BlackBerry from the center console, and picked up her briefcase. Out of the corner of her eye she saw Julia Holden rushing to catch up with her. She and Julia had worked on the same team during her first year with the company, but now Julia worked on the beverage-development team while Dayna worked on the low-calorie snacks team.

"Hi Dayna, how are you this morning?"

"I've been better," Dayna said as she mentally prepared herself for the day.

"What's the matter?"

"Oh… it's nothing. I just have to make an important decision today and I have no idea what I'm gonna do."

"Why don't we go up to the café and grab a coffee. We don't have to be in the office until 8:30. Need someone to listen?"

"Yeah, that would be great. Are you sure I won't be a bother?"

"Not at all, let's go get some mochas and chat."

The women walked into the café, purchased their coffee, and found a quiet table in the corner. Dayna explained that she had been asked to join the ClarksonCareers program, but wasn't sure if she was going to accept the invitation. When Julia asked why she didn't say yes immediately, Dayna told her that her formally appointed mentor was Michelle Richards.

"Oh." Julia said knowingly, "Well…that'll do it."

"Yeah… I just don't know what to do. I hated working for Michelle. When I first got here everyone said that I needed to work closely with her because she could teach me so much, but I just feel like she used me to get ahead. I did all the work and she got all the credit."

Michelle and Dayna had worked together on a few highly successful projects. At first, the pairing seemed great. Both women were go-getters who aimed to complete work tasks as quickly and efficiently as possible. Dayna hated sitting in endless meetings generating idea after idea when everyone already agreed that the first few suggestions were great. She believed that when a good idea presented itself, you needed to run with it rather than talking it to death. When Michelle echoed these sentiments ending their first meeting together early because enough ideas had been generated to keep everyone busy, Dayna thought she and her team leader would get along just fine.

After the women had completed their first project together, things changed drastically. The once pleasant Michelle seemed to have morphed into a highly competitive and manipulative being. Michelle would talk down to Dayna in meetings, and when work assignments were given out, Dayna always seemed to get a disproportionately large amount of work as compared to her peers. It wasn't that Dayna minded working hard—she knew she had to prove herself if she wanted to move up in the company—her problem was that her hard work seemed to equate praise for Michelle. People knew that Dayna was on the team, but after watching Michelle get praised for the development of products that she was 100% responsible for, Dayna had had enough. She was prepared to go to her group leader and complain about the situation when Michelle was promoted to a group-level manager as well.

Knowing that her days of working with Michelle were over, Dayna kept quiet and had not thought about those first few months at Clarkson until her conversation with Mr. Martinez a few weeks back.

"I just don't know what to do. I want to move up in the company, but I don't trust Michelle. I won't kill myself to advance her career. Not again. I would just ask to be paired with someone else, but Martinez made it clear that she picked me. I can't complain about her now, two years after the fact."

"You're right, you can't. Even if you asked to be paired with a different executive, Michelle is still on your supervisory team. If she took credit for your ideas, I don't want to see what she does when she finds out that you specifically asked not to work with her."

"I know. What I am wondering is if I even need to join this program to get ahead. I have been doing just fine. Sure, this seems like the easier route, but I can make it there on my own. Can't I?"

"I am sure you could, but having a mentor can sometimes be a good thing. I have learned so much about how to do my job from my mentor. Nick is always willing to share his ideas, talk about the development of my career, and even let me help out on some of his projects. While working with Nick is great, I can only imagine how beneficial it would be to work with someone who was already at the senior level. Nick and I are both team leaders, he has just been doing it longer. If you want the executives to notice you, you need to be working with one of them."

Dayna knew Julia was right. In one of her college classes, she had been told about an organization that conducted research about women in the workplace. Her professor had assigned some of their reports and she enjoyed reading them so much that she continued to read new reports whenever they came out. She knew that having a mentor at the executive level, especially a female one, should be an advantage. Not only would Dayna be more visible with an executive mentor, but she would be able to work on more challenging projects, gain access to new networks, and maybe even learn how to handle some of the unique problems women face as they move up the ladder.

"I don't know what to tell you," Julia said as the women walked to their offices.

"It's okay; I still have a lot of thinking to do."

TO MENTOR OR BE MENTORED

Dayna walked onto her floor at 8:25, and sat down at her desk. She started reviewing the proposed packaging design for a new low-calorie, portion-controlled snack. Because the product was being added to an established line, approving the design was a formality. While the packaging looked great, she knew she had to check with the food scientists about the nutrition label. Before she could give her stamp of approval she needed to make sure the nutrition information and ingredients were all correct. She could just email the proof to the labs, but she knew that her best bet was to go over in person. She needed to have the packaging approved by noon if she was going to have samples made up for Friday's staff meeting.

As she walked across the campus to verify the information on her labels, she chuckled to herself. Usually, this task was a hassle, but spending time away from her cube was a welcome distraction today.

Once at the labs, Dayna passed the proof off to the Kari, the food scientist who helped her perfect the product recipe, and she took a seat in Kari's office. As she was fumbling through emails on her BlackBerry, Sundeep knocked on the window behind her.

"Hi Dayna! How's it going?"

"Same old, same old," Dayna replied not wanting to talk about her problem with anyone else today.

"Hey, I heard you got asked to join ClarksonCareers. Consider yourself lucky. My two years in the program were the best. When do you start?"

"I haven't said 'yes' yet, but if I do we will start at the beginning of next month."

"Okay, well you really need to do this. When I joined the program I was excited about becoming a protégé because I thought it would make it easier to get promotions, which would of course lead to a higher salary."

"Well I don't know about your salary, but you did seem to get the promotions soon after joining the program."

"Yeah, I thought that would be the best part, but it really wasn't. The best part is actually the opportunity to mentor other people. At first I thought it would be a time drain, but it is so rewarding to be an ally for a developing employee."

"Really?"

"Definitely, and you learn so much by working with other people. I know I am not that much older than some of the people I work with, but that doesn't matter. We both learn from each other, and it's awesome."

"That's good to know."

"Beyond that, the company does a lot for the mentors that get asked to work in the program. I just got done doing a mini-seminar on effective mentoring; it was great. But hey, I have to get going," Sundeep stated. "Let me know if I can give you any other advice. I already have a protégé from this class, but I am sure we can talk, too."

Dayna hadn't thought about the subjective benefits that would come from moving up the ranks. While she did consider herself an informal mentor to some of the members of her team, she would really like formal training and the opportunity to work in an organizationally sanctioned mentor-protégé relationship. This trip was supposed to take her mind off of her decision, but instead it just made her more confused.

THE CLOCK IS TICKING

As the day drew on, Dayna got more and more nervous about her pending decision. She knew that turning down this opportunity might amount to career suicide, but she also knew that agreeing to work with Michelle might end her career at Clarkson, too. Julia was right; mentors could do so much to help their protégés' careers, but what do you do when your mentor is more concerned with advancing her own career then helping you with yours? How much effort would she have to put into her work to remain visible if Michelle continued to take credit for all her ideas? If Sundeep had to take mentoring training, did Michelle? Would the training even make a difference?

Dayna had still not made her decision when she got a call from Mr. Martinez's administrative assistant. George informed Dayna that Charles wanted to meet with her at 4:30 that afternoon.

As Dayna made the trek to the Bailey building her mind was going 100 miles per hour. This time around she didn't notice her lush surroundings; she just silently sat in the lobby.

"Ms. Reynolds." George stated, "He'll see you now."

Dayna walked into Martinez's office and sat down.

"So," Martinez asked, "are you joining this program or not?"

DISCUSSION QUESTIONS

1. Dayna seems to think that joining the formal mentoring program is the only way to advance at Clarkson. Would you agree or disagree with Dayna? How else might Dayna take advantage of the benefits of mentoring without participating in the development program?

2. Dayna recalls having read information about how female protégés stand to benefit from having executive mentors, especially if those mentors are female. What are some organizational challenges that women (and minorities) face? How might a mentor ease some of those challenges? In what ways might having a female mentor be beneficial for a woman?

3. Dayna's fear of working with Michelle stems from some negative mentoring experiences from the past. In what ways might negative mentoring experiences affect a protégé? A mentor? An organization? What can mentors, protégés, and/or organizations do to lessen the damage caused by a negative mentor/protégé experience?

4. If you were Dayna, what would you do? What information/experiences would you consider to be the most salient as you make your decision?

KEY TERMS

Mentoring, gender, decision-making, excessive careerism

CHAPTER

15

Friendly Fire

Franziska Macur

EDGEWOOD COLLEGE

"I don't trust him. We're friends."
— *Bertolt Brecht*

ABSTRACT

Nelly and Ava celebrated their "girlfriend-business" until Nelly dropped a bomb on an unsuspecting Ava. Is it time for Ava to fire back, change her business approach, or give it a second try?

Ava stared absently out of the window. Her accountant, Trevor Adler, shifted uncomfortably in his seat. For a while, these meetings were energizing. Ava remembered the confidence that Trevor had in those early days.

How had it gotten to this? she thought to herself.

She and Nelly were business partners. They had a successful consulting firm, which skyrocketed since it opened two years ago. And now, they were sitting here fighting over a printer cartridge. It was a sad picture. It took everything she had to keep from getting emotional.

Nelly was leaving the firm and was very determined to get her share of the cost of a cartridge that was still in its box. Ava would use it in the business and Nelly "just wanted her fair share." Nelly was done contributing. It was her time to get some money, and even more … some respect.

THE BEGINNING

Ava and Nelly met working at a big consulting firm. They made a great team. Two young, career-oriented women, ready to conquer the world. Clients noticed, and together they quickly started to build a substantial book of business.

They didn't really consider starting their own business until one of their clients asked them point blank why they were not starting on their own. He also offered to follow them and be their first big customer. Nelly and Ava took the step into entrepreneurship. And even though they had to work even more hours, they quadrupled their income.

The business took off. Soon they hired a third full-time person, Coleen. Clients kept knocking on the door of their stylish downtown office. Work was great. Life seemed to be great, too.

THE MIDDLE

Perspectives on balancing work life with personal life started to differ. Nelly's boyfriend, Matthew, moved to London. She took more and more time off, arguing that she could work from the distance. Those absences started with occasional long weekends, but recently they extended into full weeks, often with short notice to Ava.

Ava tried to be supportive. After all, she and Nelly were not just business partners—they were friends. That's how it felt. That's what made the business so much fun for Ava. They worked hard, yet they also had fun together. After a thirteen-hour work day they would go to the gym together. For relaxation, all three of them would go sailing for a weekend on Ava's parents' boat. They started to take cooking classes during lunch breaks. And of course, Nelly and Coleen were at Ava's wedding. They liked to describe themselves as a business of girlfriends. They all seemed to enjoy those blurred boundaries—after all, wasn't that what everybody dreamed of? You start your own business, you earn a lot of money, and you do all this with friends who discuss ... not only marketing strategies but also the newest fashion trends and boyfriend troubles.

But Ava struggled with those boundaries when there was conflict. For example, she wasn't sure how to handle Nelly's work attendance patterns. After all, Nelly still did a lot of work. But many client meetings and weekend events had to be covered by Ava (alone) or with Coleen, which opened up another delicate area. Coleen was not a partner. She started to ask for more money now that she began to cover more of Nelly's duties. Ava didn't feel good about this. She didn't like negotiations to begin with, and she hated them when friends were involved. So she tried to find a way around them, cushion hard decisions whenever possible, and emphasize even more the "fun things" to do together. It seemed to be working out somehow. The business was going great and they really enjoyed doing what they were doing. That's at least how it looked to Ava ...

THE END

They all took a week off between Christmas and New Year, even though, as Ava described it, "You never have time off when it's your own business." But most businesses slowed down during this time—so it really seemed like a little vacation. Ava felt refreshed and motivated to go back to work and start on an exciting project that they just took over.

When she entered the office Nelly was already there. She seemed to be very focused on something.

Coleen wasn't there. Ava remembered that she had asked to have two more days off. No problem.

She tried to strike up a conversation with Nelly, asked her how her week was, not that she anticipated to hear anything new. Of course they had texted each other during the week, exchanged Christmas and New Year's greetings and shared some new gossip. "Business as usual," Ava thought, "or was it personal as usual?" Ava pondered this notion for little while and moved on.

She had a hard time drawing boundaries. But it fit her personality. She liked it. She didn't want to work with people who were just there to get the work done. She needed the personal touch.

She started looking through the mail and organized her desk. Her email was up to date. (She slept most of the time with her blackberry.) Yet she got two new messages from clients. One of them asked for an update of the current project. The other one had a new project that he wanted them to take over—"if they had enough people to handle it." Ava shook her head. What did he mean? He knew that they had three fulltime people plus a few student workers helping them out here and there. The project seemed to fit their company perfectly. She told Nelly about it, who agreed. Ava remembered that they had talked about hiring a fourth person soon. The time seemed to be right to continue the business' expansion.

Nelly came over to show Ava some slides. "Do you have time to do dinner?" she asked. Ava nodded.

After work, they went to an Italian place around the corner, Mazzuchelli's. They got a window table on the second floor that looked out over the state capitol building. Snow was falling in big flakes and the holiday lights on the trees shimmered softly. The flood lights on the capitol dome made the façade glow. It was a perfect scene.

They both ordered wine. There was something relaxing about the simplicity of the house Chianti. Ava kept her eyes closed and let the first taste linger on her tongue. It was a wonderful escape and she felt her shoulders immediately relax. She let out a soft, but audible exhale and smiled. Nelly didn't seem to notice.

They both studied the menu. It seemed to take Nelly way longer than usual. When she finally looked up at Ava, something seemed really off.

"What's wrong?" Ava asked.

Nelly starred at her. Her eyes got big and she started to cry. It seemed like forever before she could say anything.

"I want out," Nelly sobbed.

Ava was shocked. "You're breaking up with Matthew? I thought things were going great for you two."

"No", Nelly shook her head, "I want out of our firm. I'm done. I can't do this anymore."

Ava was stunned.

"What? What? Why?" she stammered and nearly toppled her water. "Why would you want to do that? What do you mean 'out'?"

"It's just too much. Too much work … too much pressure … responsibility. I can't take it anymore."

"What do you mean? This is what it takes to run a business. We talked about this when we started."

Ava was emphasizing each sentence by poking the table firmly.

"We were excited … YOU were excited. You didn't want to have a boss anymore. What … what do you mean 'out'? We wanted to be in charge of us and we are! Do you think clients pay us to walk in and look good? What about this isn't what we expected and talked about from day one? We talked about our first week for a year, for God's sake." Ava took a breath, but not a long one before continuing, "We were on such a high from working 100 hours … it was like we were in heaven. Do you … do you remember all that? Do you remember the first check we got? You're still carrying the $1,000 Prada bag! Was that all just bullshit?"

"Yeah … I know … but, I need my space … you're just consuming me night and day."

"Wait … I'm consuming you?" Ava's pulse quickened and she shifted from stunned to irritated. "You need your 'space'? What the hell does that mean?"

Ava struggled to keep her voice and composure in check, but it wasn't working well. Out of the corner of her eye, she saw the waiter approach and retreat.

"I had some appointments with my doctor about my stomach cramps," Nelly said, looking down with her hands clenched in her lap. "She said it was stress and that I was moving to an ulcer."

"And that's my fault?"

Silence. Ten seconds of silence that seemed like ten hours. Ava glared. Nelly avoided.

Ava waited for something … at least some form of apology. It didn't come.

"I can't do this anymore," said Nelly, and she got up and left the restaurant.

Ava still stared at her as she walked away and disappeared down the stairs. She shook her head and replayed the conversation fifty more times.

The waiter approached cautiously.

Dinner for one.

THE MORNING AFTER

To say that the first moments were awkward was a gross understatement.

All conversations had buried emotions. All sentences were short. And most of the time the reply was, "Fine."

Ava and Nelly tiptoed around each other for the many weeks. Nelly had agreed to stay on for six more months. This way, they could finish all the projects started together and plan accordingly for new ones. The business felt like work all sudden. Ava was glad when she could escape to an onsite meeting or a business trip.

They had also agreed not to tell Coleen for a while. Nobody should get too worried before it was necessary, especially the clients. Yet all the sudden Ava could see the need for boundaries. Was it her duty to tell Coleen? She was, after all, a friend? Or was it fair to handle this as strictly business?

Ava wished somebody would wake her up from a bad dream. The worst part was probably that she still couldn't understand Nelly. She felt like she had worked with a stranger for the last two years. *Why didn't she notice the mental stress? Why didn't Nelly tell her? Was all the friend stuff just fake? As a partner, wasn't Nelly obliged to talk to her about those issues before she made a final decision, friends or not?* Ava had never thought about those kinds of business rules. Because things were going so well, she didn't have to.

After a while Ava started to see positive aspects of the situation. She would be her own boss. She would make more money. She could make decisions without always asking for Nelly's approval. The fact that it was very difficult to work with Nelly these days made it easier to see the bright side, even though Nelly did handle herself very professionally.

Nelly, Coleen, and Ava went for their lunch. It was time to tell Coleen. Maybe she could get the raise after all. Coleen took the news rather calmly. She hugged Nelly and asked if there was anything she could do to make it easier for her. Ava felt left out. Really, Coleen felt sorry for Nelly? Shouldn't her priorities be with the company?

Coleen's priorities were apparently not with the company. Two weeks later she shared with Ava and Nelly that she was leaving—to work for a competitor. All the sudden, the bond between Ava and Nelly seemed to get stronger again. They had to fight for what they built together. This meant keeping Coleen from taking any customers over to her new employer. It seemed to be an exhausting task. The struggle and disappointment with Coleen made Ava sometimes forget about Nelly's leave. Once in a while she even thought Nelly would change her mind, especially when she saw how important the company was to her. But Nelly didn't change her mind. She got more and more involved in planning her life after work. She started to take more time off. And she finally requested to meet with Ava to talk about finances.

Ava felt unprepared. She knew Nelly was a good negotiator. And Nelly knew that Ava wasn't. Bad starting point. However, Ava didn't see much need for negotiation. The equipment they had purchased together was rather limited. A few computers, printers, a projector, some smaller office items. They could easily split those. Maybe there wasn't anything to negotiate. It would be more than fair if Nelly would just leave it all to her, to the company that she, after all, still valued. But Nelly's agenda was different.

THE BITTER END

Ava was the first to enter the conference room. As she turned on the lights, she just shook her head. The room felt so different today. *How many times had clients signed contracts right here? How many times had the two friends put their feet up on the table at the end of a long day of a long week and celebrated?*

Nelly came in and sat directly across from Ava.

"She always sat next to me," Ava thought.

Nelly began, "I want $20,000 for the market value of our brand."

Ava swallowed. "I beg your pardon?!"

Nelly didn't blink.

"$20,000. We both know," Nelly calmly stated, "that we built something great, and you get the honor to keep going with it. That is worth something."

Ava tried to keep her calm. She never yelled. She never got angry. She just didn't know of any other reaction that would suit this request.

Nelly continued. "We built … together … something that has tremendous potential. We built … together … something that has value. This amount is a fair share representing my contribution to the company that you will be able to run, because I helped us get here." Nelly took a deep inhale and sat back in her chair, looking calmly at Ava.

Well coached, Ava thought.

Ava shook her head. Finally, she reacted: "You're leaving. It was your decision. You are leaving me to deal with all the work and all the problems that might surface with your departure. You are devaluing our brand with your departure. You are hurting our friendship. You are thinking of nobody but yourself. And you want me to pay you $20,000 for that?"

Nelly started to look angry, but took a quick breath and composed herself. In a shaky voice, she asked, "Why can't you acknowledge that it is something grand we built? Why can't you show me any *respect* for that? Why in the world can't you have a decent business negotiation without playing the friendship card? This has nothing to do with our being friends. It has everything to do with our being business partners. I'm leaving you the company. Did you really anticipate that I would leave it for nothing?"

Silence … again. Ava excused herself saying, "I will consider this."

Ava left the meeting almost in tears. She would have cried if this would have happened earlier, but it seemed that the times where she would cry in front of Nelly had passed. You don't cry in a business meeting. That was a rule she knew.

It was one more month before Nelly would leave for good. Ava was going back and forth about her request. Nelly seemed to be obsessed with the financial side of the business. She made sure that Ava looked at all the updated reports that showed in what a good financial standing their company was. It was annoying to Ava. And she hated it. After debating if she should just keep the company under a different name or pay Nelly the $20,000, she came to a conclusion. She would pay her the amount requested and be done with it. She didn't have the energy to fight anymore. She wished Nelly had never been a friend. But she wasn't probably, anyway.

PARTING SHOTS

The accountant shifted, obviously uncomfortable. The two women he had known for a while always seemed very cheerful. Today they barely looked at each other.

Ava spoke. "I will agree to the $20,000 buyout price."

But Nelly was not satisfied. "I wish you would just say that you value what we built and show me some respect," she said to Ava. She repeated this sentence like a mantra.

Ava didn't respond. She looked at the accountant and tried to make an apologetic face. She would like to sign and leave. But Nelly was not done. She presented a list of all of the assets of the company. The total was $12,645.74. The last item on the list was an $80 printer cartridge that was sitting in its original box. On the bottom of the last page was some simple math:

$$\$12,645.74 / 2 = \$6,322.87 \quad \text{Final Settlement for Property and Equipment}$$

Ava got up from her seat. "I'm sorry we are taking up so much of your time, Mr. Adler," she said. "I'm sure you have more important things to do. I will pay Nelly $20,000 plus $1,200 for equipment. If she wants anything else, I will meet her at the courthouse." She shook his hand and left. Never once did she look at Nelly.

The fresh air felt good. Is this what divorce felt like? Ava felt like a burden had been lifted from her shoulders. The last six months had been exhausting. It could only get better. She wasn't sure how the business would continue. She needed some time to sort things out.

THE FUTURE OF THE FUTURE

It was 6:30 AM when Ava arrived at the office. She walked by the now deserted office of her former partner, paused, and closed the door.

She went into her own office and surveyed the scene... papers and folders everywhere. The whiteboard had some notes in Nelly's handwriting.

A few days later, she ran into Monica. Monica was a friend of her husband's and worked in the same field as Ava. She always liked Monica and enjoyed chatting with her at occasional get-togethers. Monica told Ava that she had heard about the business and the split with Nelly. Monica said that she stopped working for her old firm and wondered if Ava wanted to get together for lunch. Maybe there would be an opportunity to work together? Ava said she would give her a call soon.

A lot went through her head while she was walking home: *What should she do next? Should she just run the firm as a one-woman show? But where would this leave the fun? Should she try to find some new employees? Maybe she should look for somebody to be her new business partner? How could she avoid ending up in the same situation again? Could a meeting with Monica be the right next step into the future of her business?*

DISCUSSION QUESTIONS

1. What questions/conversations should Ava and Nelly have had prior to launching business? What were the main issues that Ava and Nelly should have dealt with?

2. What are the advantages and disadvantages of starting a business with a friend?

3. How could Ava and Nelly have protected themselves against an eventual falling out?

4. Was Nelly justified in asking for the $20,000 plus the $6,322.87 in her settlement package?

5. What would you do if you were Ava?

KEY TERMS

Workplace friendships, partnership dissolution, professional boundaries

CHAPTER 16

The Ballad of Bloomfield Academy

Robyn Fink, Caitlin Hamryszak, Adrienne Sliz, and Sarah Upperman

ITHACA COLLEGE

ABSTRACT

After a teacher doesn't like the annual review he receives, he finds the principal in an apparent compromising position with a new, younger teacher.

PERFORMANCE REVIEW

History teacher Seth Phillips enters the main administration office at Bloomfield Academy. He anxiously awaits his performance review results during a meeting with Victoria Middleton, principal of Bloomfield Academy. As I peek into Victoria's office to see what's keeping Seth waiting, I spot the new music teacher Blaine Clark.

Blaine, popular with the faculty and even more so with students, joined Bloomfield Academy from the music industry where he was most recently a guitarist with a popular pop group. When his band broke apart, he decided a career change was in order. Honestly, it was probably a good thing. I've heard a few of the band's songs and they ain't nothing to write home about. After finishing college at the age of 28, his first employment is here with us at the well-respected Bloomfield Academy. The students seem to really enjoy him—especially the female ones.

While waiting for his review with Victoria, I initiate small talk with Seth to ease his nerves, but our conversation ends when we hear laughter from Principal Middleton's office. Peering into the office, we both see Victoria poised atop her desk with legs crossed and a jovial expression smeared across her face. Giggling, she leans forward as Blaine, sitting right in front of her, gingerly caresses her leg. As the duo concludes their conversation, Blaine exits Victoria's office with a smirk across his face.

Waiting for an invitation to enter Victoria's office, Seth watches as Blaine leaves the main office area and strides down the hallway toward his classroom. Moments later, Victoria calls for Seth, instructing him to enter her office. As Seth enters, Victoria motions for him to take a seat as she crosses the room and positions herself behind the desk. Her void expression matches her reputation for professionalism in the workplace. Seth, who I've heard has a history for mediocre reviews, clamps his hands on the chair and tries to keep his composure. As the door shuts, I watch as Victoria begins shaking her head, much like a disappointed mother reprimands her child.

I hope Seth survives because he's an honest teacher and forces his students to clean up his room at the end of each day. Luckily for me, administrative assistants don't have to undergo the same rigorous review process. "Score one for the little guy," I chuckle to myself as I continue to type a letter the principal has going home later that week to all the parents.

WELCOME TO BLOOMFIELD

Behind my perch in the main office, I hear it all and I see it all. I've been with Bloomfield Academy for 10 years; as the Administrative Assistant to the principal, I've answered the phone as helicopter parents inquire about their children's lackluster grades, complain about their children's dress code violations; and answer questions about our institution to the parents of prospective students. I have my role down to a science.

Bloomfield Academy, located in Bloomfield, NY, is a private co-ed high school. Bloomfield serves as a preparatory school for nearly 1,000 of the best and brightest students in the greater New York area. In addition to catering to the highly educated student body, there is a high level of parent involvement in the school, culminating with the 15-member governing body, The Parent Advisory Board (PAB). Leading the PAB is Rhonda Carlisle, infamous wife of a prominent New York City plastic surgeon (she was close to being a cast member on "The Real Housewives of New York"). The powerful Mrs. Carlisle is also involved in several philanthropic efforts, including The Sustainability League. Fittingly, her two children are superior students and athletes at Bloomfield Academy. In addition to various other roles, the PAB is responsible for analyzing staff performance reviews, and helps to assess the effectiveness of the school's principal, Victoria Middleton.

VICTORIA MIDDLETON, PRINCIPAL

I watch as Victoria sits at her desk awaiting the start of a busy school week. Because of the well-behaved student body and elitism of Bloomfield Academy, Victoria rarely deals with disciplinary issues. Instead, her responsibilities include serving as the school's fearless figurehead, and maintaining the integrity of the program. Though she enjoys her job, I know she dislikes conducting semi-annual performance reviews.

While Bloomfield Academy was built with strong minds, the walls appear to have been built with grade F cardstock—I hear everything through the walls. From my desk, a few feet outside of Victoria's office, I've overheard her complaining about the bureaucracy of the performance review process during after-hours phone calls.

Because of the private-school structure of Bloomfield Academy, it is Victoria's responsibility to assess each teacher at one of two review periods during the academic year. She then brings her findings to the PAB for their review. These PAB meetings tend to be especially tense, as the PAB has a reputation for being tough critics of faculty members. New to the principal position, Victoria is anxious for the performance review reports, hoping they will pass without incident.

"Malena," she asks me quickly, "can you pull the phone messages from the weekend and grab the file of staff performance reviews for me? I need to review all of them in anticipation for the PAB meeting later this month."

"Not a problem, Victoria," I respond. Attempting to alleviate tension, I ask, "Did you and Howard have a nice weekend?"

Howard Middleton, Victoria's husband, has been a beloved teacher at Bloomfield almost as long as he's been married to Victoria. Twelve years Victoria's senior, he is a technological guru and his presence at the Academy helped Victoria secure the highly coveted principal position at Bloomfield Academy.

Victoria grabs her coffee mug and begins pouring while rehashing an abbreviated version of her weekend discussion with Howard.

"Yes, we did, but we spent most of it talking about our future," Victoria answers while adding cream and sugar to her coffee. Victoria continues, "Howard is planning on retiring within the next three years, so we're trying to figure out the finances. As for me, I'm too much of a career woman to retire. I have way too much energy, and it'd be silly for me to retire at 45."

As Victoria walks into her office, she grabs the files from my desk. "Howard's so loved by the faculty and students," I quickly remind her. "It'll be a shame to see him go. Someone will have big shoes to fill."

"More like size eight Birkenstock's," Victoria laughs as she walks into her office.

Administrative Assistants are the oil of this academic engine, or at least that's what I always tell myself. As long as I show up on time, do what is told of me and laugh at the boss's jokes, I won't be replaced.

"Haha, good one, Victoria!" I yell before returning to the daily absentee list. Who is she kidding? I think to myself—he might be a bit older, but he's still cute.

LUNCH

Lunchtime, a twenty-minute break from the chaos of demanding and overachieving high school students, is welcomed by all faculty and staff members seeking a break from reality. As an extra perk at the prestigious school, faculty and staff are able to eat in a plush room filled with couches and served daily with catered sweets and coffee. It's another added benefit from the PAB to keep workers happy and motivated (or at least full) while working at Bloomfield Academy.

Per usual, I am sitting alone eating and reading a Jodi Picoult novel. At the table to my right, Victoria is seated—cucumber and cream cheese sandwich in hand and skinny chai tea latté by her side—when Blaine enters the room and slides into the seat next to her.

Victoria inquisitively looks up from her sandwich. In all my times eating lunch in the same room with Victoria, she doesn't often welcome lunchtime chatting, but she smiles and acknowledges Blaine's presence. It's well known among faculty members that she admires his enthusiasm for the job and she respects the industry knowledge he brings to the position.

"Hey Vic, what day works for you for those guitar lessons?" the suave new faculty member asks, not even acknowledging my presence in the room. Without waiting for a response, he adds, "I was initially thinking we could do it after work one day this week, but I know you're busy with the kids. So what about Columbus Day? We'd have more time for our solo jam session."

"Sounds great, Blaine," Victoria smiles. I've never heard anyone but Howard, her husband, call her "Vic."

"Hey, before I peace out, you have a little something uhh," Blaine says as he leans closer to brush the crumb off of her face, "right there."

As Blaine leans forward to help out Victoria, Seth Phillips, a history teacher, enters. Noticing the two, he looks at me and shakes his head. With a quizzical look and furrowed brow, he asks Victoria, "Hey, how's that husband of yours doing?"

Blaine, noticeably embarrassed, mutters, "Vic, see you at 10 AM on Columbus Day for those lessons. Can't wait."

As he strides out of the room, he finally notices me. "Oh, hey, Malena." My heart stops.

With Miracle Whip on the edge of my lips, I can only muster a quick "Hi, Blaine." I'm almost positive I'm blushing.

"How are things in the world of office bureaucracy?" he politely inquires. *Seems pretty good between you and Principal Middleton,* I think to myself.

"Parents, files, students, parents—fun, fun, fun!" I respond with forced enthusiasm. Did I just really say that? Why do I revert to a 13-year old boy-band fan when I'm around him? My eyes dart to Principal Middleton. I guess I'm not the only one.

TENSION ON THE LINKS

My husband, Jerry, is principal at a neighboring all-boys school, so we often socialize with various faculty members from Bloomfield. That weekend, Jerry and I had a foursome scheduled for Saturday morning at 9 AM at the country club with Howard and Seth. Victoria was never a big golf player, so she usually stayed at home and worked on who knows what while the four of us golfed. After 17 holes of golf, the four of us were enjoying what may be the last warm day of the season. We're all avid golfers, and we've been friends ever since I started working at Bloomfield in the principal's office five years ago.

"So, what's the family up to today?" I ask Howard as Frank is lining up to hit his golf ball down a long fairway.

"You know how it is—the kids have rowing practice and Vic's getting guitar lessons from the new music teacher, Blaine," Howard explains.

"Oh wow, not working for a change?"

"Yeah, I know," Howard says with a hint of sarcasm in his voice.

A few minutes later on the final hole, my husband lines up at the tee and banks his shot to the left. A quick curse word slips out of his mouth under his breath. Thankfully, I think I'm the only one who hears it. As we're heading toward the green on the 18th hole, I accidentally overhear a different conversation going on between Howard and Seth.

"I heard about your performance review, Seth. Sorry Vic's such a stickler for rules and authority. I'm sure when she brings the report to PAB next week, she will have nothing but nice things to say," Howard said to Seth.

"Well, thanks, but she really shouldn't be saying things to you, Howard," Seth said, clearly upset. "Your wife should remember basic protocol here. And maybe stop play favorites all the time! Of course, maybe she likes playing favorites with Blaine."

Now both men were visibly shaken and neither man was able to concentrate enough to sink their easy shots.

THE BOARD MEETING

When the much-anticipated quarterly PAB meeting arrives, faculty members are apprehensive about my performance review presentations. Strangely enough, though, I look forward to watching Victoria promote the faculty's achievements to the highly critical PAB. It's a challenge that Victoria fully embraces.

Entering the boardroom with confidence, Victoria takes her usual seat next to Rhonda near the head of the table. Though she's only been a principal for a year at Bloomfield Academy, her longstanding personal relationships with PAB members make her feel at ease. Victoria smiles and establishes eye contact with the members as Rhonda asks for a call to start the meeting.

I, of course, get the opportunity to sit in the meeting with my netbook, taking the minutes. I've been to these PAB meetings more times than Victoria, so I know how tense these meetings can sometimes become. Of course, as an administrative assistant, I get to stay out of the firing range and just watch.

"As usual," Rhonda begins, "we'll start the past quarter's performance review meeting with a report from Victoria about the faculty's progress."

Victoria begins her well-rehearsed spiel about the successes of her faculty. Heck, she practiced this speech three times in the mirror before leaving her office. Focused on delivering a flawless presentation, she passionately relays the performance of new faculty members. She begins with Blaine Clark, detailing his industry experience and how well he connects with the students—and her professionally.

Finally, she concludes the forty-minute presentation, which she believes has accurately explained the accomplishments of individual faculty members, while maintaining the integrity of the school. Thankfully, she provided me a copy of her address earlier that morning, so I really don't have to type anything while she's speaking. Instead, I watch the facial expressions on the various PAB members. When she mentions Blaine, I definitely saw a few eyebrows raise. I don't think Victoria noticed, though.

Rhonda acknowledges her report and mentions that the PAB will be discussing the findings in full executive session, where decisions will determine raises and the budget for the next academic year. Rhonda asks the PAB members to direct their attention toward the Comment Box, explaining, as per proper PAB protocol, that the box is available to all faculty, staff, parents, and community members as a way to respond to concerns about the school and its activities, curriculum and administration. With a highly involved community and active parent group, it's not uncommon to address at least one comment during each of the PAB meetings. Rhonda opens the box and directs her attention to the first three comments, and then she reaches inside and grabs the final comment.

Pausing before reading, Rhonda becomes flushed and requests that the last note be addressed privately in a more appropriate setting.

Victoria is clearly annoyed and eventually pressures Rhonda into reading the note, "Rhonda, it is policy that all notes are read aloud," Victoria reminds her. "Whatever this concerns should come to the full attention of all PAB Members."

Rhonda uneasily begins reading the message:

Stunned, I put my hands over my mouth to keep the surprised from escaping my mouth. Victoria, turns a shade of green I had never seen before. Rhonda looks up at the Board, and then her eyes meet Victoria's.

"Victoria, how do we proceed?" is the last thing I heard before Victoria slumped in her chair and closed her eyes.

Additional contributions by Kyle M. Woody

DISCUSSION QUESTIONS

1. If you were a member of the PAB, how would you proceed?
2. Based on the material you read in the case, do you think Victoria was behaving inappropriately? Why or why not?
3. If you were Victoria, how would you react to being publicly humiliated in this fashion?
4. In this case, we have an instance where a supervisor, Victoria, also associates with many of her colleagues socially. Should supervisors ever socialize with their colleagues?
5. Should someone talk to Blaine about appropriate versus inappropriate workplace behavior?

KEY TERMS

Workplace relationships, cognitive dissonance theory, expectancy violations theory, nonverbal communication, supervisor-subordinate relationships

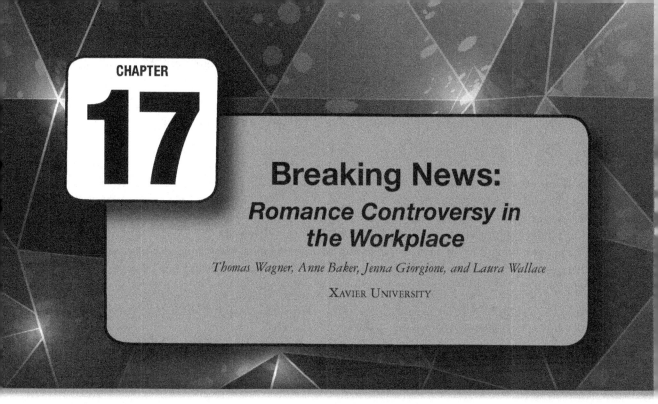

Breaking News:
Romance Controversy in the Workplace

Thomas Wagner, Anne Baker, Jenna Giorgione, and Laura Wallace

Xavier University

ABSTRACT

Bev Andrews, the Editor in Chief of the Dayton Times *has begun dating Steve, a copy editor. What obligation do they have to reveal their romantic relationship to their workplace HR?*

"Yes, what do you need? I am very busy!" Bev says as she winks at Steve.

"Bev, you know I can't stand waiting! Come on, please, am I the new Sports Editor or not?"

"Steve, you know the announcement is going to be at lunch tomorrow."

"And that announcement will be?" Steve asks as he rubs Bev's shoulders.

"Ok, ok, Congrats! It was a tough decision, but you were the best candidate for the job."

"Thanks! I only had to sleep with the boss to get it," jokes Steve as he kisses Bev on the forehead.

"That is not funny, Steve," replies Bev sternly. "We could get in serious trouble if the Human Resource Department thought that you were promoted because of our relationship. Speaking of which, I have been thinking that maybe we need to tell Human Resources about us. It is company policy, after all. I am stressed about this, because our relationship has moved fast and now I feel like we should have filed with HR sooner!"

"Relax Bev! We're fine! How about dinner tonight to celebrate my promotion? We can talk about it then."

Bev agrees, gives him a quick hug, and then orders him with a loving smile, "Now scoot, out of my office. I have very important business to finish! I'll see you after work. Pick me up at 7:00."

Steve, originally from Dayton, moved back to the mid-sized city from New York City a year ago in order to care for his ill mother. In New York, Steve was the Assistant Sports Editor at a large national newspaper. Although Steve was over-qualified, he took his current position as Copy Editor with the *Dayton Times* just to keep active. Given his previous experience in New York, Steve wanted to be the Sports Editor when the previous editor announced his retirement. After developing a strong friendship for a little less than a year, Steve and Bev began dating two months ago.

Bev, on the other hand, has been with the *Dayton Times* for twelve years and served as the Editor in Chief of the paper for the past five years.

Later that night, Bev is touching up her makeup as she anxiously waits for Steve to arrive. *It is 7:15. Of course, he is late; being on time would be a miracle for Steve.* At this moment, she hears knocking at the door.

"Right on time!" Bev sarcastically proclaims to Steve when she opens the door.

Steve shrugs his shoulders and says, "Sorry, there is always traffic on I-75; you know that." Steve gives Bev a kiss on the cheek, apologizes one more time, and declares, "Come on babe, let's get out of here. I'm starving!" Bev smiles and grabs her jacket as they walk out the door.

They arrive at O'Toole's, their favorite restaurant and bar, and sit at their regular table, next to the window. After ordering drinks and food, Bev says, "Steve, I think we need to disclose our relationship to Human Resources. How do you feel about that?"

Steve looks at Bev and admits, "I don't think we should tell them. It's none of their business. This relationship is between us and it hasn't affected our work. You know that we are a great team."

Bev grabs Steve's hands and says, "Listen, you have to see it from their point of view. Our relationship does affect workplace culture, and they want to be able to deal with any negative perceptions."

"What? You actually think people would think I got promoted because of 'us'!? Bev, I was totally joking earlier about sleeping with the boss to get the promotion! Geez!" Steve says defensively.

"Steve, our relationship had no impact on the decision of choosing you for the Sports Editor position, but as I said, I do think that we need to reveal our relationship to Human Resources."

After a moment of contemplating, Steve finally nods his head, "Fine. Tell the Human Resource Department. But, I do not think we need to tell the entire office. It's no one else's business." He continues, "I really do like working with you though, Bev. I am much happier, and I am more creative and open with my ideas around you! Oh, by the way, did you notice that we were nominated for a Pulitzer Prize for our piece on Mill Creek Valley?"

"I know! You're right. We're a great team!" Bev proclaims as they raise their glasses together in a toast to a successful relationship.

"Thank god, work is over today! I so need a drink," Holly Smithers says to her girlfriend Cheryl as they walk into O'Toole's. Holly and Cheryl both worked on the Ohio desk at the *Dayton Times,* so after the congressional session ended in Columbus that afternoon, the two had raced back to the office to file their stories before heading home.

"Look, isn't that Steve?" Cheryl exclaims spotting Bev and Steve sitting in the window seat. Holly turns around and sees Steve and Bev holding hands while they patiently wait for their food.

"It looks as if they are on a date!" Holly says rather loudly to Cheryl.

"Oh wow! It sure does. He just kissed her hand! He can't keep his eyes off her! Too cute!" admires Cheryl.

Unbeknownst to Cheryl, Holly had been looking to get off the Ohio desk for a while now, and saw her opportunity when the sports editor position opened. Holly was a former Ohio State basketball player who even had a two-year stint in the WNBA on the Indiana Fevers before a serious knee injury took her out of the game. With her professional experience and deep ties to Ohio athletics, Holly thought she was perfect for the editor position. For Holly, seeing Bev and Steve was anything but "cute."

Holly had been anxiously awaiting the decision tomorrow afternoon about the editor's position, but the sight of Steve and Bev together made her think the decision had already been made. Holly began working for the *Dayton Times* as an intern seven years ago during journalism school, and took a position as copy editor immediately after her injury. After landing on the Ohio desk, She has been unable to move anywhere in the paper, due to a lack of turnover. Holly had often thought of leaving Dayton to take a sports writing position at another Ohio paper, but she had come to make Dayton her home, so she really didn't want to move anywhere. The Sports Editor position would result in more meaningful work and a raise. In addition to her company loyalty, Holly believed she was more qualified than Steve because she knew Ohio athletics and had a popular sports blog with a national following.

Avoiding eye contact with Bev and Steve, Holly steers Cheryl out of O'Toole's. Outside, Cheryl finally looks at Holly and questions, "What's wrong?"

"Let's go down to Mackers and I'll buy you a beer and explain everything," Holly says, clearly angry but trying to contain her emotions.

While enjoying a beer at Mackers, they begin discussing Bev and Steve's date. Holly finishes her first beer and bangs the bottle on the bar. Then, she expresses how she truly feels, "I think Steve is dating Bev so he can get an edge on the Sports Editor job. I can't believe this! I thought I was being evaluated fairly. He better not get the promotion over me."

Cheryl waits for Holly to stop and breathe for a minute. Then she places her hand on her shoulder and responds calmly, "Listen Holly, Steve is qualified for the job but so are you. I am sure Bev will keep it professional. Don't worry, just keep working hard, and you'll get promoted!"

However, Holly is not paying attention to Cheryl because she is too distracted by the thoughts of how she might get cheated out of a promotion. "It just isn't fair," Holly mumbles to herself.

After a long night and champagne to boot, Bev barely makes it to work on time the next morning. She strolls into the building, grabbing a cup of coffee from the vendor in the lobby before heading to her office. As she approaches, she finds Holly sitting, waiting for her.

"What can I do for you, Holly?"

"Well, I thought I would tell you about something really interesting I saw last night at O'Toole's"

"What do you mean?" Bev says nervously.

"Was that a romantic celebration last night Bev? You cannot honestly think that you can promote your boyfriend. I'm pretty sure that is against company policy and just isn't fair," Holly says firmly.

"What are you talking about?" Bev says with shock.

"You know exactly what I am talking about and I am not the only one who knows about you two," Holly says with an upset but confident tone.

Nervous, Bev states, "Steve and I... um, look Holly, our work relationship..." Bev responds stumbling over her words. Bev stands up and says "The announcement isn't until the lunch today so, I'll see you then Holly."

"See you then!" Holly says frustrated and walks out of Bev's office.

Bev buries her head in her hands and takes a deep breath. She had no idea how Holly found out about her romantic relationship with Steve. She had tried to keep it quiet but the sneaking around wasn't fun. Now she risked the accusation of sexual favoritism. This is exactly why she wanted to disclose her romantic relationship with Steve to Human Resources. Exasperated, she calls Todd, the head of Human Resources. It is a call that she hates to make and she blames herself for the situation.

"Hello Todd"

"Hi Bev. Ready for the big announcement of the new Sports Editor this afternoon?"

"About that, Todd, listen, we need to talk. Can I stop by your office?"

"Sure, I'm free."

"Ok, see you in a few minutes."

Bev grabbed her cup of coffee, *I'm going to need this. I think it's going to be one of those days.* She headed over to the elevator bank and went down two floors to where Human Resources was located. She wormed her way through the labyrinth of offices and finally found herself at Todd's door. She quickly rapped on the door and her Todd yell, "come in."

"Hi, Todd. I have something we need to talk about," says Bev entering into Todd's office.

"Sure, sit down." replies Todd. Bev sits down in a black, leather chair opposite from Todd.

"Well," says Bev, "I'm in a mess… I don't even know where to begin."

"Start at the beginning?"

"Steve and I have been seeing each other for a couple of months now."

"What?" Todd suddenly becomes unfriendly and scolds, "You know, you really should have reported this earlier. Company policy states that if employees begin a romantic relationship, they must report it to Human Resources immediately. Is there a reason you did not report this earlier?"

Bev defends, "Well, we had just started dating, and we didn't know where our relationship was going. We had heard of another couple who was terminated right after reporting an interoffice romance, and we weren't ready to sacrifice our positions for a relationship. This relationship has not affected our work negatively. If anything, it has improved our work! Steve motivates me, and we work very well together. We are even nominated for a Pulitzer on the Mill Creek piece! What we do on our own time is not the company's business."

"OK, I can see some of the logic in what you're saying."

"Well, the problem is, Steve is one of the candidates for the Sports Editor. And honestly, I think he's the better candidate."

"Listen, Bev, we have a bigger issue here. If he had an unfair advantage because the two of you are dating… you really should have reported your romance earlier. As the Editor in Chief of this newspaper, you know the corporate policies and I am not going to debate them here with you. The policy states that all romantic relationships between coworkers must be disclosed and that no romantic partners can be in direct supervision of each other. Why didn't you follow the policy?"

"Well, I'm the editor. I'm in direct supervision of all reporters. By policy, Steve would be unable to work here in any kind of reporting capacity," Bev responds. Upset and nervous, she takes a deep breath to calm her nerves. She did not expect Todd's reaction would be so much of a reprimand. She says nervously, "You are right. I should have reported it earlier. I am truly sorry. Honestly, though, my relationship with Steve had nothing to do with his promotion. After all, you were there for the decision. Todd, we discussed the strengths and weaknesses of every candidate and made the hire decision together. Steve really was the better candidate for the position. He brings experience that is more diverse. Being a Sports Editor at a bigger newspaper gave him an edge. Additionally, he and I work together better than Holly and I do. Holly's work is good but Steve and I inspire each other, and our relationship, even though we kept it a secret, has had a lot of positive impacts on the company. If I thought that our relationship was going to cause problems,

I would have reported it immediately. I thought we were actually improving the company with our more creative work."

"Well, I cannot argue with the fact that the two of you have done great work. Since you and Steve have begun working together, your columns have improved greatly. However, there are bigger issues here. I am still not convinced that the promotion was fair, and you should have reported your relationship as soon as it began. It's your call, Bev, but you know if you give Steve the promotion..., just certain people might think he had an unfair advantage. You should not be supervising someone you are romantically involved with."

Bev sits in silence forces a half smile and says, "Ok, see you at lunch Todd. I'll make the announcement."

Bev is dreading explaining any of this to Steve. She looks at her watch. It has already been a long morning and there is only an hour before the lunch meeting. She calls Steve but he is out of the office. She doesn't want to communicate the change over the phone. She sends a text message to Steve, "See me before lunch today."

With just minutes before the lunch meeting Bev is trying to keep her composure. Steve finally stops by her office.

"Hey babe, ready for lunch?" Steve says with a flirty smile until he sees the somber look on Bev's face and says, "Hey, Bev, what happened?"

"Steve, people know. Heck, Holly knows about us, and I am worried that I shouldn't promote you now."

"Ok, not funny," says Steve perplexed, and then more directly says "You are serious?"

"Yes I am serious! I told you we should have disclosed to HR! Now I am worried about how this will all look if I promote you and the implications it could have for the company since we didn't follow policy."

"No, this isn't fair! What are you talking about?! I worked hard for that position and I am the best candidate." Steve says defensively.

"Fair? Steve give me a break. I feel bad about this too but we are the ones who are skating on thin ice here." Bev explains.

"What? Thin ice? Do you hear yourself?" Steve asks sarcastically.

"Steve! Stop it. I told you over and over we should have disclosed our relationship. Did you ever read the policies in the employee handbook? Look, I have some thinking to do. I'll see you at the lunch."

Steve walks out of Bev's office upset and Bev stares at her desk and takes several deep breaths.

A few minutes later Bev walks into the conference room late for the lunch meeting. Holly awkwardly shakes Bev's hand. The situation is uncomfortable, with Bev experiencing a tight knot pulling on her stomach. Steve is awkwardly standing in the corner with his arms folded. "Excuse me, everyone. I have an announcement to make," proclaims Bev. This was the announcement the whole office had been waiting for. After holding the office in suspense for a moment, Bev clears her throat and says, "The new Sports Editor will be... ."

DISCUSSION QUESTIONS

1. At what point should Bev and Steve have disclosed their romantic relationship?
2. How did the organization benefit from the romantic relationship?
3. Was Holly justified in her action to confront Bev?
4. Do organizations have the right to investigate and interfere with romantic relationships? Why or why not?
5. What is the most ethical decision Bev's can make regarding promotion?
6. How does a workplace romance affect the whole organization?

KEY TERMS

Romantic workplace relationships, supervisor-subordinate relationships, sexual harassment, organizational justice

CHAPTER 18

Mascots Gone Wild:
An Exploration of Workplace Harassment Ethics

Shannon M. Brogan, Erin E. Gilles, and Le'Artis W. Allen, II

KENTUCKY STATE UNIVERSITY

ABSTRACT

A family-owned theme park is opening a new location. The new park is scheduled to open in two months. A small team has been assembled in Omaha, NE to prepare for the opening. To cope with the stress of the impending grand opening, the Director of Park Operations from the Aurora, IL location, decided to send a humorous email to the Nebraska team. The recipients all responded in different manners to the email, which contained sexually explicit images. One upset employee emailed the COO with their concerns. The COO must now decide to how handle this manner without disrupting his team and without putting the company's reputation in jeopardy.

Clicking on the first picture, Shamarla couldn't believe her eyes. Park employees wearing the park mascot costumes, Boxy the Dog and Roxy the Cat, were contorted in a sexual position. As her mouth hit the floor, she debated whether to open the next images. Surely Jamal, someone so well-respected in the company, wouldn't be sending other employees such inappropriate images. Hesitantly, Shamarla opened the second and third jpegs, finding more images similar to the first. She had no idea how to respond.

Imaginarium Fantasy Parks, owned by Brolles Productions, opened their first theme park in 1994 in Charleston, SC. They maintain their corporate headquarters at this location. Due to the success of the first park, and the growth in the U.S. entertainment industry, Brolles Productions opened two additional parks in the U.S. The second location was opened in Dallas, TX in 2000, the third in Aurora, Ill., in 2006, and the fourth would be opening in Omaha, NE, later this year. Imaginarium Fantasy Parks are known for their extreme roller coasters, which are designed by the world's leading engineers. The roller coasters are just the beginning; the adrenaline-filled guests also experience cutting-edge arcades with 3-D, immersive gaming experiences. Younger guests enjoy the musical productions, featuring the famous mascots Boxy the Dog and Roxy the Cat. In the portions of the park designed for youths under the age of 10, guests can enjoy smaller-scale roller coasters, themed merry-go-rounds, roaming mascots, face painting, and much more.

The first park was opened by Jim and Kathy Brolles, and over 15 years later the company was still family-owned and operated. The Brolles' family initially hired 50 employees, and now employs 535 people over their four locations; Charleston, Dallas, Aurora, and now Omaha. Key infrastructure of the new park was already built, but minor difficulties with some of the computerized features were holding up the opening date. In addition, finishing design details such as interior paint, furniture, and decorations were still not in place.

With the opening scheduled in two months for the upcoming summer season, new director of Park Operations Stacy Velarde and the director of the design team Shamarla Bailey were concerned about finishing everything on time. The onsite people kept telling Stacy and Shamarla that the opening date was still on-track, but rumors from the ground just didn't support that viewpoint, so Stacy and Shamarla decided to conduct a surprise visit to Omaha. Upon arrival, they quickly met with Lance Thompson, the director of public relations, who was already on-site in Omaha gearing up for the pre-opening day publicity blitz. Obviously, Lance is frustrated that the opening day may need to be pushed back, which is halting his public relations team from promoting the new park.

After meeting with Thompson, Stacy and Sharmala decide that they need to have an immediate video conference with Matt Prescott, in Charleston; the regional manager Paka Kamau in Dallas; Jamal McGregor, the director of park operations of the Aurora park; and Jim Brolles, Jr., the chief operations officer in Charleston. Stacy and Shamarla schedule the meeting for the next morning.

On the day of the meeting, Stacy, Sharmala, and Lance gathered at the park's business center at 8:00 AM EST to review their list of concerns and complete the progress report. Thankfully, the park's business center was one of the few places that seemed to be completely operational. When Thomson arrived at 8:00 AM, Velarde had already brewed coffee and set out donuts and fresh fruit. As Lance reached for a piece of cantaloupe he was startled as Shamarla slammed the door behind her.

He turned and said "Good morning, Shamarla. Is everything OK?"

As Shamarla turned and glared at Thomson she said, "It would be a good morning if the construction crew was working on the Eastern Pavilion like they are supposed to. What in the hell are we paying them to do?"

Thomson smiled and said, "At least we will not have to pay them their early completion bonus."

Stacy overheard the conversation and said, "The park better open on time because a late opening is a reflection of me and I'll look bad."

"Let me get the contractor on the phone. I bet Brad, the site supervisor, took the guys out drinking again last night," Shamarla answered.

Thomson spoke up before Shamarla dialed Brad's number and said, "As fired up as you are now, I would not want to be Brad."

Finished with her call and pacified that the crew would be there in thirty minutes, Shamarla rejoined the group as they prepared for the videoconference later that morning. The team worked quickly to make up for the lost time that they spent dealing with the missing construction crew. They completed their list of remaining tasks before opening and the list of obstacles that their tech installers were encountering. The team faxed the lists to all of the locations about ten minutes before the meeting was scheduled to begin. Five minutes before the meeting Shamarla, Lance, and Stacy logged into the video conferencing software to check their microphones, cameras, and to check for any additional problems that may occur.

A minute later, there was a hiss of static and Paku Kamau, the regional manager in Dallas Texas appeared on the screen.

"Greetings from Texas, y'all!" Paku said.

"Good morning," the Omaha team said in unison. Just then, the screen flashed again and Jamal McGregor, the director of the Aurora park operations appeared on-screen.

"Hello, everyone," Jamal said. "Nice to see you all again. Remind me after the meeting to send some funny pictures to you. I think you need something funny to brighten you day. From the grumblings I'm hearing from Omaha, you all need a pick-me-up!" As was he speaking, the Charleston team, which included Jim Brolles, Jr., COO, and the VP of project management, Matt Prescott, joined the conversation. Greetings were quickly exchanged, and the meeting was underway.

Jim began the meeting by asking how the Omaha project was going. After Stacy informed him about this morning's construction crew issues, discussion turned to the to-do list and solutions for the technology hold-ups. Seventy minutes later, the corporate office ended their transmission, and the virtual meeting was over. Before Jamal logged off, Sharmarla reminded him to send her the funny email. Jamal agreed and said, "I can't wait to see what you think. Have a good day, and let me know if you need anything." It was back to work in the real world.

A SCANDALOUS EMAIL

Before Jamal left for lunch, he sat down to forward the email to the whole group. He opened his "My Pictures" folder, and selected a folder called "Company Mascots." Although the folder contained more than 200 images, Jamal picked the three he felt were the most humorous. Two minutes later the pictures were uploaded and the email was zipping through cyberspace on its way to Shamarla, Stacy, and Lance.

At 3:14 PM Shamarla returned from her meeting with the construction contractor, Brad, about the progress on the Eastern Pavilion. The crew was completing the finish work on the drywall, and would begin painting the day after tomorrow. Brad assured her that despite this morning's setbacks, the project was still on schedule for the projected completion date. Tired, she dropped into her office chair, and opened her email. As she scanned through her emails, she saw Jamal's email, titled "ROFL with the interns," with a red flag indicating high importance. Shamarla knew from her teenage sons that ROFL stood for "rolling on the floor laughing," and was common chatroom and text message lingo. A click later and the brief message with three attached pictures popped up.

ROFL with the Interns

To: Stacy Verlarde; Shamarla Bailey; Lance Thompson
From: Jamal McGregor
Date: Wed. 3/2/2011 11:53 AM
Attachments: Intern1.jpeg; Intern53.jpeg; Intern147.jpeg

Hi Omaha Team!

Attached are the funny pictures I was talking about earlier in the video conference. Hope u get a laugh.

Lemme know what you think,

Jamal

Jamal McGregor, MBA
Director of Park Operations
100 Theme Park Blvd.
Suite 204
Aurora, IL 60507
jamal.mcgregor@brollesproductions.com
(630) 555-1929
(630) 555-1930 (Fax)

Clicking on the first picture, Shamarla couldn't believe her eyes. Park employees wearing the park mascot costumes, Boxy the Dog and Roxy the Cat, were contorted in a sexual position. As her mouth hit the floor, she debated whether to open the next images. Surely, Jamal, someone so well-respected in the company wouldn't be sending other employees such inappropriate images. Hesitantly, Shamarla opened the second and third jpegs, finding more images similar to the first. She had no idea how to respond. This infuriated her and made her feel very uncomfortable. She remembered that the email talked about interns, and she wondered what was happening with the high school and college students that the park often hired for summer work. Suddenly, Shamarla dreaded any further interactions with Jamal. She hoped that he wouldn't bring up the email in their future discussions. Shaking her head, Shamarla hit the delete key, and tried to direct her mind back to work.

As he headed down the hallway toward his office from the lunchroom, Lance rubbed his eyes. He could feel a tension headache forming as he thought of the mountain of tasks ahead of him. His emails from the PR team were piling up as they were gearing up for the big opening. However, Lance had been dreading giving his team the green light on some of the projects because of the construction delays. Lance knew he couldn't avoid the backlog of emails much longer, even though he was spending hours every day walking through the various construction sites throughout the park. After grabbing a couple of aspirin and his third coffee of the day, Lance reluctantly opened his e-mail. He was in a bad mood, and the 38 unopened emails did not improve the situation. A red flag caught his eye, and he clicked on Jamal's email. Jamal's friendly message with the three attachments filled the screen.

Lance recoiled as the first image popped up. He actually felt sick, and his hand shook as he quickly closed the first picture. Lance was deeply religious and he hated anything pornographic. Lance detested seeing women shown immodestly. If the next two pictures were anything like the first, they were surely more of the same disgusting smut. Such inappropriate material was not anything to circulate at work. Lance realized that Shamarla and Stacy got the same email. How could a man with any honor send something like that to women? Lance was furious. Should he email Jamal back and address him directly, or should he just go straight to Jim Brolles, Jr.? Lance jumped up from his chair and began pacing behind his desk. *Someone was going to hear about this today,* Lance thought.

A DIFFERENCE OF OPINION

After grabbing a fresh mug of coffee from the breakroom, Stacy stopped by Shamarla's desk to get the latest copy of the inspection reports.

"Hey, Shamarla," Stacy said. "Do you have the latest progress report from the construction firm?"

"Yeah, right here," Shamarla replied, handing them over.

"What did you think of those pics from Jamal?" Stacy asked. "Weren't they a hoot? I remember doing some crazy things when I was an intern, but never in a mascot costume!"

Shamarla looked at Staci's enthusiastic, 31-year-old face, and suddenly felt old. Was she out of touch? Those pictures weren't funny to her. She could only think that those kids were someone's children, and now they were part of an email joke to be forwarded around an office.

"I saw them, but I just didn't really find it funny," Shamarla said. "I deleted the email. It's not like I'm a prude or anything, but I wonder if those kids might regret those pictures one day. You know, a lot of companies check Facebook before they hire. Plus, if those leak out, it could be a PR nightmare for us."

"Oh, I didn't think of it that way," Staci said. She looked a little bit embarrassed. "It helped break the tension of all of those stressful work meetings. And, that's that kind of stuff we always did at parties when I was in college. It reminded me of my sorority days. I guess that's why I thought it was funny."

"Don't say that!" Sharmarla cried. "My oldest is rushing next year."

"He'll be fine, Shamarla," Staci said. "You raised him very well."

Shamarla smiled gratefully, and soon the conversation turned back to work topics.

THE CONCERN GOES TO CORPORATE

It is almost quitting time and Lance is still fuming over Jamal's email. After thinking through several options, he decided that the company should take immediate action due to the severity of the content of the email. Therefore, he decided to email Jim Brolles, Jr., the COO, and CC: Jamal.

FW: ROFL with the Interns

To: Jim Brolles, Jr.
From: Lance Thompson
CC: Jamal McGregor
Date: Wed. 3/2/2011 4:53 PM

Dear Mr. Brolles:

I received a very disturbing email today from Jamal McGregor. After careful consideration, I felt that I must bring this to your attention. Below is a copy of the email and the attachments. Please note that Stacy Verlarde and Shamarla Bailey were also sent this email.

I was so disturbed by the graphic nature of the image that I only viewed the first attachment, called "Intern1." Although I cannot speak to the content of the other two attachments, I feel that this should be addressed immediately. As a Christian, I feel that this has created a hostile work environment. In addition, as the Director of Public Relations for the Omaha Park I am concerned about the potential damage to our reputation were these images to become public. As you know, Brolles Productions is a family friendly company and has worked hard to maintain that image. Such desecration of our innocent mascots shatters what we have worked so hard to build.

I felt that you needed to be aware of my feelings regarding this matter. Thank you for your concern.

Sincerely,

Lance Thompson

ROFL with the Interns

To: Stacy Verlarde; Shamarla Bailey; Lance Thompson
From: Jamal McGregor
Date: Wed. 3/2/2011 11:53 AM
Attachments: Intern1.jpeg; Intern53.jpeg; Intern147.jpeg

Jim Brolles, Jr. was working late, as usual. It was not uncommon for him to be in his office past 7 PM most nights. Especially with the new park opening in Omaha, there was always more work to do than hours to do it in. Luckily, his wife was equally devoted to the business. She knew that, from late February to early September, the theme park business was in full swing and could demand your full attention.

Looking up from the quarterly earning spreadsheet, Jim saw an email from Lance Thompson, whom he knew was on the Omaha team. The title caught his attention immediately because it was strangely informal for Lance, who had always impressed Jim as being very proper. As Jim began reading the email Lance's forward Jim's concern quickly increased. Three sentences in, he stopped reading to open the picture attachments. His heart sinking, Jim quickly grasped that Imaginarium Fantasy Parks could be on the brink of a nasty problem.

Lance may be a bit uptight, Jim thought, but he was right. If these pictures got out, irreparable damage could result. In the age of Twitter, YouTube, and Facebook, bad press can spread like a virus. Jamal was a brilliant PR man and a workhorse, but he already had a negative letter in his HR file for hitting on an intern several years ago. Maybe he hadn't stopped his philandering ways. *If Jim fired Jamal, would Jamal distribute these pictures in spite? Were there more of these pictures? Was Jamal partying with the interns?* Jim knew that the company hired both college and high school interns for summer work in the parks. Some of these kids may be minors, and the last thing Jim wanted was to be fielding angry calls from parents or potential lawsuits. Lance was upset, as well. Jim had no idea how Stacy and Shamarla felt about this email. With the grand opening of the Omaha park just two months away, Jim needed his team to concentrate on the new park. *This email fiasco is not the kind of distraction that they need right now.* With a sigh, Jim picked up the phone. He called the only person he could think of that would know what to do, someone who had been working in the theme park industry for decades.

"Dad, we've got a problem," Jim said. "I need your advice…"

DISCUSSION QUESTIONS

1. Do you consider forwarding "sexy" images of mascots a form of sexual harassment?
2. How would you approach Jamal about the forwarding of the email?
3. How would you approach Jamal about the creation of the pictures in the first place?
4. If the images were leaked, what kind of damage do you think they would do to Imaginarium Fantasy Parks?
5. If you were Jim Brolles, Sr., what advice would you give to your son?

KEY TERMS

Sexual harassment, technology, internal communication, crisis communication

—PART IV—

COMMUNICATING DIVERSITY

CHAPTER 19

Somebody Different

Jeff Youngquist

OAKLAND UNIVERSITY

ABSTRACT

When a new, unskilled heavy-machine operator named Curtiss starts working he seems different, but not just because he's the first Black employee of Myrdal Engineering. As diversity takes center stage, the organization must learn to face a variety of factors related to diversity.

Bjorn was happy to be back in the field. The Spring sun had warmed the morning air and, even though he was standing in the middle of the construction site, there was something beautiful about his surroundings. The heavy machinery was not yet running, and the focus and intensity of the typical workday had yet to arrive. Through the stillness, Bjorn could easily hear the voices of one of his clients and two of his employees on the other side of the building foundation, talking about last night's game.

"How about those Celtics? Can you believe he missed that free-throw. I swear, I don't know why I bother staying up so late. They're just gonna lose anyways."

"No kidding. It's pathetic. These guys get paid millions and they can't even sink a lousy free-throw. I mean, come on, this is stuff your coach teaches you in the 3rd grade. Let me play on the team. I'll sink that free-throw and they won't even have to pay me."

Bjorn smiled. He'd seen the game and it was pretty bad.

Bjorn was the president of Myrdal Engineering. He'd built the organization from the ground up and it hadn't been an easy road. But, over the years he'd learned a great deal and he'd come up with a system that seemed to work. A significant component of this system was hiring the right employees.

There was a sameness to the employees of Myrdal Engineering. Part of this sameness was by design. Bjorn had certain criteria in mind when he hired his employees. He looked for people that were able to understand the job and were able to understand very clearly what he wanted from them. But, on the other hand, he expected these people to act independently. He couldn't follow all of his crews out into the field every day and monitor their every move. So, he put together crews that could function independently without his presence. Without having to manage, he had more time to meet with his clients and court possible new clients. And, it certainly didn't hurt if his employees knew how to golf. He loved golf and he had developed strong bonds with his employees by golfing with them and taking them on golf trips. Over the years, he had accurately assessed most of the employees during the hiring process. However, he did occasionally make mistakes.

Though some of the sameness in his employees came from Bjorn's actions, some the sameness also came from the broader culture. That is, Myrdal Engineering was located in the working-class town of Pinetown and the company was deeply involved, every day, in the local construction projects. These men (and they were almost always men) that worked at Myrdal Engineering had a lewd, crude, tough, fun-loving, masculine way about them. They spent much of their time outside and in the dirt. They worked hard and took their jobs very seriously. There was no tolerance for slackers. But they played hard, too. They were drinkers. They loved sports, especially the local teams. They talked big. Traditional stereotypes of other people were easy targets for jokes, mockery, and poking fun. They teased each other frequently and sometimes mercilessly. And his employees were entirely White. It wasn't that Bjorn only hired White guys; he just never had anyone else apply. He considered himself open-minded and had worked with people from all races throughout his career. However, Myrdal Engineering was located in a community that was almost entirely White and almost everyone that applied for a job was White.

IN WALKS CURTISS

Curtiss had come to Myrdal Engineering about a year ago. He'd literally walked in off the street and asked if Myrdal Engineering was hiring. This was a little unusual for Myrdal Engineering, but not unheard of. Curtiss had never worked construction before but he was desperate to find a job and willing to learn. He didn't know this at the time but his timing was perfect. Bjorn, who'd always tried to be selective and thoughtful when hiring, was in a situation where he needed a body, anybody. He'd simultaneously lost several employees, experienced a surge in work, and had several deadlines that were looming. So, Curtiss walked in the door and Bjorn hired him.

Curtiss was different from the typical Myrdal Engineering employee in a couple of ways. First of all, he was Black. Second, whereas most of the Myrdal Engineering employees lived somewhere near the company's office, Curtiss actually had to commute about 45 miles from Linden, a larger community on the coast.

Curtiss was different in other ways, too. For instance, he did not own a car. He hitched a ride to work every day with people he knew and who were going his way. He always made it to work on time, though. Most of the other guys owned pickup trucks or SUVs of one sort or another. Their vehicles were, in a way, an expression of their masculinity. Most of the employees either had wives and children or girlfriends and Curtiss did not. Curtiss was not currently involved in a relationship and he wasn't about to tell anybody at Myrdal Engineering about his past relationships. Many of Curtiss' coworkers had a college education focusing on civil engineering or surveying or they were currently in college. Curtiss had graduated from high school but had no interest in going to college. And, his coworkers had extensive work experiences in these fields, whereas Curtiss had worked in a variety of retail positions and other odd jobs. He felt that he would someday pursue some sort of career; he just didn't know yet what it was.

Overall, Bjorn thought Curtiss fit in pretty well at Myrdal Engineering. He was outgoing and talkative and people typically seemed to like him. Even though he was clearly different in some ways, he tried to connect with the other employees. Though he didn't have the education or work experiences of many of the others, he was always trying to learn, and he learned quickly. After a year with Myrdal Engineering, Curtiss knew everything he needed to know to do his job and to do it well. Above all else, Curtiss worked hard and he did it with a good attitude. For these reasons, Bjorn found Curtiss to be an invaluable employee.

THE BREAKING POINT

Curtiss was just one of the Myrdal Engineering employees on the job site with Bjorn on this morning. The other one was Mike. Mike loved his job. He'd started at Myrdal Engineering as an intern during college and joined the company full-time after he'd graduated. Mike was big, burly, loud, and gregarious, and he loved to throw out his opinions in a friendly but challenging way to see how people reacted. Of course, he was like this most with his friends and people he felt comfortable with, but even in a crowd of strangers, he was a noticeable presence. Mike had grown up in a hard-working, traditional family that some might call "old school." Pinetown was where he had been raised, just like his parents had, and he had never traveled much. The problems of the big cities and the world beyond Pinetown were scary and bizarre but also very distant. The biggest experience he'd ever had beyond Pinetown was when he'd transferred to the state college to finish his degree. He was happy at Myrdal Engineering and life seemed to be going in the right direction. His career was on track and he liked the people he worked with.

As Bjorn started to walk around the building foundation on this beautiful morning and approach Mike, Curtiss, and the client, he noticed that Mike and Curtiss were talking.

"Hey Curtiss, how's it feel to be the token Black?" Mike questioned with a mischievous smile, "Myrdal Engineering has met its quota." This wasn't the first time Bjorn had heard Mike make a comment like this.

Without skipping a beat, Curtiss retorted, "I may be the token Black, but that must mean that you're the token 'mentally challenged' employee."

Mike paused for a second, and then let out a big laugh before punching Curtiss in the arm. "Well, at least you're not gay, man!" Mike continued, "That would be un-ac-cept-a-ble". Mike enunciated each of the syllables of "unacceptable" in a comic and exaggerated manner to make it clear just how unacceptable it would be to be gay. "We don't let no gays in Pinetown," Mike said. "Hell, would you come here if you were a fag? I know that if I were…"

"What the hell is your problem, Mike?!" Curtiss erupted as he quickly got up in Mike's face, "Do you have to be such an ass all of the time?!"

Bjorn watched Curtiss as he clenched his fist, clearly on the verge of decking Mike, "HEY!" Bjorn yelled. "What the hell is going on here!?"

After yelling, Bjorn watched as Curtiss' head swiveled in his direction. In that instant Bjorn saw a man about to attack. "Curtiss, in the car! Now!" Bjorn bellowed.

Curtiss paused, then spun on his heels and headed towards the main road.

Mike was just standing in the construction site dumbfounded, "What? What did I do? You're so sensitive. Maybe you *are* one of those gays?"

Bjorn watched as Curtiss turned around and hurled his tape measure at Mike's head before storming back towards the road. There were a few moments of silence as everyone else, stunned by what had just happened, looked at each other with their jaws dropped. Eventually, the conversation resumed as those remaining said things like, "What's up with him" and watched Curtiss disappear down the road.

Bjorn came in early the next morning and immediately went to the table in the back where he often worked (he had an office but he seldom used it). Bjorn had been looking over some plans but his thoughts had been distracted by the previous day's events. Curtiss had ridden to the job site yesterday with Mike in one of the crew trucks and, when he'd gotten mad, he'd just walked off the job site and headed back towards town on foot. Bjorn just let him go, figuring he'd be back when he cooled off. But, Curtiss never came back and when Bjorn returned to the office later in the day, Curtiss' was not there either. He hadn't been sure if Curtiss would show up this morning and, if he did, he wasn't sure what to expect from him.

When Curtiss did show up, he was a bit late. Most of the crews and some of the engineers had already headed out to the field, including Mike. Curtiss headed straight back to Bjorn's table.

"Hey Boss", said Curtiss, "We need to talk. I've kept my mouth shut for a long time now but I can't put up with this crap any more. You've got do something about Mike or I…I'll…I don't know what I'll do."

"Yeah, what was up with that yesterday?", asked Bjorn, "Why'd you get so pissed at Mike?"

"Boss…", Curtiss said hesitantly. He was the only one at the company who called Bjorn "boss" and he did so respectfully. "Boss, maybe I should have told you this a while ago but I'm gay."

In that moment, the impact of everything that had been happening to Curtiss' over the last year came together for Bjorn. He'd heard some of the things Mike had said in Curtiss' presence in the past and he'd just cringed. Prior to Curtiss' arrival, he hadn't thought twice about Mike's comments. Somewhere deep inside, though, he'd known there was something wrong about what Mike was saying, he just didn't really mind. What Mike was saying was about other people, after all. Now he had a real problem on his hands and he wasn't sure how to respond. He had been aware of the potential impact of the racial comments coming from Mike. Had Curtiss reacted to these earlier, Bjorn would not have been surprised. But Curtiss didn't react, so Bjorn didn't intercede. He knew now that he had been naïve in his hopes that Curtiss hadn't been affected by these comments. And, after this revelation from Curtiss, all of Mike's comments about gays and homosexuality took on new meaning. Curtiss had been quietly absorbing all of this over the last year and yesterday his emotional armor had finally cracked.

As Curtiss continued to describe to Bjorn why he was so upset, Bjorn began to consider how to respond to this conflict. The company was much too small to simply move either one of them to a different location. All of the employees had to put up with each other every day. One of the benefits of Bjorn's typically thoughtful approach to hiring was that everyone *did* get along so well. And, Mike's behaviors were so ingrained in him and so much of a part of Mike's personality that Bjorn knew it was going to be extraordinarily difficult for him to change. And, he could not simply ask Curtiss to ignore Mike. Doing that would be almost impossible and not fair to Curtiss. As he thought about either one of them trying to accommodate the other, he could just imagine the resulting tension. An alternative possibility would be to get rid of either Mike or Curtiss. But, he didn't want to fire either one of them and he didn't think he had any real reason to fire either one of them. Mike had always done his job well. The way he acted yesterday was basically how he always acted. And, his behaviors were very similar to the typical behaviors of many of his friends, family, and coworkers with whom he spent most of his time. Curtiss, on the other hand, clearly did not fit in with the organizational culture. Bjorn now felt that hiring Curtiss was probably a mistake and, in this sense, he felt responsible for what was happening. Curtiss, though, had really done nothing wrong.

Bjorn was sure that this conflict was just the beginning. If everything else stayed the way it was, the conflict between these two would not go away and might even get worse. Bjorn did not know how to solve this problem but he did know that he had to do something, and he had to do something now. Curtiss had stopped talking and stood across the table from him, waiting for a response.

DISCUSSION QUESTIONS

1. What are the sources of the conflict between Mike and Curtiss?

2. Could this problem have been prevented? How?

3. What are the strengths and weaknesses of the culture that has developed at Myrdal Engineering?

4. Is organizational diversity a factor in this story? In what way?

5. How should Bjorn respond to this situation?

KEY TERMS

Diversity, conflict, organizational culture, workplace violence

20

Innocent Comments at IF Industries

Anastacia Kurylo

MARYMOUNT MANHATTAN COLLEGE

ABSTRACT

Liam Yi Kwon has eagerly accepted a well-compensated position at IF Industries. While the organization seems to value and promote diversity, Liam's interpersonal interactions in the organization suggest this part of the organizational culture might not be internalized by its employees. When his yearly review is not as strong as he expected, Liam ponders his value to the organization and its value to him.

"Where are you from?"

"New Jersey," Liam answered not really thinking about what else it might have meant.

THE ORGANIZATION

International Food Industries also known as IF Industries is a Fortune 500 company whose focus is organic sustainable globally produced and marketed food and related products. IF Industries has locations in five countries and in seven major cities within the United States alone. Like all organizations of its size and stature, it houses its own technology division. Although small, this division is integral to the daily functioning of IF Industries because it is responsible for installing, monitoring, and updating all computer software and hardware used by its 4,500 employees.

THE EMPLOYEES

Liam Yi Kwon is an employee at IF Industries who successfully interviewed last month for the position of Director of Technology at its New York headquarters. Liam had anticipated most of the topics discussed during the interview. He was surprised, however, that diversity was one topic mentioned in great depth. He listened to the interviewer discuss affirmative action, and that discrimination and sexual harassment policies were strictly enforced. He understood why this was important because although he had never been a victim of discrimination that he knew of, he had friends who had been in unpleasant situations that had resulted in their leaving their organizations in undesirable circumstances.

The company wanted to ascertain whether Liam shared a similar outlook on issues of diversity and how these should be handled within the company. Liam answered several questions related to diversity:

- Why do you think we place a high value on diversity in this company?

- In what ways have you fostered diversity within previous organizations at which you have worked?

- How would you handle a situation in which you overhear one of your employees making an overtly biased remark to another?

- When is it appropriate to inquire about the marital status of an employee?

- When it comes to issues of diversity, who are your role models?

A considerable amount of time and energy was expended on discussing issues related to diversity. In his head, Liam questioned whether the company was simply trying to cover themselves from lawsuits or whether they were legitimately concerned about these issues. Either way, he accepted the position happily and after a few rounds of negotiations secured an exceptional compensation package. After a few weeks on the job Liam already seemed to fit well in the corporate culture, work well with his fellow workers, and adjust well to the position itself.

COMMUNICATION WITHIN THE COMPANY

Liam found that establishing personal relationships with peers and employees was taking longer than he anticipated. Liam's team was focused on their technical work, which required little personal interaction. Moreover, the organizational culture was not conducive to casual conversation, and no one really seemed to "hang out" after work. Liam's normal interactions at work often involved formal meetings in conference rooms behind closed doors with large agendas in which little time was available for chit-chat. At these meetings, the conversation was topic-focused, and unrelated commentary was discouraged by being cut off or quickly guided back on point by saying some version of, "How do you think that relates to the topic at hand?" Everyone, including Liam, knew extraneous conversations meant the meetings would last longer, and no one wanted that because they saw these conversations as a waste of valuable time.

Liam, like all of the employees, worked in cubicles that allowed everyone to see and be seen. However, Liam found that these were not positioned well to be conducive to face-to-face conversation. Instead, most communication took place through email or instant messaging, even if the person was in the adjacent cubicle. Typing on computer keys was often the only sound heard except for the occasional brief burst of conversation. Liam had quickly become used to the white noise of typing on keyboards that faded into the background throughout the day.

Because the communication was constant and meetings were regular, few internal formal memos were disseminated. All employees, including Liam, had received the large spiral bound policies, procedures, and benefits manuals that are typical of a company the size of IF Industries. Reiteration of, clarification about, or changes to these policies, procedures, and benefits were expressed at meetings.

Many of the internal units of the organization interacted with each other regularly through teleconferencing in order to maintain consistency and clarity between domestic and international employees and their divisions. In Liam's division, for example, some of the IT work such as programming was outsourced to an Indian company. Though not always the case, the language difference had caused miscommunication in the past that was consequential for the company. To prevent miscommunication, employees tended to speak clearly, state their ideas simply, become familiar with cultural norms and expectations, and avoid colloquialisms, sarcasm, and humor that might offend inadvertently.

Chit-chat did take place at the "water cooler," in the communal kitchen area, or while waiting for the elevators. Typically, these conversations involved comments on the weather, local eateries, recent sport events, and family updates for the sake of keeping the environment friendly and welcoming.

THE ELEVATOR RIDE

One Friday evening while Liam was waiting for the elevator, his colleague struck up a conversation with him. Liam hadn't previously had much opportunity to chat with Sarah because he worked on the other side of the floor and usually worked different hours. Sarah worked closely with Liam's direct supervisor, and he had seen them go to lunch together whenever the supervisor was in town, which was about once a week so. Liam assumed they were friends. He was eager to begin to establish a similar close relationship and he thought, *This is a great opportunity to speak with her.*

Liam was happy when Sarah initiated the conversation by asking, "Where are you from?"

When Liam heard her question, however, he wasn't quite sure if he understood it. So, he provided what he thought was a typical answer not really thinking about what else it might have meant. "New Jersey," he answered.

Then Sarah restated the question by saying, "No, are you Filipino? Korean? Chinese?"

Feeling a little awkward, Liam quickly answered with an awkward smile, "I was born in America, but I'm Chinese," and then patiently waited for the elevator. Liam hoped it would come soon so he didn't have to continue the conversation. This wasn't the case, instead, the elevator seemed to take forever.

Sarah asked Liam more questions about his culture noting to Liam that it is no wonder that he was already doing so well at the company. As Sarah spoke with him, it seemed to Liam that Sarah was being cautious about the words she chose and the tone that she used. Although she was pleasant, it was still an awkward conversation for Liam, because she seemed to give off an aura of "I am better than you are" even when she complimented him. As the conversation continued Liam felt a little defensive because he wasn't sure if Sarah was being friendly and trying to start conversation, or was trying to belittle him. Liam remembered conversations from his past when she had been both friendly and belittling. The conversation came to an end when the elevator finally arrived. Liam turned to Sarah and smiled politely as he said goodbye. She returned the gesture.

In the elevator, Liam rewound the conversation in his head. He found it ironic that he was still offended, although it was obvious that Sarah was trying to keep the conversation casual and polite, presumably in fear of offending Liam. Although her original inquiry appeared innocent enough, her question hurt Liam because it invoked a stereotype of Asians. To Liam, not only did it state that he was a foreigner, but it also meant that he was not American. He knew Sarah did not mean to hurt his feelings and was only trying to make conversation, but it hurt nonetheless.

Liam also thought that it was ironic that he, a generally assertive and proactive person, was downright demure in the conversation with Sarah, speaking only when asked questions and keeping his answers concise and polite. Liam realized that he had acted like the stereotypical Asian person—quiet, considerate, and naive. Liam mused that he had managed to communicate in a way that confirmed another stereotype of Asians even though he was offended that his colleague had brought up Asian stereotypes in the conversation.

WHAT BROUGHT YOU TO THE U.S.?

Liam put the incident with Sarah out of his mind over the next couple of weeks until the next time something similar happened, this time with John.

Liam contacted John, one of the other supervisors, to discuss a compatibility issue between a software program needed by the users and a security setting required by the company. Having never met John, Liam decided to make an appointment rather than to drop by John's office unexpectedly. Liam arrived promptly at the appointed time. John welcomed Liam into his office and began the conversation with the requisite small talk.

"How are you doing?"

"Fine," Liam answered, "and you?"

"Doing well. It's beautiful outside, isn't it?" John commented.

"I hope we have more weather like this," Liam responded.

"How was your weekend?" John asked.

"Too quick. Yours? Liam asked.

"Good. I spent it with my family." Then, moving to more personal conversation, John asked, "So, what brought you to this country?"

Liam realized that John had misjudged him because of his foreign sounding last name and the way he looked which led John to assume Liam was from somewhere outside of the United States. Liam was offended by the assumption and immediately answered in a sarcastic way, "Do you mean New Jersey?" The supervisor apologized for his mistake, but it was too late. The remainder of the conversation involved Liam and John discussing business in a cold, stiff atmosphere. Liam was so upset by the stereotype that he even forgot to mention a few minor issues related to the project. When he returned to his desk, Liam made sure to email John about these relevant issues.

For a long time after the conversation ended, Liam contemplated the stereotype that John communicated. Upon reflection, he realized the supervisor was probably trying to break the ice. Nonetheless, Liam concluded that this intent backfired because the stereotype was based on weak and impersonal evidence (Liam's last name) and that John's stereotype alienated Liam rather than making him feel more comfortable. Although Liam was angry at first, he soon after began to feel depressed. He knew the supervisor did not mean to offend him and had merely made a mistake. Yet, this mistake was prevalent throughout Liam's life in the form of this foreign, un-American stereotype.

Liam loved working at IF Industries. The benefits were great, everyone around him was dedicated as much as he could expect and were, for the most part, hardworking. He was encouraged to initiate new projects and had a support staff that allowed him to follow through on these. The following month his reviews were good but not great and his bonus was satisfactory. Liam was confused that the feedback he received indicated concerns that could have been easily fixed had someone told him about these earlier. He was unclear why his overall review wasn't stellar.

The conversations in which his peers communicated Asian stereotypes still lingered in his mind. As pro-diversity as the organization seemed to be when he interviewed, he couldn't help but wonder how his cultural identity impacted how others perceived him and whether it had interfered with his review. Increasingly, he pondered these issues and they didn't sit well with him, although at times, he also wondered whether he was just making a big deal out of innocent comments. Liam did not want to spend the year trying to improve based on feedback that he found unclear. So, Liam was left with a decision to make on how to proceed.

DISCUSSION QUESTIONS

1. At times, Liam questions whether he is overreacting to the stereotypes that people in the organization have communicated to him. Does Liam have a legitimate reason to be concerned? Why or why not?

2. In what ways does the organizational culture, including its emphasis on diversity and its communication patterns, play a role in Liam's dilemma at the conclusion of the case study?

3. What are the benefits and problems associated with communicating stereotypes in an organizational setting?

4. Considering Liam's dissatisfaction with his yearly review and his concerns about the comments from his peers, what steps might you advise Liam to take in order to proceed?

KEY TERMS

Stereotypes, diversity, internal communication

The Best of Intentions

Diana L. Tucker

Walden University

ABSTRACT

Assets Insurance has a new Diversity Committee to develop and engage in programming concerning diversity issues. But what happens when the programming ends up segregating rather than bringing people together?

Casey Handelman, a computer programmer for Asset Insurance, Inc., dropped her bag on her kitchen counter and let out a long sigh. Snickers, her 4-year-old Lhasa Apso, nudged her right leg and let out a "Humpf" as if he understood her frustration. Casey grabbed a light beer from the fridge, collapsed on the couch in the family room, and began to flick through the channels on the remote without much enthusiasm. Snickers jumped up on the couch with her and climbed into her lap for a head scratch. "I wish a nice little head rub would help me forget the day I've had," she said to Snickers. He grinned, licked her face, and proceeded to curl up into a ball and fall asleep.

As she surfed through the 1300 or so channels she had, Casey contemplated the issue she was facing at work. When Casey had asked to be the IT department's representative to the Asset Insurance Diversity Committee, she had done so because of her love for other cultures and her interest in learning about other people. She was genuinely excited that Asset Insurance was taking this step and implementing such a committee. In addition, Asset was doing so because of employee interest, not as a reactionary measure to some racist or sexist incident at work. Since Asset Insurance was based in Dayton, Ohio, they tended to employ more individuals who were born in America, and were raised within a 200-mile radius of their city. So the makeup of the company was not really that diverse. Getting the largely Caucasian employee base to think about their African American, Asian, and Hispanic coworkers' cultures was something Casey thought to be important. There was also a bit of a "men's club" atmosphere at times that she hoped this committee might address, as there were actually more women than men who worked at Asset Insurance.

THE DIVERSITY COMMITTEE

The Diversity Committee met once a month to discuss and implement ideas for programming about diversity issues at Asset Insurance. They had been meeting for a little over a year and had planned and executed three well-received programs. Their first program had been a book club, which met once a month during lunch. The club chose one book a month, by an author from a country outside the United States that had been translated into English. She attended most of these meetings and had really enjoyed the discussions. This program looked like it would be sustained and popular for quite a long time.

Another program had been an intercultural food fair. The committee had worked with outside vendors from around the city who each made cuisine from another culture. They had Chinese, Japanese, Italian, Indian, and Mexican food at the event, and most attendees remarked that they would like to see the program again, with even more foods available from around the world.

The third program had been a "diversity fact sheet" that the committee had put together with statistics on the diversity of the United States and quotations about diversity. These had been sent out to each employee via email and then copies were hung on billboards and in the elevators throughout the building. Once again, they received only positive comments.

A NEW PATH

Today, the Diversity Committee had met to discuss what they might do for their next program. Meetings tended to be jovial and sometimes got off track with people telling stories about their trip to Spain or their gaffe when ordering sushi at a Japanese restaurant. But Casey had been nervous going into the meeting today because of the request she was going to make to the committee members.

After receiving the Diversity Fact Sheet last month, Casey's coworker and friend, David Reinhart, stopped by her cubicle this morning before the Diversity Committee meeting.

"Do you have a minute?" David said.

"Of course, what's up?" replied Casey. David came all the way in and leaned casually against her desk.

"You know I think that all the programs the Diversity Committee are doing are great, and I am really happy to see these things happening here at Asset" he said and then paused as if trying to think how to say what he wanted to say.

"Yeeesss…" Casey prompted.

"Well," he continued, "it is great, but you really have only been doing things concerning race and nationality."

Casey looked at him quizzically, "Yeah, so?"

"Well, you do all realize there is much more to diversity than someone's race or nationality, don't you?" he quipped.

"Of course we do, David" she snapped. "There are just so many different countries and people from them out there that we haven't even scratched the surface there. And every one really seems to like our programs so far. I mean, you just said you liked them."

"Yes, I do, they are good. But don't you think that it is time to address another aspect of diversity?" he asked.

"Like what?" she said.

"Well, you know, like BGLTQ issues," he said while looking at her and holding eye contact.

"What issues?"

"BGLTQ, bisexual, gay, lesbian, transgender/transsexual, queer…"

"Oh, yeah," Casey said a little sheepishly. David was gay and while she knew this and had no problem with gay people, it was not like they talked about it or anything. "I guess I never really thought about being gay as being 'different' in terms of diversity."

"Well, it is," he said flatly.

"Of course it is," said Casey. "I am really sorry David, of course you are totally right. We should try to broaden the programming a bit."

"Well, I know you have a Diversity Committee meeting today; will you broach that subject in the meeting?" David asked.

"Yes, I will," Casey said hesitantly. "But there may be a little problem."

"Why?" asked David.

"Well, there has already been talk about having a foreign film night or an international fashion show next. People on the committee seemed to really like those ideas. I am not sure they will easily take on such a shift," She hesitated again. "And unfortunately, not everyone on that committee is as open-minded about such things as you or I might be."

"Oh, don't I know it."

"Well, would you help me brainstorm ways I can bring up the subject in the meeting and some possible ideas for programming that I could suggest?" Casey asked. "That way I will have some ideas for them to work with and not just throwing the need for BGLTQ programming out there without anything for them to contemplate."

"Good point, yeah, let's come up with something," David responded.

David and Casey spent the next thirty minutes developing a strategy for how Casey could broach the subject in the meeting and then ideas for programming she could suggest to the committee. Ultimately, deciding that the best thing would be for her to try and broach the subject right from the start of the meeting so that she got the ideas in before the group started to go off track. They thought up some ideas for programming such as having some people from the area BGLTQ advocacy organization come in and have a question-and-answer panel. Or they thought that if the Diversity Committee seemed really determined to have a movie night, maybe they could have some BGLTQ issue films played instead of international films.

THE MEETING

Casey was a little nervous going into the meeting because she had never really been one to suggest new things at these meetings. She tended to be a little reserved, and only added comments when she had had a lot of time to think them out and be sure they would sound coherent. She just didn't think of herself as an instigator.

As the committee members filed into the conference room, she began to have second thoughts about her and David's plan. She just could not figure out how she could possibly start off the meeting by talking first. But suddenly she had an idea; why not ask the chair of the committee, John Sparks, for time at the beginning? That way John could sort of "introduce her" and give her an opening to discuss the issue.

She quickly scanned the room for John; he wasn't there yet. "Perfect," she thought, "I can catch him in the hall before we start."

John Sparks was a quiet man himself and was also very diplomatic in how he chaired the meetings. He was a middle manager in the IT department and seemed to be well-liked and respected by everyone. He always seemed very aware of people's body language and made sure everyone got a chance to say something about a decision before the final choice was made in the committee meetings.

He was amenable to letting Casey speak first in the meeting and agreed with her that the committee should broaden their view of diversity and that bringing in BGLTQ issues might be just the ticket. Casey was very relieved to hear this and gained some confidence knowing that John "had her back" in this meeting.

As John started the meeting, the ten members of the committee settled down into their seats and oriented themselves toward John at the head of the table.

"Thank you all for coming," John said, "I think we all look forward to discussing what our next diversity programming possibility might be. I think we have done a great job so far and it seems that our coworkers think so too. However, Casey had a good point about our programming and I thought we'd start by listening to what she has to say. Casey?"

"Thanks, John. Well, it was brought to my attention that as great as our programming has been, and people do consistently tell me it has been great, that it really only covers one aspect of diversity," Casey explained.

"What are you talking about?" asked Bev Layton, an auto insurance specialist.

"Well, we have only looked at international aspects of diversity. You know, like only people from other countries," Casey answered.

"Well, what else is there?" asked Bev.

"Well, our own country has many different ethnicities and races, and while they may be based on nationality, some people have never even been to the country their ethnicity tends to be acquainted with," John piped in.

"Yeah," said Trent Reddick, an African American man from the claims department. "I have never been to Africa."

"I've never been to Mexico," said Joaquin Lopez, who was a second generation Mexican American and worked with the customer service department.

"Exactly," said Casey. "But it goes beyond even these ethnicities. I am talking about cultures within our American culture that so far we haven't addressed. This would include gender, religion, and sexual orientation. Specifically, I think it would be great to create a program surrounding BGLTQ issues."

"What's that?" asked Trent.

"BGLTQ stands for Bisexual, Gay, Lesbian, Transgender/Transsexual, and Queer. Sometimes the letters are turned around to be LGBTQ or GLBTQ too. But the words are the same," explained Casey.

"What, are we gonna have a drag show?" questioned Dean Standish, who was also a middle manager like John, but in the Home Insurance department. He tended to make inappropriate remarks in a joking manner, and often side-tracked the group on tangents. Casey believed it was because he had not been elected as the chair of the committee.

John quickly answered, "While I suppose that could be a possibility, drag show culture is really a very small part of the gay culture and is certainly not representative of the culture as a whole. I think something more formal and informative would be more beneficial."

"I am just not comfortable with this," Trent stated dogmatically and crossed his arms. "Being homosexual is going against God's will. As a believer, my religion is too important to me to be a part of something like this. Yes, this is very uncomfortable! And frankly, I don't know if I want to be associated with a committee or an organization that condones the homosexual lifestyle."

"Your religion makes me uncomfortable," quipped Joaquin, "And while I may not be gay, my sister is, Trent. So your bigoted 'lifestyle' makes me uncomfortable there, Trent!"

Casey could see that this was quickly getting out of hand. "Trent, you would not personally have to be involved with this particular program. But I think it would be important to have something like a panel where we bring people from the local BGLTQ advocacy group in to discuss various issues facing BGLTQ people. A panel might be helpful for dispelling myths and stereotypes. Don't you think? Later we could do another such panel on religion or something, you know? I just wanted us to broaden our horizons and start opening up to areas of diversity other than nationality."

"I just don't think anyone would go to a panel like that. One, it sounds boring, and two, we just don't have that many people here interested in stuff about homosexuality," said Dean.

"But does it have to be this BGLTQ topic? Why not start with religion?" asked Trent.

"Why not start with both?" asked Linda Wang, a receptionist for Asset Insurance.

"How do you do that? Have a drag show with priests?" Dean said snidely.

"Noooo…" Linda rolled her eyes. "I mean have a number of panels at the same time. That way people could go to the panel about the diversity topic that interests them."

"Yeah, we could have a panel on religious issues, one on that BGLTQ stuff, one on African American issues, and so on," Bev said enthusiastically.

"Okay, I think we might have something here that will make people of all backgrounds happy," John said. "So what would be our next step in developing this idea?"

"Wait a minute," Casey piped in, "while this may solve some of this committee's issues with people being uncomfortable with discussing BGLTQ issues, doesn't it actually perpetuate the problems of diversity?"

"How so?" John asked.

"Well, it is segregating people by their affinities. It is not asking people to open their minds to issues that other groups have to deal with because most likely only BGLTQ, friendly people will go to the BGLTQ panel; only people interested in religion will go to that panel. In other words, this idea will be akin to segregation, not bringing people together," Casey pleaded.

"Oh please," said Trent, "you don't know the first thing about segregation. That was a forced practice. These panels are just allowing people to be with like-minded individuals to discuss issues they care about. There is nothing sinister about it."

"Yeah Casey, I think you are putting way too much emphasis on this issue of diversity issues," Dean said. "Really, this is a good solution."

Many others at the table chimed in their agreement and John looked at Casey, shrugged his shoulders and said, "Okay then, that is settled. We will have a day where there are a number of panels about a variety of diversity issues. Maybe we could do them over the lunch hour and call them 'Brown Bag Diversity Panels.'"

Once again many people chimed in agreement and they began to work out details. Casey knew when she was beat. Of course, as they were deciding who would be in charge of which panel, she was given the BGLTQ panel to work on. They also decided to have a panel on Religion as a Culture, African American issues, Asian American issues and Hispanic Issues. She realized that she could bring up that they were missing many other types of cultures here, but decided not to because it would just perpetuate the segregation. She took her "assignment" and left the meeting without ever saying another word.

Now, as she sat on her couch drinking her beer, scratching Snickers' head and flipping through the channels on TV, Casey realized that her fellow committee members really didn't see the problem here. She knew they had the best of intentions when developing the idea for having all the different panels, but she was not sure whether David and others would see their good intentions. Furthermore, she really didn't know what she would tell David tomorrow and how (or whether) she would proceed with the panel planning.

Now Casey had some decisions to make. *How should she tell David about the turn of events? Could she get David and some others excited about this multiple panels idea and really help to make it great? If so, what kinds of things could they do on this panel to make it stand out and help bring people together? Or should she stand her ground and try to get others on the Diversity Committee to see how the multiple panels idea was a segregation-type practice? How would she go about doing that? Or, should she take the issue to someone above the committee?*

DISCUSSION QUESTIONS

1. Why do you think so many corporations focus their diversity efforts on topics like race and nationality?
2. Do you think having multiple diversity activities targeted for different diverse groups is a good idea?
3. Can fostering diversity actually lead to more segregation in an organization?
4. If you were in Casey's shoes, what would your next steps be?
5. How do you handle when one person's religious is diametrically opposed to someone else's sexual orientation in the workplace?

KEY TERMS

Diversity, culture, marginalized groups, workplace learning

Isolated Native

*Rui Liu, Shireen Kaur Ghawri, Nhung Nguyen,
Yao Li, and Jiuzhen Shen*

ITHACA COLLEGE

ABSTRACT

In the research department of FunChip & Co., a change of working environment occurs subtly after the manager announced the "English only" policy. What should the manager do with his team of scientists coming from diverse cultural background? How can he achieve the casual and flexible office atmosphere he intended to encourage innovation and productivity?

NEW YEAR, NEW POLICY

"Hey, hey, hey, everyone! What's up!?" Sam pushed open the door of the conference room and quickly attracted everybody's attention with his enthusiastic voice and brighter-than-the-sunshine smile.

"Hey, Sam!" Mike Moore, the manager of the research department at FunChip & Co., an innovative software designing and manufacturing company located in Silicon Valley, greeted Sam happily. "How's Nebraska?"

"Better than South Dakota!"

Sam and Mike then high-fived. "Classic Big Bang Theory joke!"

Kim, Yoshi, and Akemi greeted Sam happily too with a wave of hand and a quiet but big smile. Like Sam, the Korean (Kim) and the two Japanese workers (Yoshi and Akemi) are all researchers in Mike's department. Although they did not quite understand where that joke came from, they appreciated Sam for always bringing humor and encouraging a relaxed work atmosphere, "Good one, Sam!"

Mike looked at his watch, "10:00 AM Time for the meeting. Guess our Bernard has a 'greasy morning' again," said Mike, shrugging shoulders with a half-smile, not really annoyed. Of course, greasy morning is derived from the French "la grasse matinee," meaning to be in bed sleeping until very late.

"Bernard, the French guy? He's in our group?"

"I'm not sure. He just transferred?" Yoshi and Akemi exchanged their doubts in whisper.

"Hard to believe, but he is." Sam joined their conversation and answered. "He spends a lot of time working at home."

"And Mr. Moore has no problem with that?" Kim asked.

At this moment, Bernard walked in and closed the door behind him. "Morning!" He greeted everyone gently, while looking for a seat.

"All right, gentlemen. We gathered here today, the first day after our lovely little new year vacation," he paused here to allow people, especially Sam, to make their ironic sound or expression, because everybody knows that today is January 2nd. "I have two new policies in this department for this new year."

At the word "new policy," Kim, Yoshi, and Akemi quickly pulled out their notebooks and leaned forward. Mike was a little bit intimidated at first by their seriousness but soon got back to normal.

"Erh... OK. You are researchers. I understand that you need comfort and flexibility to get your work done. So I will no longer check on you every day like I used to do. The company also assigned a lounge for all of you to relax, talk, and do all other things. As some of you might have noticed, Bernard spent most of his time working at home last year while being quite productive... It is highly recommended that you come to your office and lab every day, so that it's easier for me to consult or talk to you when needed, but I'll give you the choice of working at home under two conditions: (1) Meet your deadline and (2) Make sure to be available when needed."

"So, Mr. Moore, do you need our home phone number to check on us when we work at home?" Kim asked.

"Of course not, Kim." Mike was surprised. "I will not check on you in any way. Also, by saying 'work at home,' I meant to work anywhere outside your office. You have the freedom to pick any location where you can work the most comfortable and productive."

Kim asked no more questions about this issue. Instead, he gave Mike a grateful nod. If there is one thing he learned in the United States, it is that people mean what they say. However, to him, this freedom was a little bit too good to be true. His intuition was soon proved to be right as Mike continued his speech.

"Another thing I want to mention is that I am going to install an 'English Only' policy. I am very proud of the diversity in our department, but I have heard that the multilinguals have built communication barriers among colleagues and decreased morale. From now on, English will be the only language permitted in the office and the lab."

Bernard nodded slightly. He seemed not fully awakened. *Whatever, I won't be here most of the time.*

Sam did not try to conceal his support of this new policy. He nodded enthusiastically to Mike and clapped his hands. *Finally, things will go back to normal.*

Kim, Yoshi, and Akemi, however, took back their grateful look and exchanged disturbed ones among themselves. They lay back against the chair and lowered their head, pretending to take notes. "If there are no questions, that's all I am going to say. You can go ahead and start your day!" Mike did not notice this subtle anti-climax in the room and concluded the meeting.

THREE MONTHS EARLIER...

Mike Moore never expected such an excellent team when he first started as the manager of the research department at FunChip. The three Asians were so diligent and hard-working. They would stay at the lab until midnight. Mike felt most of his supervision job had been done to make sure that they would go back home and take some rest. Sam was smart and funny, a good buddy. Bernard was nice too.

Everything went well until one day Sam rushed into the manager's office.

"Mike, I don't know if I can work like this anymore!"

"What happened, Sam?"

"You know, Mike. Kim, Yoshi, and Akemi—they formed a clique. I feel isolated."

"Really? But I thought you all get along well. They do like your jokes right?" Mike says, attempting to calm Sam down.

"To be polite! They laugh at my jokes to be polite! They always do that—smiling and nice, bringing gifts to Bernard and me on our birthdays, giving me the impression that we are friends... and completely dump me out of their little clique!"

"You don't have to feel bad about it Sam. You know, we covered it during our diversity orientation that Asian people care about being proper and polite. That's just who they are and we have to respect that."

"Oh, Mike, I know the theory!" Sam groans unhappily.

"Tell me, Sam. Does their 'clique' activity interfere with your work or anything?" Mike questions drawing air-quotes as he says the word "clique" to add emphasis.

"Yes and no, Mike. The problem is they always talk in Japanese, even Kim! I guess it's a happy surprise for him that his elementary level of Japanese is enough for him to understand Yoshi and Akemi with minimal effort. Hey, you know what? I think Kim has a crush on Akemi…"

Mike looks at him, amused and perplexed.

"OK, Mike. I know that's not my business, the office romance, I know. But they talk about EVERYTHING in Japanese! Even work. Sure, when I ask their opinion on my projects, they will speak English with me, very nicely. But you know how things work in lab right? We feed each other's idea by brainstorming and casual exchange of ideas! How can I do that when we are speaking a different language? It's so unfair. They understand me, but not vice versa!"

Mike nodded. He remembered on multiple occasions Sam would come and talk with him about optical fiber. *There were some exciting arguments,* Mike said to himself. *Sam is really good at asking questions and getting the most from the answers. He always managed to squeeze out the essence from my optics background. Oh, and that one time when he needed to make a decision about which car to buy. He just talked almost all by himself and somehow figured out which one to buy…* Mike's memory was interrupted by Sam's continued complaint.

"Now they feed off of each other's ideas by sharing thoughts and get a lot of work done. But that's not the most important part. You know my project is not going so well these days right? All those negative results from my experiments…"

"It's OK, Sam. It's normal in research, and we understand that your project is pretty cutting-edge. We can give you more time if you need."

"Thanks Mike." Sam squeezes a weak smile, looks frustrated and continues, "Maybe I just imagine things, but this morning I got another negative result and Kim was just next to me so he saw it. I'm not ashamed of that for, as you said, it's normal in research. However, he saw it and turned to Yoshi and Akemi and they started to talk in Japanese. I have a feeling that they're talking about me because they constantly looked in my direction…I don't know…I felt so bad that I yelled 'Shut Up!' to them. Then I rushed to you…"

ISOLATED WHO?

After the announcement of the new "English Only" policy, the three Asians ended up rarely talking at all. They showed up to the office less. Sometimes, they didn't even speak at all during the working hours and then disappeared together at 5:00 PM sharp, heading to one of their apartments or a bar to hang out.

"Mike, I think I made a mistake complaining to you the other day." Sam mentioned it to the manager one day during lunch hour. "The 'English Only' policy seems to be making my colleagues rather uncomfortable…"

Mike noticed that, too. He also noticed that Kim's work had been stagnating for a while and as far as he observed, Kim is not making any effort to catch up. Mike did not expect this minor language policy, which he intended to encourage conversation and communication to create a sense where no one felt comfortable speaking at all. After several weeks, Mike felt the need to ask Kim what was going on.

"I don't understand, Kim. You speak decent English. So does Yoshi and Akemi..."

"It's not just about the language, Mr. Moore. Clearly, you're not happy with us talking Japanese, so no Japanese, Sir. It's your call. We wish you could have at least mentioned about this regulation with us before enforcing it."

It's true. It suddenly occurred to Mike that although he leaves his office door open and encourages all kinds of conversations, Sam seems to be the only one who takes advantage of this friendly freedom. Still bewildered, Mike asked, "But you're always welcome to my office to talk or even complain..."

Yoshi suddenly looked up at him, surprised and confused. He never expected his boss to offer opportunities to complain. At the meantime, as loyal and hardworking as he is, neither did he expect to be blamed for not talking or complaining.

Mike, of course, has no idea what's going on in Yoshi's mind, proceeds, "I heard that you, Akemi, and Yoshi have formed a little group within yourself. You know it makes the other colleagues feel excluded."

"But, Sir," Kim started speaking, "we stick together, because it seems that you and Sam have an especially good relationship. It seems that the two of you are friends instead of supervisor and subordinate... so we stick together. I'm sorry if we offended anyone. We just don't want to be isolated."

Mike is confused, "Sam and I are colleagues and so are you and me. We never meant to isolate anyone."

"In our culture, our supervisors don't socialize with their subordinates. We keep a distance. We only socialize with colleagues of the same level," Kim explains.

"Oh, I think we have a misunderstanding here! There are no barriers between us. We just have different roles in the company, that's all!" Mike explained, stretched out his arms to show sincerity.

Kim frowned, wondering to himself, *What kind of manager is that if there is no distance and authority?* "Mr. Moore, we are just showing our respect to you by keeping a distance and working hard. If any colleague thinks we excluded him or her," Kim added, trying not to make it a personal accusation, "it would be the colleague who breaks the respect first!" He kept calm and polite while talking, but Mike can see the emotional turmoil from his eyes.

At this moment, Kim's phone rang and he quickly excused himself, leaving Mike alone in his office. "What should I do?" Mike asked himself out loud. "Who is the isolated one?"

DISCUSSION QUESTIONS

1. From the perspective of Sam and the Asians, why do you think they both feel isolated?

2. According to you, what are the implications of this case to workplace friendship?

3. If you were Mike, what would you do differently?

4. In your opinion, what factors influence the workplace friendship in an organization? In this case, what are the barriers that prevent the mutual understanding among the colleague?

5. Why do you think the "English Only" policy doesn't work in this multi-nationality department?

KEY TERMS

Communication networks, workplace isolation, workplace friendship, diversity

CHAPTER 23

Personal Foul:
Contract Interference

Caryn Quinn, Tim Pearce, Brent Hogan, and Allison Burritt

ITHACA COLLEGE

ABSTRACT

Ben Williams, a recent hire at Pro Sports Management, is given the opportunity to sign one of the top NFL wide receivers, Mike Smith. The contract takes a turn for the worse when Ben introduces his boyfriend (or male partner) at dinner. Will Ben's decision impact the signing of the contract?

THE GAME PLAN

Ben Williams, an independent sports agent who was recently hired by Pro Sports Management (PSM) to run their NFL division, was intrigued when he heard his boss call him into his office.

"Ben, you are never going to believe who I just got off the phone with," Scott said with great enthusiasm. Scott Henry, the CEO of Pro Sports Management, is the head of the largest sports agency on the east coast, which is located in New York City.

Ben quickly replied, "Who?"

"The all-time leading receiver in the NFL for the last two years, Mike Smith," Scott said.

For the past several months Scott had been pursuing NFL wide receiver Mike Smith from the Atlanta Falcons in an attempt for PSM to represent him as his new agent.

As an independent agent, Ben specialized in recruiting NFL athletes, and he knew how much of an asset Mike could be to the agency if he were to be signed. As a new hire, there was no question as to whether or not Ben was going to accept Scott's proposal.

"Ben, I know you're new to the agency, but we are well aware of your track record, and I feel there is no one more qualified than you to meet with Mike and convince him to sign with us," Scott said.

Ben replied, "I couldn't be more excited to take on the challenge, and I have full confidence that I'll be back with a signed contract. So now where do we go from here?"

Scott said, "We are flying Mike and his wife into New York City this weekend and we need you to show them a good time. Perhaps you can make reservations at Masa, one of the most expensive restaurants in New York City? Mike will be bringing his wife, so make sure you bring your spouse," Scott said noting Ben's wedding band. He continued to explain to Ben that if he is able to sign Mike, he'll be promised a six-figure bonus.

The two conclude the meeting and as Ben walks away from Scott's office he turns around and shouts, "I won't let you down!"

A RED FLAG

Ben is already seated at the table with another man, when Mike and his wife Allison arrive at Masa. They both stand to greet Mike and Allison.

Ben shakes Mike's hand and says, "Mike, I want to thank you for taking the time to sit down and meet with me. This is my husband Joel Lopez." Mike and Joel exchange a handshake.

Mike responds, "It's my pleasure. I am pleased to meet both of you, and I appreciate your taking us out to such an amazing restaurant. My wife Allison has never been to New York City before, so we're excited to be here."

The four of them sit down for dinner and proceed to get to know one another. However, the conversation soon turns to business.

Ben explains, "As you know, we are one of the largest sports agencies in the business. Because of our size and expertise, we offer a variety of benefits that you are not getting at your current agency. Not only can PSM get you the money that you deserve, but we also have the capability to set you up with sponsors, commercials…you name it."

Mike responded, "Don't get me wrong, I see the appeal of signing with a big agency such as PSM, and I wouldn't have met with you if I wasn't seriously interested. But at the same time, I think my wife and I also need a little more time to discuss this matter further before we make any final decisions. I appreciate your taking us out to dinner; it was great. You guys really know how to pull out the red carpet. For now though, why don't we just talk football and carry this conversation over to the bar."

"No problem," Ben says.

The four of them sit down at the restaurant bar and order cocktails.

Mike and Ben begin to discuss the interest that the New York Giants have in trading for him during the off-season. Mike explains that his wife is concerned about moving to New York City, because both of them have lived in the South all their lives and they have two small children to worry about.

"I have heard horror stories about crime in the city and I really want to make sure that my children are safe," Mike explains further. "Is there anywhere else outside the city that you can recommend for athletes who work in New York but want to raise a family outside the city?"

Ben replied, "Actually, a lot of athletes live in New Jersey. Joel and I just moved into a one-bedroom townhouse in a gated community in Lyndhurst and we love it."

After pausing for an awkward silence, Mike finally responded, "Oh, interesting."

Ben noticed Mike giving his wife a strange look and wondered if he had said something wrong. Shortly thereafter, Mike and his wife explained that is was getting late and decided to return to the hotel, but told them they would be in touch. Ben left feeling like the dinner went well but was unsure about whether or not he sealed the deal.

OFFSIDE

The Monday following the meeting, Scott's assistant tells him that Mike Smith is on the phone.

Scott answers, "Hello Mike! Great to hear from you! How did dinner go the other night?"

Mike paused for a second before answering and said, "The dinner was delicious, and I want to thank you for treating my wife and me to one of the nicest restaurants in New York City. However, at the end of the night, it was brought to my attention that the man that Ben brought along with him, Joel, together live in a one-bedroom townhouse. When I discovered what type of relationship they have with one another, I was completely caught off guard and felt very uncomfortable after that. I'm sorry Scott, but I don't agree with their lifestyle, and as a result, I don't feel comfortable signing with an agency that endorses homosexual relationships."

Scott was completely shocked and at a loss for words after hearing what Mike had just told him. He eventually responded and said, "I'm sorry to hear that, and I can assure you that I had no intention of making you or your wife feel uncomfortable. I hope you will reconsider."

Mike explained that he understands but his mind is made up and he will be signing with a different agency.

As soon as Scott hung up with Mike, he called Ben into his office in a rather discerning tone.

"Ben, we need to talk," Scott said, as he closed his office door shut. "I got a call from Mike today and he said that he decided to go with different agency. He explained that he was not comfortable signing with an agency that endorses homosexual relationships."

Scott looked to Ben as if confused, "What is he talking about, Ben?" Ben paused for a moment to gather his thoughts and said confidently, "My sexual orientation is none of the company's or anyone else's business. I took Mike and his wife out as I was instructed to, and as far as I was concerned he seemed ready to sign with our agency."

There was a moment of tension in which both men spoke at once but then Scott proclaimed, "Listen, what you do inside the comfort of your home is of no concern to me, but when it interferes with my money we have a problem. Mike was a huge contract. You should have explained to me that you were in a gay relationship. If I had known that I would have sent someone else. You know I could care less that you're gay, but some of these southern boys aren't New Yorkers like I am."

Ben was furious. He tried to maintain his composure but his voice became increasingly aggressive as he proclaimed, "You asked me to bring my spouse and I did. I shouldn't have to explain or defend my actions. I didn't think it would have affected the signing, and if I thought it did, I wouldn't have done it."

Scott paused to take a breath, "Ben, again, I could care less who you're married to, but you just cost me money. I am going to have to reconfigure your role inside this company to something more suitable. Needless to say, you didn't sign the deal, so I can't give you the bonus we discussed."

DISCUSSION QUESTIONS

1. Was it Ben's responsibility to inform his boss that he was in a non-traditional relationship before meeting with the client?

2. Was the outcome of this case a result of discrimination? If not, what was it?

3. Should Ben go to human resources and report the incident or take legal action? Why?

4. If Ben does take legal action, what are some possible outcomes? Could there be further consequences for Ben?

5. Should Ben have handled the situation differently? If so, how?

KEY TERMS

Workplace discrimination, external and internal communication

24

The Three R's:
Religion, Rights, and Responsibility

Alfred G. Mueller, II

MOUNT ST. MARY'S UNIVERSITY

ABSTRACT

Dr. Joan Hawking, chair of the faculty senate at Small Midwestern Public University, wants to investigate the actions of students in a Christian student club, who reportedly have been harassing students of other faiths and pressuring faculty to amend their courses. Repeated attempts by the Dean of Students to investigate these actions have had no effect on the students' behaviors, which he and the students regard as protected under their First Amendment rights. Are the students within their rights to evangelize on campus, or is this a case of religious discrimination couched in rights talk?

Dr. Joan Hawking is beginning her term as faculty senate chair at Small Midwestern Public University (SMPU). Dr. Hawking, an associate professor in the department of history, has already served on a number of campus-wide committees, chaired several of the standing committees of the faculty senate, and chaired a number of faculty search committees in her eleven years at SMPU. She is widely respected as an excellent teacher, has published in several top journals in her field, and enjoys the support of students, staff, and faculty alike.

About two weeks into the new academic year, Dr. Carol Nguyen, an assistant professor in the biology department, stopped by Dr. Hawking's office to talk about something that was bothering her. "Joan, this morning in my biology lecture class, I overheard two students talking just before class got underway. From what I gathered, a young Muslim student was telling his friend that a small group of students tried to convert him to Christianity, telling him that he needed to convert to avoid 'burning in hell,' as he put it."

Dr. Hawking said, "You're kidding!"

"No. That's what he said," Dr. Nguyen said grimly.

Dr. Hawking pressed, "Who were these students?"

Dr. Nguyen said, "I needed to start class, so I asked him to see me after class and tell me more about the situation. But he left along with his friend after class finished."

"That's too bad," Dr. Hawking groused.

Dr. Nguyen handed Dr. Hawking a paper. "Here's his name and email address. Why don't you contact him and have him come talk to you?"

"Thanks, Carol. I will. I might also ask Jon to sit in."

After Dr. Nguyen departed, Dr. Hawking called the Dean of Students, Mr. Jonathan Mosley, and reported the incident. "Jon, in my opinion, this issue is more properly a student affairs matter than a faculty concern. Do you want to handle it?"

Mr. Mosley said, "I do, Joan. Thank you very much for this report. My staff and I will get right on it."

A few weeks later, Dr. Hawking was teaching a class about the early Christian period in world history. During a group exercise designed to elicit reasons why Romans would not be sympathetic to the Christian worldview, a male student offered the idea that maybe the Romans were another type of Christian and their group didn't like Catholics. Taken aback by the response, Dr. Hawking asked him, "Why would you say that, Brian?"

Brian said, "Last week, I attended a meeting of the new Christian student club on campus and they told me that I wasn't welcome there."

"What Christian club?" Dr. Hawking asked.

Another student named Cheryl chimed in, "It's called the Society for Justice and Truth."

"That doesn't sound like a religious group," Dr. Hawking mused.

"I know," said Brian. "That's why I went to check it out. I saw a flyer about the club and I decided to attend a meeting to find out what they do. I was hanging out with the other students before the meeting started, and one of the girls there asked me what church I attended. I told her that I go to St. Mark's. That's when one of the officers was like, 'That's a Catholic Church. Are you Catholic?' And I'm like, 'Yeah.' Then another one of the officers says to me, 'Then why are you here at this meeting? Don't you know that this is a Christian club?' That kind of irritated me a little, so I'm like, 'Well, what do you think Catholics are?' That's when this guy said, 'Catholics aren't Christians. They are members of cults.' I said, 'Yeah, right,' and so I figured I better get out of there."

Dr. Hawking asked him, "Would you be willing to repeat that story for the Dean of Students?"

Brian said, "Yeah, sure."

Immediately after class, Dr. Hawking visited Mr. Mosley's office in person. She reported to Mr. Mosley what the young man had reported to her in class. Mr. Mosley was surprised to learn about the student's experience, and promised that he and his staff would look into the situation.

During the next faculty senate meeting a few days later, when the group reached new business, Dr. Richard Okeke, the Chair of the Department of Finance, reported that a Muslim female student had reported to him that she was being vigorously pursued by a small group of students affiliated with the Society for Justice and Truth, determined to convert her to Christianity. "As a Muslim myself, I find such behavior disturbing," Dr. Okeke explained.

Dr. Nguyen chimed in, "Remember that young man that I notified you about?"

Dr. Hawking said, "Yes. I passed his contact information on to Jon Mosley."

Dr. Nguyen continued, "He told me that this group was even pursuing him in the dorms, telling him that if he doesn't convert he's going to burn in hell."

Dr. Hawking vowed to resolve the issue immediately.

After the senate meeting, she again went to visit Mr. Mosley in person. As she was entering the Office of Student Affairs, she noticed a flyer on a table in the waiting area, announcing a meeting of the Society of Justice and Truth (SJT). SJT would be bringing in a minister from the local community to talk about alternative spring break programs that gave students experience in evangelizing among those dispossessed by Hurricane Katrina. The flyer noted that the Associate Dean of Students, Mrs. Annette Knott, was the club's adviser.

Dr. Hawking proceeded to Mr. Mosley's office and reported the information that had emerged during the faculty meeting. Mr. Mosley sighed audibly, "I assure you, Joan, I will look into these reports personally."

Dr. Hawking said, "Look, Jon, I'm a bit frustrated by this whole thing. What have you discovered by talking to the two young men I notified you about so far?"

Mr. Mosley said, "I met with the affected students personally and spoke with the club officers about their behaviors. The officers indicated that they felt they were merely exercising their First Amendment rights to free speech, freedom of assembly, and freedom of religion. It turns out that the young Muslim man whom Dr. Nguyen reported attended their club meeting by accident. That's where they tried to talk to him about their strong feelings for Jesus Christ."

"What about Brian's story?" Dr. Hawking asked.

"It was an ignorant comment that the officer made. I had a discussion with all of them, instructing them how Catholics really are Christians."

Dr. Hawking, a bit more relieved, replied, "Good!"

"I know. What can you do? Generally, though, I am inclined to agree with the club officers that the First Amendment protected their efforts at evangelizing since the officers acted within the context of a club meeting. But with these new reports that the club members pursued students outside of club meetings, I see I'll need to revisit the situation. I'll have another meeting with the club officers and instruct them on the difference between a club meeting and the public areas of the campus."

Dr. Hawking said, "Thanks, Jon. After you meet with the students, I would appreciate it if you give me a call to update me on the issue so I can report back to the senate at next month's meeting."

"I will, Joan," Mr. Mosley said.

After two weeks had elapsed without any call from Mr. Mosley, Dr. Hawking called him to inquire what had transpired during his meeting with the club officers. Mr. Mosley said, "I talked to the officers and they assured me that they were not to blame for following the students around campus. They suggested that it might be rank-and-file members of the club who were engaging in the behaviors or even students unaffiliated with the club. Nevertheless, the officers agreed to discuss the issue at their next club meeting and explain to all of the members what constitutes proper behavior and what doesn't. Frankly, barring any further reports, I am considering the matter closed."

Dr. Hawking said, "I hope you're right, Jon."

Less than one week later, however, Mr. Harold Eugene, an adjunct faculty member in sociology, approached Dr. Hawking. "Dr. Hawking, I had a very odd encounter last night in my sociology course. Two students approached me after class. They were each wearing SJT sweatshirts. They noted that, according to the syllabus, next week's topics focused on sexual attitudes, beliefs, and behaviors. I assign a reading on homosexuality as a socially constructed sexual identity to supplement the chapter on social construction of self. The students informed me that such a reading was contrary to their religious beliefs and that they would therefore like equal time to present a Christian perspective on homosexuality in class."

Dr. Hawking asked, "What did you say?"

Mr. Eugene said, "I turned down their request."

"Good," said Dr. Hawking. "Religion is not a justification for not performing a reading assignment. Part of our job as educators is to introduce students to views that might make them uncomfortable."

"But," said Mr. Eugene, "the students then threatened to go to my department chair and report to her that I was not respecting their First Amendment rights. This is the first time anything like this ever happened to me. I am using the standard department syllabus, so I do not know what to do about this."

"What kind of reading is it? I mean, is it *that* provocative?"

Mr. Eugene said, "Students in the past had actually found the reading to be laden with sociological jargon and therefore quite boring."

Dr. Hawking frowned. "Harry, I think you did the right thing. If I were you, I'd talk with your department chair about the encounter. That way, she's prepared for it if they follow through on it."

When she returned to her office, Dr. Hawking decided that she had to act as faculty senate chair since going through the official channels of student affairs was having little impact on the situation. She was going to appoint an *ad hoc* faculty committee to look into these events. She sent out an email to the faculty listserv, explaining the reason for the new committee and asking for volunteers. Within an hour, she had fifteen faculty names for the committee. So she sent another email to the listserv, explaining to the faculty that she had more than enough volunteers already.

Looking over the list of names, she decided to winnow the list down to seven faculty members by eliminating multiple people from the same department and trying to achieve gender and disciplinary balance. The final committee had four women and three men drawn from the departments of art, computer science, English, physics, philosophy, religious studies, and psychology. She arranged to meet with them after the faculty meeting the following week and give them an official charge.

The next day, Dr. Hawking noticed two emails marked "URGENT" in her list. One was from Mr. Mosley and one was from the art professor named to the *ad hoc* committee, Ms. Kira Rogers. Mr. Mosley wrote, "Joan, late this afternoon, I discovered that you were appointing a faculty committee to investigate a student affairs matter. I do not understand how a student affairs issue suddenly became a faculty issue. If you go ahead with forming this committee, I insist that I be named as chair of the committee. If not, I have no intention of cooperating with the committee's work, since I regard it as an attempt to interfere in student affairs. Please contact me at once to explain what is motivating your effort."

Ms. Rogers, meanwhile, wrote, "Joan, you'll never guess what I found out. I was cleaning out a file cabinet drawer and found a roster of religious affiliations of various members of the SMPU community from back when we had that Interfaith Council operating on campus. According to that list, the Dean of Students, the Associate Dean of Students, and both of their administrative assistants are all of the same religious denomination as the students in SJT. Don't you find it odd that ALL of the members of an office on campus are of the same religious group? I mean, given that we are a public university, I bet you won't find that kind of coincidence in any other office on campus. This is definitely something for the committee to pursue."

Dr. Hawking had planned to begin drafting the committee charge that morning, but given these two emails, she did not know how best to proceed.

DISCUSSION QUESTIONS

1. What exactly does the First Amendment guarantee to us? What limits has the Supreme Court placed on our First Amendment freedoms? What further limits exist if one is attending a private college or university with a religious affiliation?

2. How does discrimination based on one's religious beliefs compare to other forms of discrimination such as racism, sexism, ageism, or discrimination based on class or sexual preference? How might such discrimination affect an organization's culture?

3. Consider the organizational theories you have studied thus far. Which ones might help Dr. Hawking identify potential solutions to her predicament?

4. What should Dr. Hawking's next step be?

5. If Dr. Hawking chooses to proceed with drafting the committee charge, what should the main components of that charge be? Should she appoint Mr. Mosley as chair of the committee? If so, how should she justify that to the faculty members? If not, how can she explain her decision to Mr. Mosley in a way that does not prevent his cooperation with the committee?

KEY TERMS

Diversity, conflict management, organizational justice

—PART V—

EXTERNAL COMMUNICATION

CHAPTER 25

A Crisis in Customer Service

Elizabeth Kranz and Danielle Clark

ITHACA COLLEGE

ABSTRACT

Larry Klein and Isaac Farley have been best friends since high school. When the two car experts join forces to start their own automotive dealership they are determined not to let anything get in their way. Since its grand opening, Klein & Farley Motors has been ranked among the most reputable automotive dealerships in the state of Texas. As the dealership approaches its 25th anniversary, problems arise within the organization due to tardiness among the employees. Will the company's previously unblemished reputation begin to falter right before its monumental anniversary?

THE CRISIS BEGINS

It was the first day of November when Larry Klein walked through the entrance of Klein & Farley Motors. It was time for his monthly meeting with Karen. These days Larry did most of his work from home. This had never been an issue because he maintained absolute confidence in the abilities of his employees. However, he always made it a priority to stop in every month to check on his team.

As Larry was walking down the halls, he noticed something seemed to be amiss. It was 9:15 AM and the only face he recognized in any of the offices was Art. Each office had an occupant, but Art was the only sales associate he could find. Larry poked his head into Serena's office and quickly introduced himself to the unfamiliar woman standing in the room. "Morning, ma'am. My name is Larry Klein. I'm afraid we haven't met before."

"Good morning, Mr. Klein," the woman said politely. "My name is Rebecca Harris. I'm here this morning to finish up my paperwork with Serena. Another sales associate, I think his name was Art, just stepped in a second ago to let me know she was running a little late. I hope she gets here soon because I'm afraid I need to get to work myself."

"I'm terribly sorry for the inconvenience, Ms. Harris. I'm sure Serena just got stuck in traffic. Please feel free to go down to our break room at the end of the hall and grab something to eat and drink while you wait. Again, you have my deepest apologies," Larry said genuinely.

"Thank you, Mr. Klein. I think I'll do that," a smile crossed her face.

Larry ducked out of Serena's office and then came to a startling revelation. The unfamiliar faces in the offices may all be clients who were waiting for the other sales associates. A feeling of panic flooded through Larry's body. He rushed down to Karen's office at the end of the hall and nearly ran into the room.

"Karen, what the hell is going on?" he could feel the alarm in his voice.

Karen was just finishing up a conversation on the phone. "William, this is the third time you've been late since the middle of last month." A wave of embarrassment came over her face when she noticed Larry was standing in the room. She continued, "You need to get in here right now. Mr. Walsh is waiting to finish his paperwork with you and he is in a hurry," she paused. "Yes, I know Francis doesn't come in before 10 now, but I already explained that he has a special circumstance," she paused again as she listened to William rant. "I'm not saying you don't work as hard as everyone else; I'm just saying that I need you to be on time for your client appointments. Please, William, just get in here now," she hung up the receiver.

"Karen, I repeat, what the hell is going on?" Larry asked with even more panic in his voice. "You know customers are the number one priority here. We cannot keep them waiting!" he was nearly screaming. "In the 24 years that this company has been functioning I have never seen a customer wait for a sales associate to show up. This can't be happening, especially now! We are coming up on Klein & Farley Motors' 25th anniversary!" he was still shouting. He then faltered a bit and his voice then began to waver, "What would Isaac think?"

Karen knew by keeping Francis' secret she had caused extreme tension between her employees. She suspected that everyone, except Art, had begun coming in late because she had never directly addressed why she pushed back Francis' schedule to 10 am. Now, she realized, her promise to Francis was putting the company's great customer service reputation at risk right before the dealership's monumental 25th anniversary. Larry Klein was not only her boss but also her dear friend. She knew she owed him an explanation.

Karen walked over to Larry and looked him straight in the eye. "Larry, I made a bad judgment call," her voice wavered. "Things have gotten out of hand and I'm afraid I have created a crisis."

A HIGH SCHOOL DREAM SET IN MOTION

In the far southeastern corner of a mid-sized Austin, Texas suburb there lays a modest looking, 12-employee car and truck dealership called Klein & Farley Motors. It may not have all the bells and whistles of some of the big city car dealers, but Klein & Farley has been rated Texas' number one automotive dealership in customer service and satisfaction for the past eight years in a row.

Larry Klein and Isaac Farley met in their high school Auto Shop class in 1954. The two young men bonded over their love of cars and quickly formed a friendship that would last them a lifetime. After high school the two friends parted ways to go to college, but they stayed in close contact and made an effort to see one another at least once a year no matter how busy their schedules were.

Larry spent many years managing service departments for some of the top-rated car dealerships in the country while Isaac worked as a regional sales manager for a large automotive manufacturer in the New York City area. While both men deeply enjoyed their occupations, they were not completely satisfied with the work they were doing. Back in high school, they had always talked about starting a business together and, even though it seemed like an impossible task, neither man ever gave up on that dream.

In 1984, while the two men were out to dinner, Isaac finally broke the ice on the subject the friends had not talked about in years.

"What ever happened to us starting our own business?" he asked. "It may have been impossible 30 years ago, but why not try it now? I know you still think about it as much as I do!" he was on the verge of shouting.

Larry paused from his dinner and a puzzled look formed on his face. "Are you serious?" he inquired. "I was sure I was the only one who still thought about that," he added. Larry folded his arms and took a minute to contemplate the prospect that Isaac had just presented him. "We aren't as young and as energetic as we once were, but I suppose we have the money and skills now to revisit our idea."

"Of course we do!" Isaac was now shouting. One of waitresses looked over at the men's table with an alarmed expression on her face. Isaac realized his excitement was agitating some of the patrons in the restaurant so he brought his voice back down to a more acceptable level. "We always talked about opening a car dealership, so what's stopping us? Even if we fail, we are both financially stable enough that we could bounce back. Plus, between our mutual love of cars, your mechanical knowledge and my experience in sales, I don't know how we could fail!"

Larry had always been less impulsive than Isaac, but even his levelheaded nature could not override his excitement for fulfilling the dream that he and Isaac had conjured up back in high school. Larry rose from his seat and pounded his fist on the restaurant table while crying out, "Let's do it!"

THE KEY TO SUCCESS

Larry and Isaac knew that customer satisfaction was the biggest element that could make or break their business. From day one, the two men vowed to do everything in their power to make sure that customers would never leave their dealership without a smile on their face.

In 1986, two years after the dinner conversation that set their plan in motion, Klein & Farley Motors opened its doors for business. Even in its first year, the company was rated one of the top five automotive dealerships in the state of Texas. This was primarily due to the staggering number of customer referrals the business received from previously satisfied customers.

Starting in 2002, *Texas Automotive Weekly,* the top selling car magazine in the state, began presenting the highly prestigious Best Customer Service & Satisfaction Award. This award was given out once a year by the magazine to only one dealership in the entire state of Texas. The award was created in order to recognize outstanding employee interaction with customers, excellent service policies for recalls and other automotive defects, customer loyalty (customers who have purchased 2 or more vehicles from the dealership), and the number of customers who had been referred by previous clients. Klein & Farley Motors has received the award every consecutive year since it was first issued. While Klein & Farley has maintained an outstanding reputation in all of the fields that the award acknowledges, the dealership most notably receives, on average, three to four times as many referrals as even the largest dealerships in Texas.

24 YEARS LATER—A YEAR OF TRIUMPH AND TEARS

Despite business being great and Klein & Farley Motors receiving the Best Customer Service & Satisfaction Award for the eighth time in a row, Larry Klein was having a tough year. Back in January, only two weeks before Klein & Farley Motors was presented with its prestigious award, Isaac Farley passed away unexpectedly due to a massive heart attack. Isaac had been in top-notch health for a man his age, so his death was especially devastating to his family and friends. While everyone at the company was deeply saddened by the death of one of their beloved CEOs, no one took the blow as hard as Larry. While the two men had experienced plenty of triumphs over their years working together Larry was heartbroken not only to lose his best friend but to lose him only one year before the company's monumental 25th anniversary.

TROUBLE BEGINS

It was a beautiful Monday morning in August when Karen Meyer, the Sales Division Manager at Klein & Farley Motors, stepped out of her car and headed toward the entrance of the dealership building. After entering the building she passed the break room and saw three of her sales associates, William, Cindy, and Serena, grabbing their morning coffee. They seemed to be chatting about something and their faces looked a little sullen. She quickly contemplated why this was and then remembered it was, after all, a Monday morning.

"Good morning, all!" Karen walked into the room with a grin on her face. They all looked up.

"Morning, Karen!" they said in unison and laughed. Karen realized years ago that she was, and probably always will be, the only morning person at the company. However, despite all of her employees not enjoying being awake before 10 AM, they had worked very hard to take on the same cheery disposition she had in the mornings.

"I'm very proud of you all. That 'Morning, Karen!' almost sounded genuine this time," she giggled. "Sorry, I don't have time to chat this morning. I have to get started on this month's financial reports. I'll catch up with you all at lunch." Serena handed her a cup of coffee; Karen waved to her friends and then headed back down the hall.

On her way she popped her head into Art's office. Art was the longest standing sales associate in the department. He had just passed his 20-year mark working for the company. When Karen started at Klein & Farley Motors 12 years ago, Art was the Sales Division Manager. However, Karen was promoted to his position only a year after she started because Art wanted to go back to just being a sales associate. Art disliked many of the managerial responsibilities and missed having the one-on-one interactions with customers. He still claims it is the best business decision he ever made.

When she stuck her head into his office, she noticed he was with a customer so she just waved. He looked up and returned the friendly gesture.

Finally, Karen decided that since she had seen everyone else she would stop into Francis' office. Francis was the only other employee who worked under her. Even though he was at least 15 years younger than any other employee in the department, he had just passed his 10-year mark working for the company. He had come to work at Klein & Farley right out of high school, and even though Karen was initially hesitant to hire him because of his lack of experience, his charisma and strong work ethic eventually won her over. Since his second year working at the company he had consistently received the most customer referrals and had the highest customer satisfaction ratings. Quite simply, he was the best sales associate at Klein & Farley.

Karen walked through Francis' door, "Good morning, Francis!" She stopped suddenly; Francis wasn't there. Just as she stepped out of his office she happened to see Art walking down towards the break room.

"Hey, Art!" she yelled down the hall.

"Yeah, Karen, what's up?" he turned around and smiled.

"Have you seen Francis yet today? Is he down in the break room?"

"Hold on a second," he said and stuck his head into the break room. After a second he shook his head at Karen. Art then made a gesture for Karen to come down and join him so she quickly obliged. "No, I haven't seen him today," he whispered. "I didn't want to yell this down the hall but I was actually just coming down here to find out if anyone else had seen him. The lady sitting in my office right now is Francis' client. She had a 9 AM appointment with him but he seems to be missing in action," he grumbled.

Karen looked down at her watch. It was now 9:18 AM While Karen was a staunch believer in letting her employees be flexible with their hours she had always been adamant that they show up to work at least 15 minutes prior to any meetings scheduled with customers so they had plenty of preparation time.

Art continued on, "I pulled Mrs. White into my office and offered to get her paperwork started but she is insisting on waiting for Francis. Apparently it is because he is the one that her grandson recommended she meet with," he rolled his eyes. "I'm not really sure what to do," he continued.

"Well, if Mrs. White insists on waiting for Francis then that is what will happen. It is our job to give the customer what they want. I really appreciate your help, Art," she placed her hand on his shoulder. "Please, just make her as comfortable as possible until Francis gets here. I'm going to go call him now."

"Karen," Art said with a little hesitation in his voice. "You need to know something," he continued. "This is the fourth time that I have covered for Francis since June. I didn't want to tell you because I like the kid a lot, but this is becoming an issue. Luckily, the last three customers were willing to do their paperwork with me, but as you can see, this time we aren't so lucky," he sighed. "Also, I don't have details but I do know Serena has covered for him at least once. I wouldn't be surprised if the other two hadn't done the same. Francis' tardiness seems to be all those three talk about in the break room anymore," he stated with a little disgust in his voice. "Not that I'm defending them for gossiping, but part of me can't blame them for what they say. We all like Francis, but picking up his slack is cutting into our own work time. The last time I covered for him, I had to reschedule one of my own appointments at the last minute, and the customer was not happy."

The truth was Karen had noticed that Francis was becoming less reliable lately. His customer satisfaction ratings were as strong as always so she didn't feel an immediate need to address the issue, but it was obviously affecting the productivity of her other workers. It was time to have a talk with Francis.

When she got back to her office she picked up her phone and dialed Francis' cell number. His phone rang four times before he picked up with a with a panicked sounding, "Hello?"

"Francis, it's Karen. Where are you? You missed your 9 AM appointment with Mrs. White and she is refusing to close the deal with anyone other than you," she said as calmly as she possibly could.

"Shoot!" he screamed into the receiver. Karen could hear the sound of children crying in the background. "Karen, I'm so sorry, can you please see if Mrs. White would be willing to reschedule for some time this afternoon?"

"Francis, are you okay? I hear crying," she asked concernedly.

"I'm fine. Things are just a little hectic today. I'll be in ASAP," he said.

"Francis, I'll take care of rescheduling Mrs. White's appointment but you and I also really need to meet this afternoon. I'm concerned about you," she said.

Other than the crying children in the background the line went quiet for a moment. Francis finally sighed and said, "Karen, I know what you need to talk to me about. Please schedule me for whatever time works for you. I'll see you in a little bit." With that last remark, the line went dead and Karen was left listening to the buzz of the dial tone.

THE CONFRONTATION

Francis sat across from Karen with a defeated look on his face. She was just about to open her mouth to speak when Francis began, "Trust me, I know exactly what this is about. Everyone probably thinks I've been flaking out lately and you have every right to believe that," he paused for a moment and looked down at his lap. After a few seconds he continued, "Karen, I should have told you this sooner but I was hoping I could manage. I hate worrying people and I don't want anyone feeling bad for me," he paused again. "Last year my wife, Becky, was diagnosed with breast cancer. She started chemo and was doing really well and the doctors were convinced she'd have a full recovery. By last November everything seemed to have cleared up but," Francis began to choke up. "In May she woke up at night and was having trouble breathing. The doctors in the ER did a PET scan and found that the cancer had recurred and spread to her lungs."

Karen was speechless. She couldn't believe that Francis had been keeping this to himself for so long. Tears began to well up in her eyes.

Francis continued, "As you know, Becky and I have twin boys, Jayden and Peter. Becky's been a stay-at-home Mom since they were born three years ago. When she was first diagnosed with cancer she was still able to take care of them because her chemo treatments were fairly mild," he paused. "I'm afraid that's not the case anymore. The chemo that she is going through now leaves her with absolutely no energy. My poor Becky is lucky if she has the energy to get out of bed," Francis began tearing up. "I've been running late so many times in the past few months because I have to feed Becky her breakfast in the morning—otherwise she won't eat. I also have to get the boys ready to take them to the babysitter. I love those kiddos to death but they are definitely a handful at this age. Most mornings I am able to get out the door on time but, as you already know, I'm not that lucky every day," he looked down again in shame.

Karen pulled herself together despite having the strong urge to cry. "Francis, I'm so sorry. You should have told me sooner so we could have worked something out. We can adjust your schedule so you don't have to come in before 10. Will that be enough time to take care of your morning tasks?"

"I'm sorry I didn't tell you sooner," Francis added. "I thought I could handle things but I obviously can't. Are you sure it would be okay to adjust my schedule? That should give me plenty of time to get the boys ready and take care of Becky."

Karen's face lightened up a bit. "Coming in at 10 would be no problem. You will just have to make sure not to schedule any clients before 10:15. I'll take care of letting the rest of the staff know what's going on."

A look of pure distress came across Francis' face. "Please, Karen, no. Is there any way we can just keep this between the two of us? It is so hard for me to talk about and I don't want everyone's pity. I'd rather have the rest of the staff just think I was being flaky for a few months."

Karen felt uncomfortable keeping this from the rest of the staff but she reluctantly agreed. "Your secret is safe with me."

DISCUSSION QUESTIONS

1. Examine the actions of Karen throughout the case and evaluate her role in the organizational crisis. As a manager, what did she do well? Is there anything she should have done differently? What would you have done in her situation?

2. Do you believe Karen is correct in labeling the situation as a "crisis"? Why or why not? Whether you decide if the situation is a crisis or not, what plan of action would you suggest Klein & Farley Motors' management take to get matters under control?

3. What lessons can individuals and organizations learn from this case?

KEY TERMS

Customer service, internal communication, work-life balance, crisis communication

Intergenerational Communication Struggles:
A Skirmish over Sales via Facebook

Marlane C. Steinwart

VALPARAISO UNIVERSITY

ABSTRACT

Sylvia, 51, is a seasoned sales manager for Orthwein Packaging, a mid-sized company whose success comes from high levels of customer service. Though they have a new online ordering and tracking system, their use of technology otherwise is not cutting-edge. Andrea, a recent college graduate and the newest member of the sales force, creates several dilemmas for Sylvia when she damages the company's customer-service reputation by conducting sales through a social networking site. Sylvia is questioning how to best use Andrea's technology talents while preventing intergenerational communication struggles in the future.

DISTURBING PHONE CALL

"Laura, I'm sorry this happened," Sylvia Wallace exclaimed. "I assure you this is not the way Orthwein Packaging usually does business. We value our customers. Please let me talk to Andrea and get this fixed for you." promised Sylvia.

"Do what you can," said Laura, president of MJD, "but I'm on a tight deadline. I have a meeting Tuesday morning with another packaging company. My customer needs our products by the 25th."

Sylvia hung up the phone, her mind racing as she looked at the clock. It was 4:45 PM on Friday. There wasn't much time to solve this problem.

ORTHWEIN PACKAGING

Orthwein Packaging is an industry leader in producing packing materials. The mid-sized company specializes in making custom corrugated boxes and soft packing material for a variety of products. Orthwein Packaging's industry success is due in large part to its attentive sales staff.

Sylvia Wallace is the sales manager at Orthwein Packaging. At 51, Sylvia has worked in sales most of her career. She has been with Orthwein for ten years and has been sales manager for four years. During her tenure as sales manager, she's seen a 25% growth in sales, which has primarily been attributed to their top-notch customer service.

Unfortunately, in the last decade, Orthwein Packaging has not been able to keep ahead of changing trends in technology. While not quite cutting edge, the organization has often adopted various technologies before their competitors, but they still seem to be behind the curve of some of the top names in the packaging industry. Initially, technology permitted the sales staff to use the computer to monitor inventory levels and track deliveries, both of which allowed them to serve their customers better. To help streamline the ordering process, Orthwein Packaging has recently begun to accept online orders directly from customers.

THE WEEKLY SALES MEETING

As she mulled over the disturbing phone call, Sylvia's thoughts turned to last Wednesday's sales staff meeting. The meeting had begun with Owen, the 35-year-old sales team lead, reporting on the two long-time customers who had started using the online ordering system. Seven years ago, Owen started with Orthwein as a junior sales associate. After two years, he became a sales associate, and three years ago, Owen was named sales team lead.

"Both Intec and Zimco placed their first orders through OrthweinOnline this week. I walked Daniel, from Intec, through the process over the phone," Owen said. "He seemed to understand it, but I sense he's relieved that we're still here to talk to him. He really enjoys discussing his options with me. I think I'm a good sounding board for him…Sandy at Zimco, on the other hand, is a different story," Owen continued. "She ordered online on Monday morning. I noticed the order just after lunch and called her to ask how it went. She seemed surprised to hear from me," Owen speculated, "as though she thought I was calling because something had gone wrong with the order. I assured her that OrthweinOnline was processing the order and she could track the delivery through our website."

Sylvia considered this information. Having been in sales for over 25 years, the fact that Sandy would find Owen's call surprising had bewildered her. What had happened to the almighty "face time" with customers that her mentors preached about? Personally, she loved technology and the instant gratification it could provide. For her, though, nothing could beat being face-to-face with a customer so she could interpret body language and really be able to read the relationship.

"Sylvia, I hate doing this, but I have a new-client meeting in about ten minutes, so I really must leave," Owen said, stacking his papers and nervously looking at his watch.

"Not a problem—go get us some new customers," Sylvia said smiling.

"Thanks, don't worry, Justin and Andrea are up-to-speed and can handle the rest of the meeting," Owen replied, nodding toward his two junior colleagues. Owen finished gathering his belongings and was out the door in a flash.

"So," Sylvia started, "Justin, what accounts are you working on?"

The 27-year-old sales associate smiled. "Things are going really well. The two new accounts I've been working on for about a month—Glowlite and Porter—finally signed. Glowlite is small, but growing. I signed them in a meeting on Monday. Porter came to us from AllPak. They left AllPak because the online system there kept rejecting their orders, and they couldn't count on their sales rep to fix the issues. They said he would tell them he'd straightened out the order, but the order wouldn't arrive at all or it would contain the wrong items. So I promised to alert them about their order status until they have the product, even though the system generates tracking messages. For a while, anyway, I think they'll appreciate that personal touch."

"Great! Thanks for your hard work, Owen. The orders from Glowlite and Porter will really help our quarterly numbers. Andrea, how are things going for you?"

Andrea was the newest addition to the Orthwein sales team. A junior sales associate out of school for just over a year, she mainly worked on servicing existing accounts that Justin or Owen had landed in the past.

"I'm doing great! I've been helping Justin and Owen with customers who are interested in migrating to OrthweinOnline. I've also been working with the IT staff about establishing our presence on Facebook and Twitter. One of Justin's customers gave us a lead on a prospect, MJD Corporation. They contacted us, and Justin and Owen agree that I'm ready to try to land this one on my own!"

"Excellent," Sylvia had replied. "I'll be happy to hear how it goes. Let me know if you need any help." After a short conversation about goals for the next meeting, Sylvia ended the meeting.

SALE IN JEOPARDY

Two days later on Friday afternoon, Sylvia received a call from Laura Hunt, the President of MJD. Sylvia thought about the industry trade shows where she sometimes bumped into Laura. Inwardly, Sylvia figured Laura was calling to congratulate her on the new account.

"Hi Sylvia, this is Laura Hunt with MJD."

"Hi, Laura. I'm happy to hear from you!"

"Well, you might not be after you hear what I have to say. My staff has been working with Andrea in your sales department to get a quote on packing materials for our products. We were really excited about working with you because we'd been hearing good things about OrthweinOnline and the level of personalized service they've received from your sales people."

Sensing a problem, Sylvia braced herself.

"Well, on Monday, my production manager Loralei called your sales office from her cell phone to ask about pricing and availability of certain boxes we need by the 20th. She left a detailed message that included her email address. On Tuesday, she received a text message on her cell from Andrea in your sales department asking what Andrea could do for her. Loralei had to visit your website to find Andrea's email address.

"Loralei emailed Andrea the parameters of the project she needed packaging materials for and its deadline on Wednesday morning. On Thursday afternoon, Andrea posted a link to the quote on Loralei's Facebook wall with the message 'here's the info you wanted…cant w8 to hear from U!'".

Sylvia cringed as Laura spelled out the exact characters Andrea had used in the wall post. *Dear God, what was Andrea thinking putting confidential pricing information in a public place?* Sylvia thought to herself.

"I understand that today's communication is fast-paced, and we all probably reach for whatever is most convenient for us, myself included," Laura continued. "However, I don't think conducting business via Facebook is appropriate. For one thing, it's too public. I don't know who else saw Andrea's post to my production manager, but I don't want other companies knowing what we're doing because they read it on a social networking site!" Laura bellowed.

"Loralei is under a tight deadline. I have another company coming in Tuesday to show me samples and give me pricing for this project. In the meantime, make sure that link is removed from Facebook."

Fuming inwardly, Sylvia promised Laura that she'd find out more about the situation and the link on Facebook would be removed, though she wondered how that would be done. She hung up with Laura and picked up the phone again to call Andrea at her desk. Sylvia did not get an answer, and she decided the situation was too important to discuss in a voicemail message. Instead, she walked down the hall to the sales staff area. Andrea was not in her cubicle, but she spotted Owen nearby.

THE SEARCH FOR ANDREA

"Owen!" she exclaimed, startling him. "Where is Andrea?"

"Um…she left a little while ago. She and some IT staff were meeting at the coffee shop next door. You can probably text her."

It was now 4:50 on Friday afternoon. Sylvia was outraged at the fact that Andrea was already gone for the weekend. Her mind raced with questions: *Does she care at all about her job? What about the company's reputation? Does she even think about our future?* Sylvia picked up the phone to call Andrea and interrupt her Friday afternoon fun, but then she changed her mind. She fired off an email: "Andrea, in my office, 8 AM, Monday" and then left for the day.

Sylvia arrived home on Friday night and found her husband Mark ready to relax.

"You are not going to *believe* what Andrea did today!" Sylvia blurted out, still steaming. She relayed her conversation with Laura Hunt to Mark.

"Isn't Andrea the recent college graduate you were so excited to bring on board for all the Facebook stuff?"

"Yes, but we also hired her as a sales associate. She's had all the sales training that we offer, and she's watched Justin and Owen for the last several months. They don't do things that way. I don't understand what she was thinking."

"Didn't you make any mistakes when you started out in sales, especially when you were just out of school?" Mark asked, somewhat timidly.

"Sure I did," replied Sylvia, "but somehow, this feels different."

"Well, if it's not working out, why don't you fire her?" suggested Mark.

Sylvia thought about Mark's suggestion. On one hand, Andrea's comfort with technology was an asset to Orthwein. She not only understood what everyone was already using, she was interested in what was on the horizon. She seemed to like learning new stuff. On the other hand, she needed to be a strong sales associate.

Sylvia reflected on her own actions when she was Andrea's age. Was she just as clueless at 23? It seemed to her that at that age she wanted to learn from the older sales staff. They were successful, so it seemed natural to want to do whatever they did. The generation gap seemed bigger, different, and more significant today. And it wasn't just about age. The real gap seemed to be in communication.

In the course of her weekend errands, Sylvia stopped at a bookstore, perusing the shelves for information on the generation gap in the workplace. She found several books and leafed through them. She wondered how much they could help, though, since they primarily dealt with the idea that there *are* multiple generations in the workplace today. She wanted to find one that had specific suggestions on *how* to deal with the differences among the generations. She needed the handbook she could read quickly to solve her problems.

On Monday, Andrea appeared, looking ashen, in Sylvia's doorway at 8:05 AM.

"You wanted to meet with me?" she asked meekly.

"Yes, Andrea, come in. I wanted to talk to you about the deal with MJD. How are things going?"

"Um…what's the problem? I gave a quote for the boxes they wanted on Thursday, but I haven't heard anything back yet."

"So you met with the MJD people on Thursday?" Sylvia pried, wanting to hear how the communication trail looked from Andrea's perspective.

"No, I didn't *meet* with them. I figured out how to use OrthweinOnline to create a faster quote for customers—even though it took a little tweaking. Plus, it will reduce the time it will take us to fill the order in the long run. Then I posted a link to the quote on the production manager's

Facebook page because I figured it was the quickest way to get the information to her," she added. "It was actually kind of fun!"

SYLVIA'S DILEMMA

Sylvia was stunned. She marveled at Andrea's discovery of a way to use the online system to reduce order fulfillment time. But at the same time, she was embarrassed about the communication method Andrea used with MJD. She was also worried about how she could help Andrea to realize that she needed to improve her interpersonal interaction skills.

Sylvia dismissed Andrea from the meeting as her mind filled with questions. Should she set a meeting with MJD, or just let this sale go? If she lets it go, what will happen to Orthwein Packaging's reputation? What should she do about Andrea? Sylvia's future sales staff will have more Andreas. How can she harness the skill set of Andrea's generation while instilling in them the value of interpersonal communication?

DISCUSSION QUESTIONS

1. What can Sylvia do to save the MJD account?
2. What could Andrea have done differently to avoid this scenario? What could Sylvia have done differently?
3. What roles, if any, do Owen and Andy play in Andrea's current situation?
4. Going forward, what should Sylvia do to prevent this problem from recurring?

KEY TERMS

Web 2.0, customer service, sales, negotiation, intergenerational communication

Mount Kenya Coffee

Jason S. Wrench

SUNY New Paltz

Doreen Jowi

Bloomsburg University

ABSTRACT

When Jonah is hired to work as a risk communication expert for Mount Kenya Coffee, he finds himself facing internal problems from management and questions of health hazards from the Kenyan Government.

"Afiya, I'm sorry but the latest research coming out from the an independent firm from the Netherlands clearly indicates that Organochlorine Carbamate isn't toxic to humans, but the perception of its toxicity is what I'm worried about here," Jonah said for the tenth time during his weekly meeting.

"I understand your concerns Jonah, but unless the evidence is conclusive, I don't think there's any reason to start warning people about a 'possible' toxin unless there is absolute proof," Afiya Omondi said flatly. "Besides, OrgCarb has been a godsend for the crop this year. We're going to have one of the highest harvest yields this company has ever seen."

"What about reassuring our growers and the local residents?"

"Please, you're talking nonsense Jonah! I don't want to hear about this again."

"But…"

"This conversation is over," Afiya said as she turned back to her computer monitor clearly indicating that the weekly meeting was officially over.

Jonah gathered his stack of research reports, picked up his iPad, took one last glance at Afiya, and left the office. *I can't believe she can sit there so smugly. How can someone not care about saving lives?*

I'M GOING WHERE?

Jonah Keating graduated with his master's degree in risk communication from Richland University, a small private school about an hour outside Chicago. After a short stint working for the Centers for Disease Control and Prevention in the United States, Jonah decided he was tired of working for the government, and started looking for more lucrative jobs in the private sector.

As a risk communication expert, Jonah was trained to help both nonprofit and for-profit organizations clearly explain what types of risks could be associated with various processes and services. Half of risk communication was being able to clearly and concisely articulate scientific information, while the other half of risk communication was understanding how the public perceives a risk. Jonah quickly learned at the CDC that many of the risks that people are scared of actually pose very little harm, while many serious threats are barely even on the public's radar.

After interviewing for a number of different positions, Jonah saw an advertisement looking for a risk communication expert for Mount Kenya Coffee (MKC). After doing a little investigating on the web, Jonah came to really respect MKC.

Mount Kenya Coffee resides at the base of Mt. Kenya, the second tallest mountain in Africa, and about 150 kilometers northeast of Nairobi, the capital of The Republic of Kenya. The mountain is home to a number of coffee farmers, and MKC was originally designed as a cooperative among several farmers to make sure their product reached an international audience. Over two decades, MKC quickly grew to be a global powerhouse in coffee retail. As such, the company quickly garnered an international reach with offices in New York, London, Hong Kong, and Sydney.

Jonah was impressed not only with the award winning coffee, but also with the progressiveness of the organization's attitude towards growers and the environment. While Mount Kenya Coffee had grown to a global powerhouse in the international coffee trade, the original owners were very particular that the larger organization kept the co-op feel of its early days. As such, local farmers participated in profit sharing to help encourage new and innovative growing techniques. MKC was also known to help struggling farmers during seasons when growth rates were not high because of droughts and other forms of crop destruction.

As for the environment, MKC had won numerous environmental awards, including the United Nations Environment Program's citation of excellence for MKC's work on organic farming and fair trade. Furthermore, MKC had a strict policy of only using natural pesticides that had been clinically proven to pose no threat to the long-term health of both the land and people.

Overall, Jonah just knew this was the type of organization he would love to work for, so he quickly sent off his resume and waited for a response.

Within a week Jonah was on a plane to New York to meet with the Vice President of Strategic Outreach, an American named Keith Clancy. The interview lasted an entire day; Keith explained the basic philosophy of MKC in detail and explained some of the new initiatives that the company was undertaking. Right after lunch, Keith called the Chief Operations Officer of the MKC, a woman named Afiya Omondi.

"Afiya, you there?" Keith asked into the video camera connecting himself to Kenya via a voice over internet protocol (voip) software similar to Skype. In a few seconds, a woman in her early 40s with shortly kept braided hair appeared on the monitor wearing a smart business suit.

"Mr. Clancy, how good to see you again."

"Afiya, I'm so glad you could join us at this later hour."

"It's only 8:30 PM here, so not too late," Afiya said dismissively.

"OK," Keith said with a slight grimace. "Anyways, I wanted to introduce you to one of our candidates for the new risk communication director position for MKC, Mr. Jonah Keating."

"Well, Mr. Keating, let me start by saying that I do not believe this position is necessary. I just feel it is important for me to forewarn you of my opinion."

"Why is that?" Jonah questioned.

"I just don't think hiring someone to 'communicate' risks is an issue. I mean we don't pose a risk to anyone here at MKC, so I think this is just another case of an American 'fad' entering into international business."

For the next thirty minutes the interview was pleasant, but Jonah could clearly see that Afiya was not going to be easily swayed to the importance of risk communication in any organization. At the conclusion of the conversation, Clancy disconnected the conferencing system and turned to Jonah.

"Here's the reality: Afiya means well, but she doesn't completely understand why we must make sure that our practices are above reproach. The fact is the Kenyan government has pretty strict policies with regards to agriculture because agriculture is one of the most important parts of the Kenyan economy. As such, we need to make sure that any potential threats are clearly communicated to avoid any kind of backlash either from the locals in the area or the Kenyan government."

"OK," Jonah said before asking, "How do you see me fitting in?"

"Well, I'm glad you asked; you would primarily be working with Safi Michieka, our chief grower at Mount Kenya Coffee and the man who oversees our operations for the Kenyan Government, Gakuru Adoyo, the Minister of Agriculture."

"OK."

"Our goal at Mount Kenya Coffee is not only to provide a world class coffee, but to promote Kenyan culture and enrich the lives of the Kenyan people through our organizational endeavors. Ms. Omondi, really means well, but often she sees getting ahead in her career as more important than the basic mission of the organization."

"Huh?" Jonah questioned.

"I may be speaking out of turn here, but I just want to be honest. There have been grumblings in the organization that Afiya is looking to jump ship and become a CEO elsewhere. As such, she has been making some decisions that have helped the organization grow, but have not clearly been aligned with the organization's values."

Jonah let what Keith was telling him sink in. Without being explicitly told what was going on, Jonah could easily surmise what was going on here. Realizing the problems Afiya Omondi could pose, Jonah carefully posed his next question, "What power or authority would I have to counteract Ms. Omondi's decisions?"

"Honestly, not much," Keith said flatly. "Look, I'm not looking to turn you off of the job, I just want to make sure I give you a very realistic understanding of what life is going to be like working with Afiya. While I may be your immediate supervisor, I'm going to be in New York and you're going to be living in Kenya, so you'll have to deal with Afiya daily."

"Oh, so I'll be living full-time in Kenya?"

"Well, not exactly. You'll be living partially in Kenya, partially in London, and partially here in New York. Don't worry about housing, the company will provide you three small apartments in each location while you're working in the different locations. I know this will involve a lot of traveling, but it really is an amazing opportunity."

The rest of the interview went off without a hitch. Later that week Jonah received a phone call offering him the job, and within the month he was staying in a small apartment at The Ark Lodge in Abadare at the base of Mt. Kenya.

PROBLEMS SURFACE

The first year working for Mount Kenya Coffee was a blur. Jonah found himself crisscrossing the Atlantic Ocean and the Mediterranean Sea so often he was beginning to imaging he was a bird migrating on a weekly basis. For the most part, working with Afiya Omondi had turned out to be much more pleasant than their initial interview had predicted.

Jonah was just settling into his job when Gakuru Adoyo, the Minister of Agriculture requested a meeting with Jonah. Meetings with the minister occurred monthly, so being asked to come for a meeting wasn't something that unusual.

Jonah arrived for the meeting Adoyo and was surprised to find Safi Michieka sitting in the lobby as well.

"Mr. Keating," Safi exclaimed, raising from his seat to shake Jonah's hand.

"Please, sit down," Jonah said as he motioned for Safi to retake his seat. "I guess you're here to see Minister Adoyo as well?" Safi nodded his head yes, so Jonah continued, "Any idea what this meeting is about?"

"I have no idea. I received a phone call that I was expected to appear for a meeting with the minister. I was given no details."

"Interesting," Jonah said running through a list of possible topics the minister may want to address in the meeting.

Just as Jonah was about to verbalize some of his ideas, the minister's secretary emerged and ushered them into the minister's office.

Agricultural Minister Gakuru Adoyo was an imposing figure. He stood 6-feet tall and weighed almost 250 pounds. His deep, booming voice always reminded Jonah of the actor James Earl Jones.

"Mr. Keating, Mr. Michieka. I'm glad you two could make it today," nodding for Jonah and Safi to take the seats in front of his desk. "According to my documents, Mount Kenya Coffee has been using a new pesticide called Organochlorine Carbamate or OrgCarb for short."

Jonah and Safi started to answer simultaneously. After looking at each other quickly, Safi nodded to Jonah for him to go first. "Yes, Minister Adoyo, we have been using OrgCarb for about a year now to amazing results."

"In fact, we've been able to almost double our yield on some plantations this year," Safi chimed in.

"Stop," Adoyo commanded. "I have reason to believe that this chemical may be causing harmful side effects to both the Kenyan people and the Kenyan land."

"What do you mean?" Jonah questioned.

"I received this research article," Minister Adoyo exclaimed handing a copies to both Jonah and Safi. "In this article by a Dutch research team, they claim that Organochloridine Carbamate can actually cause a spike in cancer among those people who are exposed for long periods of time, and can actually cause a depletion in soil chemicals."

"Oh my," Jonah said. "No wonder you asked us to come here today."

"What do you have to say to these allegations?" Minister Adoyo commanded.

"Well, Minister Adoyo, I really cannot say too much about the allegations without actually going over the article itself and possibly reaching out to my contacts in the scientific community," Jonah replied.

"You have until next week to provide an official response," Minister Adoyo said and then without skipping a beat he nodded his towards the office door, saying, "Good day."

SMALL SPARKS TURN INTO FOREST FIRES

Jonah spent the rest of that week reading through the research article and finding that the study linking OrgCarb to cancer was conducted primarily in rats. As for the chemical leeching nutrients from the ground, the article actually didn't exactly say this. Jonah read the paragraph again for the fourth time:

One possible side effect of Organochlorine Carbamate could be the leeching of soil nutrients like zinc and iron if the chemical is exposed to high levels of radiation. However, in our current analysis, we were unable to find the exact level of radiation exposure that would be necessary for this to occur. We hypothesize that a nuclear blast could theoretically alter the Organochlorine Carbamate to the point where leeching may occur.

Working with the legal department, Jonah crafted a one-page analysis and sent it to Minister Adoyo, Keith Clancy, and Afiya Omondi. As a follow-up precaution, Jonah decided that he should probably start preparing a risk communication campaign to clearly articulate the possible side effects of OrgCarb, to reassure not only the Kenyan Government but also any local farmers or residents in case the allegations were made public.

During their weekly meeting, Jonah raised the idea of creating the risk communication campaign with Afiya, who quickly struck the idea down. After getting back to his office, Jonah sat in his office wondering what steps he should take next, if any.

DISCUSSION QUESTIONS

1. Would you consider Afiya Omondi an excessive careerist based on what you've read? Why or why not?

2. Do you think Keith Clancy made the correct decision in providing Jonah Keating a complete and realistic job preview? Why or why not?

3. How would you tackle the risk communication campaign?

4. Based on the information within the case, what should Jonah do next?

KEY TERMS

Risk communication, external communication, branding, excessive careerism

CHAPTER 28

A Road to Nowhere

Jason S. Wrench and Lauren Jensen

STATE UNIVERSITY OF NEW YORK AT NEW PALTZ

ABSTRACT

When a social media expert is brought in to help a Broadway show plagued by problems, he quickly realizes that the show is a public relations nightmare both on and off the stage.

"What are you, a few clowns short of a circus!?" screamed Danielle Tillman, the show's acclaimed director.

"Maybe, but this whole show is an exercise in artificial stupidity at this point!" responded Carl Lightman, the show's producer.

"My show is artificial stupidity? Apparently, I'm the only real artist working today!"

Ben Weber leaned against a banister on the other side of the atrium watching the two get louder and louder as onlookers walked past them. The new Broadway Musical based on the British best-selling novel, *A Road to Nowhere,* had been plagued with press controversies, questions about the suitability of the material, high-profile exits of the two leading actors, and a recent injury involving one of the prop pieces. And now this, the very public spectacle occurring before his eyes between the director and producer during the intermission of a Wednesday Matinee.

Ben noted an audience member with a smart phone recording the whole episode out the corner of his eyes. *As the show's newly hired director of social media, I should have an usher stop the guy, but why bother. I've been hired to polish the railings on the Titanic!*

Against his better judgment, Ben caught an usher's attention and directed him toward the young man illegally recording the argument. The usher walked over to the guy and had a brief encounter with him. After a few seconds, the usher flagged Ben over to the conversation.

Not really wanting to leave his ring-side seat for the fight of the century, Ben reluctantly waded his way through the afternoon matinee crowd and approached the two saying, "What's going on?"

"Mr. Weber, this gentleman was recording the conversation between Ms. Tillman and Mr. Lightman."

"OK."

"I tried to stop the recording, but he's already posted the video to YouTube."

Ben sighed, *not surprised,* looking at the young man, "You do realize that any flash photography or recording of the show is strictly not permitted?"

The young man looked at Ben with a defiant look on his face, "But I wasn't recording the show, I was recording the fight!"

"Technically, from the moment you enter into a Broadway theater, everything you see and hear is proprietary, so you have violated the productions copyright. I'm going to have to delete the file from your phone and request you delete the YouTube file or face being banned from this theater and any other theaters associated with this production organization." Ben wasn't completely convinced that what he was saying was 100% legal, but the guy handed over his smart phone and Ben quickly deleted the file. Thankfully, they had the same model phone, so making the deletion was very easy and Ben had the guy back in his seat before the second act.

The rest of the show went off without a hitch. Once the theater was cleared he pulled out his phone and looked at the RSS (really simple syndication) feed he'd set up for the show. Immediately, the list started loading, and the mentions of that afternoon's fight was the only part of the show being discussed. Everything from Playbill.com to BroadwayWorld.com to AllThatChat.com were all over the fight. Even the *New York Post* theater writer, who notoriously hated the show, had already written an op-ed about the conflict.

ALL ABOARD

Ben graduated from college with a major in organizational communication and an emphasis in organizational uses of social media. During his final year in college, he had worked for a local non-profit organization helping them fine-tune their social media campaign to entice new donors. The success of the new campaign was beyond any expectation the CEO had.

Shortly after the conclusion of the campaign, the CEO asked Ben to come to her office one afternoon. When Ben arrived he was introduced to the CEO's brother-in-law Paul Hohne, the CEO of a digital media consulting firm in New York City called Amica Consulting. Amica stemmed from the Latin word *amicabiliter,* which roughly translates in English as "social."

"It's nice to meet you, Ben," Paul said motioning towards a chair in the room, "my sister in-law here has been telling me all about your campaign. I've checked out your producibles and was quite impressed with your level of skill and sophistication. I've already talked it over with my senior partners, and we want to extend a job offer to you. As soon as you graduate, we'll give you a month off to move to New York City and then you can start working in the big-leagues if you're interested. Oh, and we'll supply you with an apartment near our offices for six months while you find a more permanent place to stay in the city."

Ben wasn't sure if he had heard all of that correctly, but he had. Three months later Ben started working at the Amica Consulting Group's offices right in the heart of Manhattan.

For the first few months, Ben worked under another project manager and learned the ropes of client proposals and project management, which were skills Ben really hadn't learned in college. Within four years, Ben even became a certified project management professional and started taking on new clients.

Ben landed the contract for Carney productions right after he was made a junior partner in the firm. Carney Productions was one of the top theater producing companies in New York City and the world. Carney Productions had garnered countless Tony Awards (the prized award for best new play or new musical granted each year to shows on Broadway) and was looking to branch out into new digital media.

To determine if Amica Consulting was the right social media firm, Carney Productions asked Ben to create a social media campaign targeted at younger theater audiences for the revival of Arthur Bicknell's play *Moose Murders.* The play was a huge success, and the social media campaign actually delivered a much younger market for the show. With that level of success, Carney Productions was set to make the Amica Consulting Group its full time social media partner.

ICEBERG RIGHT AHEAD

Two days before the contracts were to be signed, Ben received a phone call from Jennifer Carney, the CEO of Carney Productions, in a panic.

"Jennifer, calm down, what's wrong? Is something wrong with the contract?"

"Forget about the contract for a moment, Ben, everything is falling apart right now!" she quickly said the words barely getting out of her mouth fast enough.

"Slow down, what happened?"

"Our new show, *A Road to Nowhere,* is being slaughtered in the media."

"I didn't think the show was even in previews yet," Ben replied referring to the period of time a show is tested before live audiences, but before critics see the show for reviewing purposes.

"It's not—we're barely into the rehearsals, but the show is already a disaster. Marty Russell at the *New York Post* has already labeled it the 'Train Wreck of the Season.' Apparently, someone in the cast has been twittering about problems with the show and a few arguments the lead producer, Carl Lightman, has been having with the show's director, Danielle Tillman."

"OK, let's not panic. The show isn't even out of previews yet, so there's still plenty of time to get the press and public on your side. First, and foremost, we need to get ahead of the social media campaign and stop whoever it is that's Tweeting."

"We kind of found out who has been tweeting," Jennifer responded hesitantly.

"What aren't you telling me, Jennifer?"

"It's Anita Sharpe, the show's lead."

"Oh, that definitely changes things," Ben said slowly. "Give me an hour, I'm going to run this up to my bosses and get over to your offices with a team today. We've got to get ahead of this thing today."

Jennifer thanked Ben and said she'd order in lunch for the team and have it ready for their arrival. Ben immediately left his office and head down the hall to Paul Hohne's office. Paul's secretary looked up as Ben approached. She was going to stop him, but something in Ben's face just led her to say, "He's not busy, just walk right in."

Ben rapped on his door and heard Paul bellow from within his office, "Come in."

Ben entered the office and just started explaining the conversation he'd just had with Jennifer Carney.

"But we haven't signed the contracts with Carney Productions yet?" Paul asked.

"Right, and I have a feeling if we can't get ahead of this thing, we may not end up signing contracts with Carney Productions."

"Did Carney come right out and say that?"

"No, but she seemed clearly more focused on this current crisis and less concerned with the contracts, which could mean that if this crisis isn't handled, the contracts may never get signed."

"I definitely see your point. Take Pennington and McDonald with you," Paul said in a tone that clearly indicated the conversation was over. "Oh, and I want a report this evening. Call me on my cell once you have a better picture of the damage that's already been done."

"Sure thing boss," Ben replied as he exited the office and set off to find Linda Pennington and Robert McDonald. Thankfully, Linda and Robert were in their offices and took just a few minutes to gather their belongings and the three were outside on the curb hailing a cab for the quick trip across town.

During the cab ride, Ben, Linda, and Robert all started following Anita Sharpe's Twitter feed.

After a few minutes of silence, Linda finally broke the silence, "Is this woman trying to kill the show?"

"If not," Robert started, "She's sure doing the job for all of the gossip columnists in the city. This woman is raking more muck than anyone has been on Page 6 for years." Page Six referring to the *New York Post's* famous gossip page.

"Linda, I want you to start scouring all of the social media sites and see what's being said. Worse comes to worst, call some of the contacts you made during *Moose Murders*. Robert, I want you to focus on traditional media. I want to know if *New York Post* is the only source reporting information or if others are picking up on the story," Ben said as the cab arrived in front of the Carney Productions office complex.

The three walked up the stairs and into the building, and were immediately greeted by a receptionist, "Mr. Weber, good to see you again. Mrs. Carney is upstairs waiting for you. She asked me to send you and your colleagues directly to the 20th floor."

"Thanks," Ben said as he ushered his team towards a waiting elevator. On the ride up to the 20th floor, Ben gave his final marching orders, "Just as an FYI, we have to be on our A game here. This contract is very important for our financial stability, so we don't want to do anything that would jeopardize the signing of those contracts. Paul picked you two because you're the best at what you do. Please, please, please don't let any of us down today. We have our work cut out for us."

HOLES, WHAT HOLES?

Over the next week, the whole affair went from bad to worse and then to complete meltdown. After being asked to tone down her twitter feed, Anita Sharpe threw a fit and quit the show all together. Of course, she had to post one final tweet as a parting shot, "Worst show in history—I'm leaving this disaster before I'm completely consumed by its fires and lose any credibility as an actor." Next thing you know, her costar feels the need to quit as well in solidarity. Of course, all of this hit social media and traditional media instantly.

As for the contracts, Carney Productions made the decision to avoid any new contractual obligations until after the opening of *A Road to Nowhere*. After the leaving of the two leads, new leads were found and there appeared to be a new sense of excitement on the set. Even the social media and traditional media seemed to quiet down for a few weeks.

On the first preview of the show, everything fell apart once again. First, the show ended up running almost four hours long because of technical glitches with the set and costume changes that hadn't been rehearsed with the union stage hands and dressers because the lead producer tried to save money during the unexpected extended rehearsal period. Second, a spotlight that was incorrectly hung in the rafters, fell during the second act, shattering next to one of the dancers. While the dancer wasn't directly hit by the spotlight, the explosion of glass left her pretty cut-up. After the horrific affair, the first preview performance was cut short as the young woman was rushed to a nearby hospital.

Of course, all of these first preview problems were captured by an audience member on her cell phone. Before the young woman had even made it out of the theater, she had posted the whole accident online.

Ben's team was meeting on a daily basis with the management team for both Carney Productions and the theater in an effort to stay ahead of the show. Of course, the constant twittering of the former lead actress still wasn't helping the show. Her latest tweet came right after the chorus-girl's accident, "I thank God for sparing me any personal harm. I pray for the young ingénue's recovery. I blame the Producer and Director—it's their fault!"

After this tweet, Ben decided it was time for him or one of his team members to attend every rehearsal and preview just to stay on top of anything that could happen before it's all over the net. They also started filming short YouTube clips with audience members after the show to get immediate audience feedback saying how much they enjoyed the show. Ben even set it up that his team could actually upload the video to the person's own YouTube channel or Facebook page with permission. The goal of this endeavor was to make the comments look as organic as humanly possible.

The first few nights went off without a hitch, and then it was Ben's turn to see the show and capture as much social media attention as humanly possible. The first act went off without a hitch. In fact, the show was actually starting to hold together. The acting was superb, the music was gorgeous, and there were no technical mishaps. From his seat in the back of the Mezzanine, Ben watched as the director and producer wrote copious notes during the performance. When the curtain fell and the lights came up at the end of act one, Ben quickly exited the theater to hang out in the atrium during intermission.

Ben's goal for hanging out in the atrium was to eavesdrop on the audience members' conversations and hear what real theater-goers were saying to each other about the show. Ben listened to a young couple of Brooklyn excitedly explain how much they were enjoying the show. He walked on and heard a group of high school students from Texas explain how "awesome" the show was.

Ben was just starting to feel at ease with the evening, when he heard a crash followed by a loud female voice, "What do you mean we have to chop 10 minutes from Act One!?" Danielle Tillman's voice echoed through the marble atrium.

"Get a grip Danielle, I've been telling you for weeks that the show was running too long. You've got to chop 10 minutes out of the first act. If you don't do it, I'll find someone who will!"

"Are you threatening me?"

Ben swiveled on his heels to see the director and producer standing with the rest of the artistic team outside the bathroom area with Danielle's clipboard lying on the floor in front of her. *I can't believe they're doing this in public!* Ben just stared at the group in absolute shock at the completely unprofessional display unfolding in front of him. Of course, the confrontation quickly went from bad to worse, which was when Ben noticed the young man recording the confrontation with his cell phone.

GOING DOWN WITH THE SHIP?

After the show, Ben slipped out of the theater and hailed a cab back to his office. In the cab he looked down at his cell phone and saw that he already had phone calls from both Paul Hohne and Jennifer Carney. He held the phone up to his ear and listened to the first call from Jennifer.

"Ben, what the heck is going on at the theater tonight? I've already received phone calls from three different papers about some video that ended up on YouTube. I thought you were preventing this kind of stuff. Call me!"

Ben deleted the message and readied himself for the message from his boss.

"Ben, I just got off the phone with a pretty irate Jennifer Carney. Apparently, you let some kid video tape some kind of disagreement between the director and producer and then let him post it on YouTube. This doesn't make sense to me. Call me. We clearly need to strategize and get ahead of this immediately."

Ben deleted the message and stared out the window as his cab traveled down 5th Avenue towards his office building. *What now?*

DISCUSSION QUESTIONS

1. If you were hired as the consultant for this show, how would you go about creating a social media campaign?
2. Is social media an effective communicative tool during a crisis?
3. What is the best way to combat negative information being disseminated when the information is disseminated through social media?
4. If you were Ben's boss, would you keep Ben on the account considering all of the problems that are occurring?
5. If you were Ben, what would you do now?

KEY TERMS

Social media, crisis communication, conflict

How to Win Friends and Influence People:
The Art of Organizational Interventions

Lynn Cooper

Wheaton College

ABSTRACT

How do you conduct an effective consultation? Non-profit organizations will always be clamoring for money, but going beyond the surface to determine the cause of problems as well as solutions beyond the obvious need is the challenge of an organizational consultation.

"We need money." The voice on the telephone was low and urgent.

"Excuse me? Are you asking for a donation?" The call caught Professor Louise Joseph off guard. It had been awhile since she had heard from Peter Bertini.

"Well, no; actually that would be great, but no. Unless you have a lot of money?" The caller sounded hopeful even as he laughed nervously. "No, really we need your students. That is, one of the board members went to a fundraising seminar. They said college students are a good resource… well, they actually said 'cheap labor' for non-profits like ours with problems. I remembered that you worked with students on consulting projects, and thought that you could help us find a good student to get us a grant or something. As I said, we need money."

Over the next ten minutes the story came out in bits and pieces. Peter Bertini was a board member for a non-profit called FOCUS. The 20-year old organization was in crisis because its major sponsor had unexpectedly cut funding. Their situation was bleak: within six months, the board would have depleted all existing funds, and would have to close shop. "Can you help us?"

Louise considered her words carefully. "Grant-writing is a special skill. It's a good and obvious source of income, but there's lots of competition for grants. Even if you can pull together a good proposal, it takes a while to receive the money. And the fact your organization is going under is not a compelling pitch for receiving the foundation's funds either. What's the board's strategy?"

"Well, we're all making phone calls…" The voice had gotten quieter, hesitant, even defensive. Little alarms were going off in Louise's head.

"Do you have information you can send me? Promotional materials I could look at? Budget information? Donor reports? How about a copy of your mission statement and goals?" Louise liked to have as much information as possible before making a decision—even with alarms sounding.

"We have a webpage. Oh, and some old brochures. I could ask one of our volunteers to send those to you." Bertini grew hopeful. "Do you think you can help us?"

Wondering why the phone call was originating from a board member, Louise asked, "Is there anything else going on in the organization at this time? Anything I should know about to help you with your situation?"

The voice became confidential and in a rush of words admitted that they had recently dealt with a sensitive personnel issue. "We're looking for a new executive director. And we're probably going to have to replace a few board members who are leaving. It's only a big deal because these people have been there a few years. Actually, George's been leading the organization for more than fifteen years. Everybody liked George. You might say some people are a little sensitive about his retirement."

Louise thought it over quickly before answering. "Send me the information you have. I'll look at the webpage in the meantime. I need to know more before I can say yes or no."

ANATOMY OF AN INTERVENTION

The Problem

Several days later, Louise reviewed the sparse materials with a sigh. It was clear that the lack of money, though a significant obstacle, was not the only problem. The easy part was determining the organization's purpose, since this was the only information that was clearly articulated. FOCUS is the agency that provides rehabilitative services to inmates in the county jail system. They offer a wide-ranging selection of classes and counseling services to help these inmates while they wait to go to trial, are sentenced, or serve their jail time. There is no competition for this market; FOCUS is the only game in town.

Louise could see that the non-profit balanced a carefully drawn relationship with its sponsor. Jail officials viewed the agency with cautious respect, since the program gave prisoners something to do. However, the presence of FOCUS meant more "outsiders" who pose security risks for the officers. Apart from the jail routine, accomplishing their mission was also challenging, since

FOCUS' client list was a moving target. Inmates might be in the jail as little as a few days, but there was usually less than a year to begin the process of rehabilitation. Business was good: on any given day, there were more than 800 potential "clients." Louise couldn't help but wonder how anyone could run a program effectively within this environment.

The mission of FOCUS was appealing. Louise liked the earnest, straightforward way its message was conveyed. However, the external communication to potential donors and volunteers was a mess. The promotional brochure was clearly out of date. The executive director listed was not the current leader of the organization. Contact information was also outdated. Louise had a knee-jerk reaction to the only image in the brochure: a stereotyped drawing of a shackled prisoner with a bowed head. The webpage wasn't much better. Its design was an unappealing and boring presentation of black and white text, and the lack of color seemed to emphasize the image of the despairing prisoner. The webpage's layout was also difficult to navigate. Links were broken and important information, such as how to donate money and how donations are used, was missing. There was some good information about the mission and history of the organization, but this was inconsistent. The list of programs offered by FOCUS was outdated. Worst of all, there was no indication that FOCUS was successful in reaching its goals. From the look of its external communication, Louise began to feel a little depressed herself.

Louise concluded that there was not a lot to inspire potential donors, and certainly none of the documentation that would establish this organization as grant-worthy. In fact, lack of money seemed more of a symptom rather than the cause of the problem. From the initial conversation with the board member, Louise sensed that FOCUS suffered from many of the challenges of an organization in its adolescence: long-term, but ineffectual leadership, an operation mentality triggered by financial crisis rather than strategic plan, and no "hard" data to determine accountability or success. In truth, FOCUS seemed to have lost its focus. Without a full check-up to determine the cause of their money problems, the organization would be facing the same crunch a year down the road. Any intervention would be limited, Louise reasoned. *We'd be putting a Band-Aid on a severed artery.*

Louise made the call, regretfully backing away from the consultation. Yes, the organization's work was important and significant. Clearly, FOCUS needed money. But it also needed a strategic plan to lead the organization beyond the current crisis to a more secure future. Louise sensed the organization's leadership was not ready or able to deal with larger issues. "If FOCUS makes it past its immediate crisis and wants to talk about long-term solutions, give me a call."

The call came a year later. The speaker was young and enthusiastic, introducing herself as Claire Darcey, the new executive director of FOCUS. "Your name was given to me as someone who might be able to help us move in the right direction."

"I have to admit I'm a bit surprised. Last I heard, things were bad and getting worse. What happened?" Louise was curious to hear how FOCUS had turned itself around in such a short time.

"Nothing short of a miracle, I assure you," Claire said with a laugh. "We were bailed out by a local foundation that gave us the money outright. It's a one-time gift that gives us two years to breathe. I was hired two months ago to handle everything."

Miracle, indeed; Louise thought it would be interesting to know how many calls Peter Bertini had to make before he found that money pot. "Well, I am interested. It would take me about a month to prepare my students for the project. I'm going to need access to information about the organization as we work through a plan of action. I'm assuming that works for you."

Claire admitted, "After two months behind bars, I'm looking forward to working with students. You just have to tell me what you'll need. Preferably that would involve a face-to-face meeting anywhere there's coffee."

"Let's set a date. Now that the 'honeymoon' period is ending, how are things going?"

Claire was surprisingly honest. "The Board liked my energy and ideas, even though I have no real experience as an executive director. Would you believe I've never even visited, let alone worked within, a prison system? They're very supportive, and I told them I was willing to give them two years. I have to say, getting used to daily security checks is challenging!" The laughter was hearty, but her words became serious. "The clock is ticking, and I think you know that our problems are bigger than money."

The Process

Louise laid out the situation to her students. "This is going to be a big project. We've already covered a month of theoretical information about how nonprofit organizations are supposed to work. This case would be a reality check. We have a little information about how FOCUS operates, and we can do a site visit to see them at work. But we don't know anything about their donors, their volunteers, or their staff. There are no benchmarks for performance in their organization's history. In fact, the way the Board operates is a bit of a mystery, too. Claire Darcey is a new leader, and she's opening the organization to us, with the Board's approval. They're eager to help her succeed. Even the jail is willing to give us access as student consultants. But I won't kid you; there's a lot to do." Knowing the answer before she looked around the team of seven students, Louise asked, "Are you up to it?"

By the end of class, a preliminary strategy was laid out: divide and conquer, with the goal of benchmarking information relevant to running an effective nonprofit organization. This meant gathering preliminary reports on organizational stakeholders. We had six weeks to collect information and report back to the organization. Work would be assigned according to student interest and expertise, with all hands agreed they were willing to help out during any creative slumps or crunch times. Louise would train students to the task they would be performing as part of a 360-degree look at the organization. She would maintain the logistical communication with FOCUS, teach students how consultants do needs assessments for strategic alignment, and supply the necessary resources to help them succeed.

The site visit was scheduled once students cleared a preliminary background check. Luckily, no one had outstanding parking tickets, moving violations, or misdemeanors! The students were more quiet than usual when they learned the average inmate in this jail was their age, noting: "They're just like us." As the deputy checked his weapon before entering the jail, he noted that 75% of the inmates were incarcerated for drug use. "We usually see the same people again and again." Students jumped as a series of doors shut behind them, and they entered the inner bowels of the jail environment. A student muttered, "We're not the only ones who have our work cut out for us." And there really was a green line to walk throughout the secured area.

The Players

Despite their sobering experience, student motivation was high after the site visit. Jockeying for consulting roles took place in the car ride back to campus. Bethel, who was an Art minor, quickly volunteered to take on the first challenge: preliminary work to improve FOCUS' external communication. "That webpage is really bothering me, and I think I could tinker around with the logo and image to make the promotional materials look more up-to-date." Bethel scheduled an extra meeting with the executive director in order to get a better sense of organizational identity. Her goal was to create several redesigns of the logo and branded image that would pass muster of the director and be acceptable to the board. She learned that the image of the shackled prisoner was drawn by a former inmate who was one of FOCUS' successes, which got her thinking about how to use that story with actual and potential stakeholders. Bethel soon discovered she would need information from her classmates to find other such stories, as well as to determine the intended audience for any persuasive appeals. Happily, Bethel developed the new webpage that could be uploaded once she had more data.

Diana, who worked part-time in the college's development office, was interested in developing a simple questionnaire to benchmark the FOCUS donor base. Despite her interest, Diana had little experience in survey design and less confidence in her ability to do the job. She looked for assistance with the project, and found this help in Oskar, an outgoing student who majored in extra-curricular activity. An avid volunteer himself, Oskar chose to find out more about the FOCUS volunteers. Diana and Oskar agreed to work together to develop a parallel survey that would be relevant and cost-efficient for both groups. Since they would have to enter the jail again to work with mailing lists, run off surveys, and stuff envelopes, "We definitely want the company!"

Informational interviews were chosen as the approach to understanding more about FOCUS' staff and leadership. Manny and Kate were self-proclaimed "people-persons" who teamed together to develop questions, set up meetings, conduct, and transcribe these interviews. Sometimes their meetings were set up in a workplace; other times the interviews took place at a mutually convenient restaurant. Their professor provided a small coffee budget for them, since "the hardest part about doing this is figuring out who picks up the check."

Stefan volunteered to work with the executive director on a client survey that would also give information about program effectiveness. A double major in Communication and Sociology, Stefan proclaimed: "I like doing research, but not the kind that involves calculating numbers on spreadsheets. Give me a library anytime!" Given logistical problems of approaching inmates, Louise recommended the benchmark study of clients and programs be outsourced. That is, FOCUS staff would distribute the survey within the prison, and give the data to one of their volunteers who knew how to enter data and produce a spreadsheet. While the client survey was being conducted, Stefan researched other programs like FOCUS for comparison purposes in order to determine what a "successful" program would look like. Hearing some initial interest from the informational interviews, Stefan also researched what a new program for "aftercare" would involve, so the last piece of data for the organizational puzzle was in place.

The editor/writer for the project was Jackson, whose involvement in athletics compromised his time toward the beginning of the project. Therefore, Jackson's job was to read and compile all the individual reports into one, and lead the group toward final recommendations. "I'm good at organizing, and I like to write." By doing a SWOT summary (noting the Strengths, Weaknesses, Opportunities, and Threats for the organization), Jackson managed a huge amount of information for the team, and ensured that nothing would get lost in the process. Once the insider's perspective was known, a strategic alignment of FOCUS mission with its leadership, personnel, donors, volunteers, clients, and inmate programs could be envisioned.

We were ready to work.

Prelude: The Client

When the next call came several weeks into the project, it took Louise by surprise.

"Hi, this is Claire Darcey. I've got news." The familiar laughter rang in the phone as Claire explained there would be a change in the consultation process. "I'm pregnant!"

"Wow, congratulations; I'm really delighted for you." Louise remembered the bigger ripples such announcements often made in the workplace. "Does the Board know?"

"I told them last night at the board meeting. They took it very well and are already launching into search mode." Claire's good mood was infectious. "Of course, nothing changes in terms of our commitment to the students' consultation. It just means you may be dealing with a new executive director, since the board is eager to fill this position quickly. With so many people out of work, I don't think they'll have any problem finding a replacement, do you?"

In fact, within a month the position was filled. Claire was busy training the new director, an older woman who was also new to this kind of leadership role. Louise made a mental note to connect with her after the transition was complete, and invite her to meet the students. However, less than two weeks after being hired, the new director beat her to the punch and set up a meeting. Louise liked her immediately. From her first comment she was assured the project would proceed with only minor adjustments.

"I think I'm going to need your help."

Stakeholder Perspective: The Donors

"Does anyone know how hard it is to get the donors' perspective without having an updated list of donors?" Diana faced the team with the first in a series of reports, obviously irritated by the fact that she was only able to get responses from 10% of the people on the list supplied by FOCUS staff. Because of her background in development, she was not impressed by the in-house data about these important organizational members. "I'm not sure how important the results of my survey are. There's no regular assessment going on, so it's hard to compare my data to anything. At the very least, they need to have a reliable mailing list." Stressing that donor care is about building relationships, Diana wanted to talk about a system of consistent communication for FOCUS. "It's not like these people need a *lot* of information from FOCUS. I'm wondering if they're getting the *right* information."

The data that was collected revealed a small army of middle-aged to elderly supporters who staunchly believed in the mission of FOCUS. In fact, no one under 40 years old had responded to the donor survey. There were a few common threads between these people besides age: many of them had church connections, and knew others who donated to FOCUS. Donors who responded tended to be well-educated, with an average income level of $50,000 per year. The vast majority said they donated money to FOCUS once a year, but fully 60% said they hadn't given money in more than a year. Diana noted that some of the donors who returned their survey included a small check with hand-written notes: "My finances are limited." "This check will save you any further expenses." "There are so many organizations asking for money; it's hard for people to make a choice."

In explaining other donor attitudes, Diana said "a strong belief in the organization's mission" and that "the money given will make a difference" were strong motivators. However, most respondents did not believe giving to FOCUS was a priority, or express an interest in further involvement. Summing up her impressions, Diana indicated the "active" donors seemed to include a small bubble of dutiful but aging supporters, giving small gifts at irregular intervals. No connection was seen with the larger group of potential donors in the community who might be interested in prison work and social justice. "Judging from this donor base," Diana reluctantly concluded, "I don't think FOCUS can sustain its operation."

Stakeholder Perspective: The Volunteers

It was Oskar's turn next. His survey questions were similar to Diana's, but there was no problem locating a list of volunteers. Every worker had to be registered and pass a security check, and only 150 people received this clearance. Oskar was excited that more than half of the volunteers responded to his survey, and they showed many of the characteristics of the donor profile. This is a well-educated, comfortably middle-class, and predominantly white/non-Hispanic group of individuals. Age again appeared as a dominant feature, with only three volunteers who took the survey saying they were less than 40 years old. Years of service varied, but more than half of the volunteers had worked with FOCUS more than 10 years. Probably due to the enforced "cap," in the last two years only ten volunteers joined the FOCUS work team. Oskar noted that the majority of the volunteers worked once or twice a month. Despite their long service, this limited time commitment is problematic, since the jail only allows 150 outsiders on the FOCUS volunteer list at any time.

FOCUS volunteers describe themselves as highly committed, enthusiastic, and appreciative of the opportunity to work with this organization. This positive attitude builds morale in a work situation that otherwise could be discouraging. However, there is no way to assess how effective the volunteers are in this role. After their initial orientation to the jail, there is no follow-up training. There is no evaluation of individual courses to provide the instructors with feedback. Even though the scheduling is done by FOCUS staff, the match of volunteer to a particular class is done by the volunteer. For example, most of the survey respondent said they worked in the area of "spiritual guidance," rather than in the often requested employment, education, and addiction recovery courses. "I'm nervous about how the programs are staffed," Oskar admitted. "Without a regular cycle of recruitment and training, FOCUS seems to be vulnerable."

Because FOCUS takes place out of the public eye, volunteers are not permitted to take photos or to film course sessions within the facility. [This policy was especially disappointing to Bethel as she planned the promotional materials.] As a result, nobody except the insiders can fully understand the work of this organization. Yet, few of the volunteers seemed to be financially involved in supporting the organization; apparently, workers see their time as their donation. FOCUS cannot rely solely on outside support to supply its financial needs. Oskar pointed out that "A bigger commitment to the mission of FOCUS should show up in more regular work shifts, promoting their experiences to potential volunteers and donors, and actually giving some of their money to the cause."

Stakeholder Perspective: The Clients

Stefan clutched the pages of information that assessed programs focused on addiction recovery support, educational programs, employment training, and spiritual guidance. "FOCUS has a well-defined clientele, which makes program development easier. With almost half of the inmates responding, we have a good idea of what these people need." Male inmates comprise three-quarters of the jail's population. The majority of the population speaks English; only 18% of the inmates speak Spanish. The race and ethnicity of the inmates is predominantly white/Caucasian; 30% are Hispanic/Latino, and 25% of the inmates identified themselves as Black/African American. Only 21% of the population is married, but more than half are parents. Nearly half of this population was under the age of 30. The majority (62% of both men and women) have a high school diploma or GED. While all faith traditions are represented, the largest group (46%) claimed Protestant Christianity as their religion, followed by 34% who were Catholics.

Inmates had a positive attitude toward FOCUS programs as well as jail services. The most notable need was for employment training and addiction recovery programs. Stefan noted that, "While men also rated employment training #1, they were equally interested in education, addiction recovery, and spiritual guidance." Stefan pitched his belief that there is a clear indication of what programs to initiate, expand, or limit. "If this information is at odds with donor or volunteer preferences, the needs of the inmate should trump any other agendas."

Ironically, while inmates are fairly aware of FOCUS programs and claim to like them, only half of the inmates signed up for classes. There are several possible explanations. FOCUS may not offering enough of the right courses at this time. Inmates may decide not to attend even if they are offered. The fit of course and instructor may be problematic. The course may be scheduled at the wrong time. In regard to scheduling, Stefan noted that men liked afternoon classes, but most volunteers teach in the evenings. If FOCUS is interested in transitioning inmates to communities after their incarceration, some kind of aftercare should be considered. Formal programs and classes around functionally defined skills (e.g., job interviews), activities (e.g., anger management), those that aid competency (e.g., English as a Second Language), or develop links for spiritual development and personal growth (e.g., Bible studies) would continue to be important even after the inmate leaves the jail.

Stakeholder Perspective: The Staff

Manny was ready with his findings about the five-member FOCUS staff. The good news was an overall positive response—toward their leader, toward their jobs, and toward the future. Everyone felt qualified and competent to fulfill the demands of the job. Staff members knew their positions well, including how their role fit in with the organization's overall mission. At the same time, employees appeared to be open to change or improvement. "Everyone felt they were able to communicate their ideas and concerns openly and honestly to each other. But—you guys knew there was a 'but' coming—the bad news is because everyone is busy and working in different parts of the jail, nobody talks much to each other." Despite their small size, Manny described a climate of self-motivated but independent workers, rather than a cohesive and interdependent work team.

There were other problems that surfaced during the informational interviews. Staff perceived a need for more diversity throughout the organization, but especially through the influence of younger, more flexible volunteers, board, and staff. They were not immune to the financial crises either, which created the stress of having too many responsibilities and perception of being stretched too thin. Because of limited resources, staff felt the quality of their work was compromised, innovation was limited, and employees were headed toward burnout.

Manny pointed out that "Even though it would take a lot more work to accomplish it, these people wanted to do more. They talked about having an ongoing relationship with inmates after their release, about finding funding which would extend the rehabilitation process." With an appetite to bridge in-house courses to after-care programs, FOCUS would have the potential to provide an innovative model of rehabilitation. Manny warmed to his subject. "We should encourage this kind of creative thinking. I think they could get a grant to develop a pilot program like this. Don't you think that providing more care for those who have been incarcerated gives more credibility to the organization's mission, too? I would donate to that kind of organization!"

Stakeholder Perspective: The Board

Representing the Board's perspective, Kate summarized the result of the interviews she had conducted with Manny: "Houston, we have a problem." In fairness, board members seemed to know their role on the board, which allowed the board to function smoothly and with little conflict. Because many of them worked together for a long time, or were friends outside of their meetings, the Board had unity in purpose. The majority of Board members seem to be very dedicated and invested in their work. There was also valuable individual expertise in fundraising, human resources, risk management, and legal matters. There were board policies, even if they seemed to be loosely structured. For example, Kate asked why so many members chose to stay beyond the set time for a single term for a board member since board policy set term limits. In fact, board policies seem to act more as guidelines, and as a result, several members have been on the board for a decade or more.

Kate's real problem with the board was their noticeable lack of depth and communication about the vision of FOCUS, as well as lack of strategic planning to develop that vision. Board members seemed content to keep the *status quo* afloat rather than incorporate a plan for the future. Once the unpleasant business of replacing a long-term executive director was accomplished and a short-term reprieve from funding difficulties was obtained, it was as if board members were content to leave it at that. Kate insisted that this board needed to go beyond crisis management to a clearly articulated plan for the future. "Vision is the work of the Board, but unfortunately, this Board seems to be locked in a defensive or passive stance, rather than taking offensive action."

Several other defining issues came up in the informational interviews. First, an uneven distribution of responsibilities was producing cracks beneath the surface; some members felt they had more to do than others and were growing resentful. A lack of diversity among its members, including a large generational and cultural gap between the board members and the inmates that they serve, is obvious, as is the absence of communication addressing that issue. Kate took issue with this lack of motivation. "They seem very content to settle into small roles, as if being a member of the Board was just something else that these people do."

Postlude: Framing Recommendations

After extensive discussion, the student consultants concluded there were several challenges facing FOCUS as this organization transitions into a period of new leadership. The students were now ready to frame these challenges into specific recommendations that will meet the immediate goals of the organization as well as generate the vision for a larger, future plan.

DISCUSSION QUESTIONS

1. What considerations need to be raised by a consulting team before starting an organizational intervention?

2. Beyond the obvious need for money, what problem(s) is this organization facing? What caused the problem(s)?

3. Discuss the various organizational stakeholders. Conduct a SWOT (strengths, weaknesses, opportunities, threats) summary for each group: donors, volunteers, clients, staff, and Board. Based on your summary, what is the organization doing well overall? What is an area of concern?

4. What recommendations would you make to improve the functioning of this non-profit? How would you prioritize your recommendations?

5. What changes in the organizational consulting process if your student team is dealing with a for-profit business?

KEY TERMS

Organizational consulting

What Is the Real Problem?

Robert Whitbred

CLEVELAND STATE UNIVERSITY

ABSTRACT

Communication Survey Analytics is completing a consulting project for Medi-tech, a medical supply manufacturing company, focused on improving the motivation of employees. What happens when the project sponsor emerges as the main problem?

Fred Williams, a junior project manager for a consulting company specializing in assessing and responding to communication problems in organizations called *Communication Survey Analytics,* is concerned. He just finished reviewing his notes from an interview earlier that day with an employee of *Medi-tech,* which is a family-owned manufacturing company specializing in medical supplies, and noticed a disturbing pattern emerge. He entered a conference room and saw his project partner Mary Houseman pouring over a series of printouts of various types of analysis. Mary looked up and said "I think we may have a problem we need to talk about." Fred poured himself a cup of coffee, sat down, and replied "You go first."

Mary Houseman has been a member of *Communication Survey Analytics* for over twenty years, and a senior project manager for ten of those. She fully understood the delicate nature of this situation, and decided she and Fred should spend some time reviewing what they knew. Mary began "When we were first approached by Roger, we understood that *Medi-tech* is a family owned operation that has recently undergone some changes. Roger is facing an uphill battle trying to replace his father. It is not just that Bill founded the company, but that many in the place still revere him. Because he died unexpectedly two years ago, it seems Roger may not have been ready to step in as company President." Fred added "In one sense, you do kind of feel sorry for him, but you are much more forgiving that I am. I have found him to be an arrogant jerk who is nearly impossible to be in the same room with, never mind work with."

Mary sighed, saying "I cannot disagree with you, but let's stick to our project. We also have to keep in mind that this is a large contract." Fred continued "When Roger first approached us six months ago, he was aware that there were problems with his company, and needed help. If you recall, he said 'Our current employees are stuck in a rut, and have not gotten over my father's passing. They have forgotten what made our company so successful for so many years—our commitment to helping people with our products. We truly do make things that better man-kind! I need an internal branding program that reminds them of why they should be proud to be a member of the *Medi-tech* family.' I also recall you emphasizing that we needed to complete our own assessment of the situation, and act accordingly." Mary responded "And that is where we are."

FOLLOW THE DATA

"There is no question that this is an ill organization. All the signs are there." Mary said, and continued "The information provided by their Human Resource office shows a dramatic increase in both absenteeism and turnover over the past year or so. People who have been there for ten years or more are deciding to move on." Fred made a sour face, and suggested they look at some of the results of a *Communication Audit* survey they collected. He said "Look at the numbers in that last column of **TABLE 30.1**. I have never seen results that lousy before."

Mary asked "Do you have the rest of the results somewhere? This audit instrument is really long, and is meant to assess all communication issues in an organization." Fred replied "Yes, you have a copy of the output, but this is the most important stuff." Mary then said "I need to keep reminding myself that this survey focuses on the difference between the amount of information employees feel they need about all these topics and what they are actually getting. It seems very clear that people do not think they are getting what they need from the upper levels of the hierarchy. Employees do not even know company policies. Most or all of these topics rely on Roger to communicate." Fred added, "You are correct. Look at the pattern. Those issues such as Roger's expectations, strategic priorities, company policies, and new products that Roger knows most about are even worse than the others—and those are bad enough."

"What about the interviews you have done?" Mary asked.

"That was what I was coming to talk to you about." Fred replied, and continued "I interviewed three people over the past two days, and am hearing some things consistently. All three mentioned how Frank is arrogant and verbally aggressive, and is very impatient when dealing with those at lower levels in the hierarchy. I even wrote down and brought a quote with me that a middle level manager in marketing said: 'Marketing and sales is always hard, but it is even more stressful in our current economy. When Roger comes in and yells at my people in such a demeaning and condescending way, it's just like air being let out of a balloon. He actually called one of us a waste

TABLE 30.1 *Partial Results of Communication Audit Instrument*

Topic	Information Needed	Information Received	Difference
President's Expectations	5	1.2	-3.8
Strategic Priorities	4.8	1.8	-3
Company Policies	5	1	-4
Problems Faced by Management	4.6	2	-2.6
New Products	4.9	1	-3.9
Employee Development Opportunities	4.5	1.5	-3
Advancement Opportunities	5	1	-4
My Job Performance	5	2.5	-2.5
My Job Duties	5	3.5	-1.5
How I Can Improve	4.8	2	-2.8

of resources. One of my most talented staff just quit because of this.'" Mary concurred: "This is very similar to the things I heard as well. One thing was particularly troublesome. I interviewed a woman who works in manufacturing who disclosed that she is a single mother. She told me that when she asked Roger for information on *Medi-tech's* tuition reimbursement program, he told her to focus on her job and her family for the time being." Fred rolled his eyes, and said "We are scheduled to interview you know who tomorrow, along with Tasha his secretary and Ned who is the director of Human Resources. I'll take Ned, you take Tasha, and we'll both interview Roger."

NEXT DAY'S INTERVIEWS

The next day, Mary sat down with Tasha in a private office and found her completely unwilling to talk; the most she would disclose was "I cannot afford to lose this job, and I will not say anything about anything." Mary was highly concerned, since Tasha had been the secretary for Bill (Roger's father and the company founder) for 15 years prior to his death and had stayed on to work with Roger. Mary said, "I fully understand why you are concerned about sharing potentially sensitive information, but let me assure you of two things. First, you are in a unique position and have valuable insights that nobody else can provide. Second, I personally guarantee that anything you tell me will be strictly confidential." Tasha then said "This job and this place has become a nightmare in the last year or so. I get it from all directions. Roger is constantly complaining about how our employees do not understand the value of *Medi-tech's* work and that they are not working as hard as they should be. Everyone else around here is constantly asking me questions about things I cannot answer." Mary prompted, "Please give some examples." to which Tasha replied, "Here is a typical conversation that happened today. Person X will ask me for a copy of his performance evaluation. I tell him to go to Ned (the director of Human Resources). Person X then tells me he already went to Ned and was told he had to talk to Roger—but since Roger is so intimidating, they instead come to me and ask me to deal with it."

Mary replied, "I thought Roger had an open door policy." to which Tasha replied "Let me tell you about that one. When Roger's father was running things, he really had such a policy, and would always make time to meet with employees as needed; he really cared. Roger kept this policy in place when he started, but has no idea what it means. When people come to talk to him, he is always raising his voice, checking email, or making phone calls...anything but talking to the person. He has even programmed our phones so he can push a button to activate this light on my phone, and I'm supposed to come into his office with some excuse to get him out of there. This does not make me comfortable."

At the same time, Fred was interviewing Ned (the director of Human Resources) and found him much more willing to talk. Before Fred could ask a single question, Ned began "I have been here for over twenty years, which if my math is correct, is about ten times as long as the little pipsqueak. He came in here with his MBA this and certification that and just started telling us what to do. The problem is that he has no idea how to run this company. He is a smart guy, but he is so damn defensive about everything and so threatened by anything that he is unwilling to listen to anyone."

Later that same day, Mary and Fred both met with Roger, who began with "I've got to tell you, I've been a bit disappointed with the pace of this project. I told you a long time ago what the problem was and what we needed to do to solve it, and you have done nothing but have my people circle numbers on surveys and answer questions. What are we going to do about getting them back on board? When are you going to start the internal branding initiative that we need?" Fred replied "An internal branding initiative focuses on improving your employees' understanding of the core values and principles of a company, and in turn your employees will then be more motivated and say complimentary things about the company to others. We are not sure this is the problem." Roger then asked, "What is that supposed to mean?"

Mary interjected, and asked Roger, "Could you talk about how you feel your employees perceive your leadership?" to which Roger replied, "I have a unique advantage over most that enter into this business. I learned from my father and I also have not only my undergraduate degree, but also my MBA. I fully understand the importance of motivating employees, and what needs to be done to do so." Fred then asked, "Have you ever thought about getting your employees' input or feedback about..." At which point, Roger cut him off with "What you are describing there is the job of the leader, which I am. My role is to set direction and be sure those who I am responsible for are aware of this. This is why we are having the problems we are having. The people here are not aware of the importance of what we do." Mary tried once more by asking, "Do you feel there are any topics or issues that you could do a better job communicating about with others?" Roger responded "there is always something that someone is unhappy with or feels they must know about. I handle this with an open door policy. I am always willing to meet with my people…"

WHAT TO PRESENT?

That evening Mary and Fred scheduled a working dinner to discuss the project and what to do next. They were both worried about the presentation they had to give in five days to Roger and the other five strategic managers of *Medi-tech,* conveying the results of the data collection and recommended preliminary action steps. Mary began "As I see it, we have three basic problems. First, while Roger is a very capable and talented person, he is also very sure of himself and unaware of the reality surrounding him." Fred interjected, "The man is a compete ego-maniac," to which Mary responded "That may be the case, but continuing on. Second, Roger has already determined that the solution to all *Medi-tech's* problems is an internal branding program around the humanitarian and beneficial nature of the products they manufacture, and this will improve the motivation of their employees. We both know there are other problems. Third, *Communication Survey Analytics* needs to keep this contract. The economy is not great, and this is a fairly lucrative project. If we confront Roger with our data and conclusions, he may just fire us."

Fred responded, "So we have two basic options. First, give the man what he wants. Putting together the branding program may not really help the situation, but it will not do any real harm either. He will be happy and is so delusional that he will likely convince himself things have improved because of it. Second, we can put together a carefully worded report that we give privately to Roger, and make him aware of the feedback we have received—and run the risk of being canned on the spot." Mary then said, "Well, there is a third and even more risky option. We could deliver a report that summarizes our findings to the manager and the group, and put Roger in the position of getting this feedback publicly. This may just protect us." Fred asked "Are you crazy?" to which Mary replied, "Yeah, that is not a good idea."

After a few moments of silence, Mary said "one thing that we have not talked about and is bothering me is the ethics of this. Tasha was nearly in tears today when she was telling me some of the things going on." Fred agreed, "I know, and you are right. There are times when I felt that people were seeing us as a way to try and improve the situation, that we are sort of a lifeline. They trusted us with their stories and with their information, and now we are debating what to do—but our debates have nothing to do with the data we collected, but with the politics surrounding all this. Mary responded, "Well, we have discussed this from a lot of angles. What are we going to do?"

DISCUSSION QUESTIONS

1. What is the leadership style of Roger, the current President of *Medi-Tech*? How does this style differ from that of his father Bill, the original founder of *Medi-Tech*?

2. How do you think the culture of *Medi-Tech* has changed since Roger took over?

3. What are some of the negative things that are occurring in the company resulting from Roger's behavior?

4. What are the pressures Fred and Mary must balance when deciding what to do next?

5. Do you think most communication consulting cases face similar challenges as this one? Why or why not?

6. Do you feel the negative feedback should be provided to Roger, even though he may retaliate against some in the organization? Why or why not?

KEY TERMS

Communication audit, organizational communication consulting, internal branding, respondent confidentiality

APPENDIX A

CASE STUDY WORKSHEET

This worksheet is designed to help you think through the decision making process in a decision based case study. The worksheet is designed to be worked through step-by-step.

Initial Analysis of the Case

Important Decision Makers: Who are the key decision makers in this case study? List them by name and identify their role in the case (add others if necessary).

Name	Role

Problem Statement: State the communication problem of the case. Try to state it in a single sentence and then expand to a few more sentences (if they are necessary). Then summarize your diagnosis: the primary cases of the problem.

Remember, you cannot attempt to recommend possible alternative until you are clear on what the communication problem is within a case. Often cases have multiple communication problems; select the one that you think is either the most encompassing or the one that is the most urgent.

Communication Problem:

Causes: Once you have clearly articulated the communication problem discussed within the case, you need to clearly look for any and all causes of the communication problem. When creating your list of causes, make sure you do not add too many causes to your list because you may end up bogging yourself down in causes that cloud the overall problem.

Cause:	Evidence/Example from Case
Cause:	Evidence/Example from Case
Cause:	Evidence/Example from Case
Cause:	Evidence/Example from Case

Applicable Research/Theory

Research and Theory: No alternative should be developed until you thoroughly understand the relevant organizational communication research/theory related to general decision being made. As such, after reading the textbook and other relevant research, what research or theories are you using to help you understand this case? How does this literature apply? What types of alternatives does the literature suggest for this case?

Source #1:

How does this research/theory help you understand the case?

How are you applying this research/theory to the current case?

What possible alternatives does this research/theory suggest for the current case?

Source #2:

How does this research/theory help you understand the case?

How are you applying this research/theory to the current case?

What possible alternatives does this research/theory suggest for the current case?

Source #3:

How does this research/theory help you understand the case?

How are you applying this research/theory to the current case?

What possible alternatives does this research/theory suggest for the current case?

Decision Criteria

Decision Criteria: Select the three most important qualitative and/or quantitative decision criteria you believe are necessary for selecting an alternative in this case.

Criterion #1:

Definition/application in this case:

Argument for including this criteria:

How you will measure?

Criterion #2:

Definition/application in this case:

Argument for including this criteria:

How you will measure?

Criterion #3:

Definition/application in this case:

Argument for including this criteria:

How you will measure?

Decision Criteria Ranking: Rate your decision criteria on a scale from 1 not overly important to 10 very important?

Criterion #1:	Not Overly Important	1	2	3	4	5	6	7	8	9	10	Very Important
Criterion #2:	Not Overly Important	1	2	3	4	5	6	7	8	9	10	Very Important
Criterion #3:	Not Overly Important	1	2	3	4	5	6	7	8	9	10	Very Important

Now rank your criteria in the order of their importance? (1) most important criteria to (3) least important criteria:

1. Most Important Criteria:

2. Middle Important Criteria:

3. Least Important Criteria:

Justification: Please provide a justification for how you ranked the criteria in this section.

Decision Alternatives

Decision Alternatives: List a minimum of three possible alternatives the main character in the case should take. Decision alternatives should be clear and concise.

Remember, all alternatives should be realistic and implementable given the confines of the case.

Alternative #1:

Alternative #2:

Alternative #3:

Decision Alternative Analysis

Recommended Alternative: State the decision you are recommending and summarize the reasons for it. Also, provide evidence from the textbook or other course readings to help support your recommended decision. Be brief!

Decision:

Justification from Research/Theories: Apply any relevant organizational communication research or organizational communication theories you have used to help you make your decision.

Application of the Criteria: In this section, demonstrate how you see the three criteria clearly applying to this decision alternative. Please remember that all three of the criteria should clearly point to this decision alternative.

Justification using Criterion #1:

Justification using Criterion #2:

Justification using Criterion #3:

Risks Associated with the Recommended Alternative: What do you think are the major risks associated with the alternative you have chosen? How will you mitigate the likelihood of these risks turning into crises?

Risk	Mitigation

Decision Alternatives Not Selected Analysis

Non-Selected Alternatives: In this section, you are going to clearly explain why you opted to not choose the other two alternatives. First, you need to make your arguments using both relevant communication research and/or theories. Second, you need to make your argument using the three criteria that you have selected.

Decision Alternative Not Chosen #1:

Justification from Research/Theories: Apply any relevant organizational communication research or organizational communication theories you have used to help you make your decision.

Application of the Criteria: In this section, demonstrate how you see the three criteria clearly applying to this decision alternative. Please remember that all three of the criteria should clearly point to this decision alternative.

Justification using Criterion #1:

Justification using Criterion #2:

Justification using Criterion #3:

Justification from Research/Theories: Apply any relevant organizational communication research or organizational communication theories you have used to help you make your decision.

Application of the Criteria: In this section, demonstrate how you see the three criteria clearly applying to this decision alternative. Please remember that all three of the criteria should clearly point to this decision alternative.

Justification using Criterion #1:

Justification using Criterion #2:

Justification using Criterion #3:

Alternative Implementation

The implementation plan is where you describe how you will carry out your chosen decision alternative within the organization.

Goal(s): What are the basic goals or outcomes that you hope to achieve by implementing your decision alternative? Additionally, based on how you decided to measure your criteria, demonstrate how you will determine if your goal is being met?
Goal #1.
Evaluation of Goal:
Goal #2.
Evaluation of Goal:
Goal #3.
Evaluation of Goal:

Action Steps: Most implementation plans have clear short-term and long-term action steps that need to be taken. What short-term and long-term steps do you feel are necessary to completely implement your chosen decision alternative?

Short-Term Steps
1.
2.
3.

Long-Term Steps
1.
2.
3.

Based on your overall analysis, how confident are you that your chosen decision alternative and implementation plan will solve the communication problem you identified at the beginning of this worksheet?

Not Very Confident	1	2	3	4	5	6	7	8	9	10	Very Confident

Why?